south island

TROUT FISHING GUIDE

JOHN KENT

REED

Established in 1907, Reed Publishing (NZ) Ltd
is New Zealand's largest book publisher, with over 300 titles in print.

For details on all these books visit our website:
www.reed.co.nz

Published by Reed Books, a division of Reed Publishing (NZ) Ltd, 39 Rawene Rd, Birkenhead, Auckland. Associated companies, branches and representatives throughout the world.

ISBN 0 7900 0824 6

Cover photographs by David Hallett
Text designed by Sharon Whitaker
Maps by Sandra Parkkali

First published 1990
Reprinted 1993, 1995
Revised 1996
New edition 1998
Revised 2002

Printed in New Zealand

south island

TROUT FISHING GUIDE

contents

acknowledgements

Information for this book has largely been obtained from personal observation and travel. However, friends, other anglers, farmers, fish and game councils and the Department of Conservation have all made contributions and I would like to thank each in turn.

I would like specifically to thank my partner and travelling companion, Patti Magnano Madsen, for her help with photography, her knowledge of New Zealand fishing and her friendship.

introduction

This book is designed to help those anglers who enjoy exploring and fishing new water. I hope it will also encourage those who enjoy fishing the same stream to branch out and widen their horizons. Many anglers fish the same stream year after year, even fishing the same stretch of water on that stream, and expect the stream to remain constant. If winter floods have changed their favourite pool, they are filled with disappointment. But surely one of the excitements of trout fishing is the experience of a new stream or lake. Strange waters increase your feelings of expectancy.

Every new stretch of water presents new challenges, and one cannot criticise an angler for doing badly on unfamiliar waters. But what if an angler does badly on familiar water? I have yet to meet an angler who didn't have a good excuse: You should have been here on Thursday! The water is too clear; the stream is too low; the day's too bright; or the wind's too strong. Most likely, the fish were simply not feeding. These days, however, it pays to look for fresh footprints, as an angler fishing a clear stream 48 hours earlier could be the reason for your lack of success.

A bad angler will rarely succeed, no matter how often he or she explores a stretch of water. A good angler is a good angler anywhere, even on strange waters. It is known that 10 percent of anglers catch 90 percent of the fish. However, one can only learn and improve through new experiences and observations. So take a risk! Try a new river. You may be pleasantly surprised. You may even have more success than on waters you fish regularly. Then again, isn't catching a fish a bonus? Angling for trout takes you to beautiful places. If the scenery is spectacular, the sun is shining and you are at peace with the world, what does it really matter if you don't land a trout? Have you noticed that when you are concentrating on fishing all troublesome thoughts evaporate? Why does the day pass so quickly? To the observant nature lover, no sport affords so much pleasure. At times the excitement can also be intense. Imagine, after scrambling for an hour up a back-country river, you finally spot a magnificent wild trout swinging from side to side, feeding in the current. There's plenty of time: no other angler is within miles. A careful plan of attack is called for.

First find a place downstream, sheltered from view by riverbank scrub, and watch the trout's feeding pattern, observing the direction of the breeze and the flow of the current. Is the fish nymphing, and if so how deep, or is it rising and feeding on surface flies? What are the insects it is consuming? Do you have a pattern in your fly box resembling these? Observe the feeding lane and estimate where you will need to cast your fly in order for it to float down close to the fish. Is there a ripple on the water that might obscure the plop of a weighted nymph or an inaccurate cast? Should I lengthen the tippet so as not to line the fish? You select a fly and notice that your hand shakes a little as you tie it carefully on to the delicate tippet. Now is the moment to put your plan into action. Keeping low, you creep up behind this magnificent wild fish, strip line off the reel and prepare to cast. Suddenly, you feel a great surge of adrenaline and become full of self-doubt. Your heart beats loud enough for the fish to hear and your mouth dries. Have I selected the right fly? Can I make an accurate first cast knowing I botched the last one? Is my tippet sufficiently strong to hold this fish? What if it turns when hooked and races downstream through the rapids? Can I avoid that overhanging beech tree? The task becomes even more daunting under the critical gaze of an angling companion. I'm sure to botch it! Maybe it's my friend's turn?

Just at the crucial moment, a cloud darkens the sky and the fish is momentarily lost from view. You wait patiently in cold, knee-deep water and ponder the words you have heard for years from non-angling friends. 'Fishing must be dull and boring.' 'I haven't the patience.' 'You've been away all day and returned with nothing. What have you been doing?' And here you are standing knee-deep in this cold mountain river, shivering with nervous tension and excitement. Who said trout fishing is relaxing?

Suddenly the light returns, and thankfully, the fish is still there feeding. You begin false casting away from the fish, carefully measuring the casting distance as you strip out line. With great care and a little good fortune your first cast is accurate and delicate. The artificial drifts down with the current and the unsuspecting fish swings across without a moment's hesitation and sucks in your fly. You lift the rod quickly and tighten the line. That is the essence of fly fishing — the moment of take. All hell breaks loose as the fish dashes madly upstream, stripping line off the screaming reel.

Wild trout in a wild river seldom give up easily. The play is only over when, after a good tussle, the fish is gently landed, weighed, photographed, and released unharmed. You watch with satisfaction as the trout recovers to slowly swim back into the depths of the pool. Now for that hot thermos of coffee, ideally shared with an angling friend. And as your pulse gradually settles down to normal you reflect on what a wonderful day it is!

I make no excuse for emphasising fly fishing in this book. Once an angler has developed fly-casting skills — and they are not difficult to learn — there's just no comparison with spin or bait fishing. The pure excitement of watching a trout move sideways to take your nymph, feeling the tug when a fish grabs your wet fly or lure on the swing, or watching it rise to sip in your dry fly cannot be matched by any other fishing method.

However, there is a definite place for spinning and live-bait fishing, especially for junior anglers. I certainly caught fish using both these methods before changing to a fly rod.

At times, a river may be totally unsuitable for fly fishing yet trout can still be caught on a spinner. As a teenager I had thought fly fishing too difficult to learn! It isn't, especially if you can find another fly fisher with the time and patience to start you off. It is much easier to learn from an experienced angler than from a book. Join a fly fishing club to get started.

One of the charms of fly fishing is that if you live to be a hundred you'll never learn it all. There are so many constantly changing parameters affecting trout environment, trout food and the trout themselves. Such variables as season, barometric pressure, water and air temperature, wind direction and velocity, light intensity, time of day, the colour and state of the water, and insect hatch are but a few of the factors affecting the catch rate. You may catch a limit one day but return empty-handed the next, despite fishing the same spot.

The geography and climate of the South Island are extraordinarily varied, with snow-covered alps, dark dripping rainforests, fertile plains, barren deserts and rugged coastlines all within a few kilometres of each other. Annual rainfall can be as high as 6000 mm in Fiordland and as low as 250 mm 60 km to the east in Central Otago. The prevailing winds are the nor'westers, which sweep across the Tasman Sea collecting water to dump on the West Coast. On the eastern side of the Southern Alps, the nor'wester is a strong, warm, dry wind. These winds usually herald the arrival of a cold front, and the development of a sou'wester after the front passes can drop the temperature by as much as 12° Celsius in a couple of hours. It pays to be aware that all four seasons can arrive on one day!

The wide variations in land forms and climate are naturally reflected by the waterways. There are sluggish rain- and swamp-fed streams meandering across farmland, clear rushing mountain torrents shaded by dense native bush, unstable glacier-fed rivers, cold spring creeks, and natural as well as artificially made lakes. Nearly all the South Island's waterways contain trout, and in some remote areas fish weighing over 4.5 kg (10 lb) are not uncommon.

With so many rivers and lakes exhibiting such widely differing characteristics, the South Island is truly an angler's paradise. Over 300 rivers and 100 lakes are described in this book, and it would take a lifetime to fish even half of the water. Some anglers may be disappointed to find their favourite spot described, but a number of small, local streams holding only a few fish have been omitted. I apologise for this, but hopefully anglers fishing 'your' stream will practise catch-and-release conservation methods. (May I suggest you pay a reciprocal visit to 'their' stream!) Many high country rivers contain small numbers of trout and on a good day could easily be fished out. It is vitally important to return the larger fish in order to protect the gene pool.

Trout populations in some of the rivers described have been assessed by biologists employed by fish and game councils and the National Institute of Water and Atmospheric Research (NIWA) using drift diving techniques. Their results are included when available, but they should be taken as a guide only. It is impossible to accurately survey a whole river, and fish tend to move both upstream and downstream according to weather conditions and the season. However, it can be reassuring to know that the new water you are exploring for the first time contains a good population of trout.

Before venturing onto a new stream, it is well worth buying an up-to-date map of the area from a sports store, a map shop or the Department of Conservation (DoC). When exploring remote rivers, there are a number of excellent tramping guides available to consult. DoC can also provide a list of campsites and huts available to use, and hut permits.

The entire South Island requires only one licence, which is readily available from sports stores, fly shops, motor camps and service stations. It pays to be familiar with local rules and regulations, which may change from season to season. I have included many of these in this book, but fish and game councils produce an annual publication with this information. There is no excuse for ignorance!

Information for Canterbury rivers can be obtained by ringing the River and Flood Infoline on 08 322-5522.

Finally, may the nor'wester blow as a gentle zephyr and the sun shine brightly on you. Good luck.

John Kent and Patti Magnano Madsen with a small spring creek brown trout

safety and equipment

New Zealand is a long, narrow, mountainous, windy country with unpredictable weather patterns. It is frustrating to the angler to carefully plan a day's fishing, then arrive to find a howling downstream wind prevents any chance of casting. I have described the general direction each stream follows and strongly recommend you study the weather map and forecast before leaving for your day's fishing. Remember, however, that forecasting the weather in New Zealand is never easy.

In the mountains, special care must be taken in planning routes, carrying survival equipment and informing others of your intentions. Do not attempt difficult river crossings, especially when the river is running high. Light a fire and camp out for the night, miss a day or two at work, but come home alive. Remember, there is absolutely nothing to harm you in the bush except your own bad judgement! Books are available on mountain safety, and accurate, detailed maps are essential. DoC can also provide you with a list of their huts and permits to use these, as well as campsites. The following inventory has been developed over many years of tramping and fishing New Zealand's back country.

Equipment for fishing and camping in the mountains

General gear
Small lightweight tent and fly. In summer, a fly alone or even a sheet of black polythene can be sufficient but be prepared to get eaten alive by sandflies or mosquitoes, especially on the West Coast and in Fiordland. The tent should be insect-proof.
Frame pack
Sleeping bag (preferably down and in a waterproof cover or plastic wrap)
Sleeping pad

Torch (lightweight)
Compass (optional, as you can use your watch)
Map
Axe (optional, but must be light)
Knife (fishing or hunting)
Cooker and fuel
Billies (2) and frypan
Knife, fork, spoon, mug, plate
Pot scrubber
Small container of biodegradable dishwashing liquid
Matches (in a waterproof container)
Fire-lighters or piece of rubber
Small towel, toothbrush, soap
First-aid kit
Sunscreen and insect repellent
Camera and film

Clothing
Boots (lightweight, durable and with a good gripping sole for river
    crossings)
Sandshoes or Teva sandals
Socks (4 pairs)
Underwear
Polar fleece or synchilla jacket
T-shirt
Shorts (quick-drying material is best, and with deep pockets)
Longs (lightweight in either polypropylene or nylon)
Woollen or flannelette shirt
Parka
Hat (with a brim)
Watch

Fishing gear
Fly rod (preferably four-piece to fit in your pack)
Reel and line
Traces and tippet material
Flies
Polaroid glasses

Day pack or 'bum bag'
Scissors
Eel line (simple line and hook, great for survival when desperate!)
Fishing licence

Food
There is great scope for variety and personal preference. I choose from the following list:
Bread (wholegrain keeps longer and is more nutritious)
Butter (in a container)
Brown sugar
Tea and coffee
Honey (in a plastic bag)
Dried milk
Wholegrain oats
Muesli
Salt
Rice and pasta
Cheese
Salami
Dried vegetables
Packet soups
Freeze-dried meals or ready-to-use pasta meals (optional)
Scroggin or trail mix

Equipment for a day's fishing

Clothing can be selected according to the season and the area visited. When sight fishing I wear neutral colours to blend in with the background scenery. Green, brown and blue are satisfactory, but yellow and red scare fish. A white hat is a disaster! Most of my summer fishing is done wearing boots and shorts, although waders are essential when fishing a stream mouth at night. I find the new lightweight waders are not very durable in matagouri scrub. Nylon overtrousers are great on cold, windy days and also keep the sand-flies at bay. Anklets keep the stones out of your boots. Other essential gear includes a brimmed hat and Polaroid glasses, a fishing vest or a shirt with large secure pockets, or a 'bum bag'. In a small day pack I carry lunch, a thermos, camera and film, matches, parka, first aid kit, knife, a survival blanket and spare clothing.

Fly fishing gear

Personal preferences obviously govern the choice of rods, reels and flies. Lightweight carbon fibre (graphite) rods have now become very popular, and have superseded the older-style split cane (bamboo) and fibreglass rods. There are still purists who cling to their cane rods, but for all-round use carbon fibre rods are hard to beat. I only use a 6 weight rod in the South Island and find it satisfactory for lakes, spring creeks and larger rivers. In windy conditions or when casting two heavy nymphs, I prefer a stiff, powerful rod loaded with a 7 weight, weight forward floating line. On spring creeks, a double taper 6 weight line is preferable. Some anglers will prefer a 3 or 4 weight rod for spring creeks, but New Zealand is a windy country and such rods are limited to optimal conditions. I also carry an intermediate or slow sinking line but seldom use it. Your reel should be capable of holding at least 60 m of backing. It is important when sight fishing not to use a brightly coloured line as this will spook fish. I favour dark green or brown, and in the past have even dyed my line to a suitable colour.

Maxima brand nylon appears to be less prone to abrasion than others, and for this reason I use it to tie up my tapered leaders and tippet. My recipe is as follows: 60 cm (2 feet) of 12 kg (25–30 lb) for the butt section; 150 cm (5 feet) of 7 kg (15 lb), 60 cm (2 feet) of 4 kg (8 lb), 150 cm (5 feet) of 1–2 kg (3–5 lb) for the tippet. The tippet length and breaking strain can obviously be altered to suit the conditions.

A lightweight, wide-mouthed landing net with built-in scales in the handle can be useful on some streams, especially those that are weedy or have high banks. However, they can be a nuisance to carry in some situations and have an amazing affinity for matagouri and briar rose bushes. Most trout can usually be beached and the hook removed without taking the fish from the water. An old nylon stocking used as a glove can be used for gripping slippery fish, and also for seining the water when trout prove to be very selective.

If the river is deep and swift or if the riverbed boulders are covered in slippery algae, a collapsible wading stick can be useful. However, it can be a nuisance when casting. Some anglers carry line dressing and dry fly floatant.

The choice of flies varies from district to district and from angler to angler, but I have listed popular patterns throughout the text. Visitors should spend time in local fly shops and sports stores and obtain as much local information as possible. Trout in New Zealand are opportunistic feeders and rarely will they selectively feed on one type of hatching insect alone. Ninety percent of their food is taken sub-surface. The following is a list of trout food, but it is by no means comprehensive: caddis, mayflies, midges, stoneflies, terrestrials; the latter includes beetles, cicadas, grasshoppers, crickets, ants, bees, wasps and blowflies.

Other food includes dragon and damsel flies, smelt, inanga, bullies, trout and salmon fry, worms, centipedes, perch, goldfish, elvers, koura, frogs and tadpoles, snails, maggots, mice, willow grub, corixa and salmon eggs. Despite this list of exotic food, it would be useful to have a selection of the following patterns in your fly box.

Caddis imitations

Caddis provides the largest portion of a trout's diet. More than 100 species of caddis have been identified, with many more unclassified. Rarely does an angler need to imitate a specific caddis, as the common nymph patterns listed are a good representation.

Nymphs (larvae and pupae) Early in the season when streams and rivers are still running full, caddis nymphs need to be well weighted. I use tungsten beads for this purpose and will sometimes fish two heavily weighted nymphs. In low water summer conditions, a single unweighted nymph can be deadly on smaller streams. Hare and Copper (Hare's Ear) in sizes 12–18, Pheasant Tail 12–18, Half Back 12–18. The last is a more true representation, and tied with green peacock herl on a curved caddis hook it can be very effective.

Adults (sedge) Newly hatched adult caddis are strong insects and do not get trapped in the surface film. Rather, they emerge and fly off the water rapidly; hence the splashy rise late in the evening signifies trout feeding on caddis emergers. Deer Hair Sedge or Goddard Caddis, Elk Hair Caddis, soft hackle wet flies.

Mayfly imitations

As with caddis, there is a wide variety of mayflies which tend to vary from district to district, and it is impossible to represent all species. Local knowledge can be useful, but presentation and fly size are more important.

Nymphs

Pheasant Tail and Hare and Copper in sizes 12–16.

I weight most of my nymphs according to the water being fished. Some are heavily weighted with lead wire in the body and a tungsten bead. Others are very lightly weighted, and are useful for low water summer conditions and spring creeks. I collect unwashed merino wool off farmers' fences and tie in a tuft for my indicator with a simple overhand knot. If there is glare on the water I add brightly coloured polypropylene. As I do not enjoy fish rising to my indicator I seldom use orange. On spring creeks, I rarely use an indicator.

Emergers

When rising fish are difficult to tempt with conventional dry fly patterns, the chances are high that they are taking emerging pupae in the surface film. There are many patterns to choose from but simply cutting the wings and most of the hackle off a small dry fly will often suffice. I like a CDC emerger, an unweighted nymph or even a Klinkhammer dry fly with no tail so the body hangs down beneath the surface film. When trout seem fixed on one pattern it pays to seine the water with your hand encased in an old nylon stocking. The insects stick to the stocking and can usually be identified. The next task is to find something similar in your fly box!

Adults (dry flies)

I like to fish dry flies that are easily visible on the water, so for this reason most of my home-tied mayflies are tied parachute-style with a white calf-tail or polypropylene post. A selection of the following should be carried in sizes 12–18: Parachute Adams, Red Spinner, Dad's Favourite, Twilight Beauty, Blue Dun and Kakahi Queen.

Midges

These tiny flies had never been an important part of my armoury in the back country until I recently found brown trout in a Canterbury high country lake feeding exclusively on midges. Only by using scissors on size 18 Adams dry flies could we tempt these fish with our improvised imitations. Midges are prolific on swampy lakes, slow-flowing rivers and spring creeks.

Nymphs Midge Pupa and Serendipidity.

Adults Griffiths Gnat.

Stoneflies

Both green and brown stonefly nymphs should be carried for those rock and stone (freestone) type back country rivers. The Perla nymph is also an excellent stonefly imitation. They should be heavily weighted.

Damsel and dragon fly nymphs

Specific patterns are available but weighted brown and olive Woolly Buggers usually do the trick. These could also be used for night fishing at stream mouths.

Corixa (water boatman)

Specific pattern.

Terrestrials

Manuka beetle Coch-y-bondhu, Royal Wulff or a closed-cell foam imitation.

Brown beetle Deer hair imitation.

Cicada and grasshopper Deer hair imitation, Stimulator, Hopper patterns.

Snail Black and Peacock.

Mouse Deer hair imitation.

Blowfly Black Gnat, Love's Lure or Humpy with an iridescent blue body.

Willow Grub Yellow tying thread on a size 18 or 20 hook.

Cricket Specific copy tied with dyed black deer hair or a black-bodied Stimulator.

Worms San Juan Worm.

Fish

Smelt, inanga or whitebait Any smelt pattern such as Grey Ghost or Dorothy.
Salmon eggs Glow Bug or Muppet.
Bullies Monsom's Bully, Mrs Simpson, Hamill's Killer.

Attractor patterns

These flies do not specifically represent any insect, but they do represent food to trout and can be very successful as a searching pattern. It always pays to have a few Humpies, Stimulators, Irresistibles and Royal Wulffs in your fly box.

Do not be intimidated by this daunting list of patterns. A visiting angler could probably do very well with a few weighted Hare and Copper and Pheasant Tail nymphs in different sizes, and a few Parachute Adams and Royal Wulff dry flies.

Spin-fishing gear

Spin fishing is a great way to start fishing. It is easy to learn and the gear is less expensive than the fly fisher's. There are many waters more suitable for spin fishing than fly fishing, and the catch rate will be correspondingly greater. This is especially true on the lower reaches of most rivers, where the water is large and heavy.

Rods

There are various lengths and weights of rods available in most sports shops. A fibreglass rod 1.7–2 m long is recommended. It is an advantage to be able to collapse the rod down so it can fit into a pack. Some telescopic varieties fold to less than 50 cm.

Reels

The old bait-casting reels controlled by the thumb have been replaced by the fixed-spool reel. These can be either open or closed face. The closed face reel is ideal for beginners but the casting distance is less than with the open faced variety. The open faced reel has a far greater line capacity and snarl-ups are easier to deal with. To achieve maximum casting and retrieving capability, the drum should be filled to capacity with line

Line
Monofilament line weights can vary, depending on conditions, from 1.5 kg to 4.5 kg. An average weight line is 3 kg.

Spinners
There are many varieties on the market and these change from time to time. A selection from Toby, Cobra, Hexagon Wobblers, Panther, Tasmanian Devil, Flatfish, Billy Hill, Rapala and Zed in different colours and weights is desirable. The smaller Veltic and Mepps spinners are useful in low water summer conditions.

It is important to vary the speed of the retrieve as some fish will follow right into shore and actually pick up the spinner at the angler's feet when all motion has ceased. Anglers using spinning gear should be aware of the regulations pertaining to stream mouths and other fly-fishing-only waters.

Boat-fishing gear

Full safety equipment is essential when boat fishing. The larger lakes, such as Benmore, Wakatipu, Wanaka, Hawea and Te Anau, can become very rough and treacherous even for sizeable craft. The same safety equipment as for offshore saltwater fishing should be taken on these lakes. This should include an auxiliary outboard, oars, flares, life-jackets, tool-kit, anchor and warp, and a bailer. A radio or cellphone can be very useful.

Fishing equipment can include boat rods, fly rods, reels and lines, flies and spinners, landing net, fish box and knife. Don't forget sunscreen as the burn time is less over water. If an auxiliary outboard is not used for trolling, boat speed can be reduced by towing a bucket or sack. Trout tend to inhabit areas close to the thermocline, the junction between cold and warm water.

When using a lead line, remember every 10 m (one colour) will sink 1–2 m. If fishing in 3–5 m of water, use only 20–30 m of lead line. At the end of the lead line, attach 6–7 m of 6.5 kg nylon and then a 4–5 kg trace 3 m long. This will enable fish to fight better and if the line should snag the lead line will not be lost. If using monofilament line, a colour or two of lead line can be used to help it sink.

When harling, use a fast-sinking fly line and let it all out, including 20 m of backing. Jigging will attract fish in some areas and can be fun.

A selection of flies recommended for harling or trolling includes Rabbit patterns, Green Orbit, Parson's Glory, Red Setter, Yellow Dorothy, Grey Ghost and Ginger Mick in sizes 2–4.

Useful spinners include varieties of Cobra, Tasmanian Devil, Panther Martin, Toby, Flatfish and Zed. The selection may change from time to time so I recommend visiting the local sports store to find out what the hot lure is.

It is wise to check your licence for regulation details as these vary for each lake fished. Remember to keep 300 m from any stream mouth, although there are a few exceptions to this regulation. The same rule applies to float tubes and 'kick boats'.

conservation and etiquette

New Zealand anglers are indeed privileged. We have some of the highest quality angling for wild trout anywhere in the world. Increasing numbers of overseas anglers are visiting New Zealand because the clear water in our rivers and lakes allows sight fishing for large trout. However, there is no room for complacency. In the past, the killing of large numbers of fish was of major concern. Now it is the angling pressure on certain streams, especially in the high country, and the degradation of our low country waterways from farming methods that threaten the fishery. Catch and release is a vitally important conservation measure, especially on rivers and lakes that are self sustaining. I have no objection to anglers taking an occasional trout when tramping remote rivers, but don't kill fish weighing over 4 kg as their removal depletes the gene pool. It is easy to weigh, measure and photograph trophy fish but please return them unharmed to the river.

Briefly, this involves the following:

- The use of the strongest practical tippet to facilitate the quick landing of fish. Long playing leads to the build-up of metabolites such as lactic acid, which kills fish even after they appear to swim away unscathed.
- Care in handling fish. Use a wide-mouthed net to minimise handling or release the fish while still in the water. Wet the hands first, avoid the gill area, do not squeeze the stomach and take care not to rub off scales. Turning the fish upside down will often prevent it struggling. An old nylon stocking used as a glove can be useful for gripping a slippery fish.
- The use of artery forceps or thin-jawed pliers for removing hooks. If the hook is difficult to remove, cut the tippet and release the fish. The hook will work itself out in a few days. If the fish bleeds its chances of survival are considerably reduced.
- The use of barbless hooks. These may be difficult to obtain but

ordinary hooks can easily be adapted by carefully crimping the barb with pliers.

- Keep the fish out of the water for the shortest time possible. Wait until the photographer has everything ready. Try not to drop the fish!
- Hold the fish in the water, pointing upstream if in a river, until it is ready to swim away. If it turns over on its side, repeat the procedure.

Anglers can assist fish and game councils and the Department of Conservation by weighing and measuring all trout taken and supplying details from their diaries at the end of each season. This is especially important for fish that have been marked or tagged. Some landing nets now have scales built into the handle to minimise the handling of fish. Tags should be returned, along with the measurements, to fish and game councils. Metal or plastic tags are usually attached to the dorsal fin. Fish can also be marked by fin clipping or even fin removal. To determine the right side of the fish from the left, look down on the fish's back with the head facing away from you. Always measure the length of the fish from the fork of the tail to the tip of the snout. Send details of species, weight, length, and time and area of capture. Angler cooperation is vital in managing a fishery.

In my opinion more back country areas, such as the beautiful Tasman Wilderness Area in the Kahurangi National Park, should be set aside as wilderness zones where helicopters are prohibited. Anglers keen and fit enough to seek out trophy fish would then face a real challenge. Wealthy overseas anglers can easily afford a helicopter, and there are very few remote rivers that have not been visited by a guide and his or her clients. The pressure on some rivers is now so great that the quality of fishing must surely be reduced. It is known that brown trout take at least one day to recover from being spooked but up to three days if caught and released. When the angling pressure is non-stop, fish have hardly any time to recover and resume feeding. Their feeding habits also become super selective and they may feed only at night. It is very discouraging to watch a helicopter land upstream from where you are fishing after you have spent three hard days tramping to reach a remote river.

A number of low country streams and rivers have seriously deteriorated in recent years either as a result of drought, water draw-off for irrigation or stock breaking down banks and polluting the water. There seems to be very little control of water extraction from the aquifers by regional councils. These aquifers supply the spring creeks and smaller rivers of the Canterbury Plains and North Otago. Traditionally these areas have been dry farms, but with the conversion to dairying, irrigation has become essential. Streams and rivers such as the Irwell, Selwyn, Harts Creek, Orari, Ohapi, Waihi, Hae Hae Te Moana, Pareora, Kakanui and Shag have all been seriously affected to the point where trout fishing can be marginal in summer. Harts Creek, an excellent Ellesmere fishery, has fortunately been rescued just in time by a small group of enthusiastic local anglers and conservation-minded farmers. It takes many years and many dollars to restore a stream once the weed beds have silted over, the banks broken down and the water become polluted. In New Zealand, we pride ourselves on our clean, green image. It is a sad commentary on our farming practices that almost without exception, the best fishing rivers arise from undeveloped country.

Anglers have a duty to care for the rivers, streams and lakes that provide so much pleasure and to exert political pressure in promoting the protection of these waterways. Do not hesitate to contact the local fish and game council when problems are found.

Anglers must extend courtesy to landowners. Please ask permission before crossing private land, leave gates as you find them, avoid disturbing stock, and offer thanks on the way out. Some farmers now charge for access across their land, and considering the increase in angling pressure on some rivers, this is hardly surprising. However, the Queen's chain must be preserved at all costs, otherwise anglers will pay large sums of money for access and some waterways will be locked away for private use only. One only has to experience fishing in Europe and the US to appreciate that New Zealand's waterways are a priceless asset that should be preserved for future generations.

The terms true right and true left are used frequently in this book when describing rivers. Both are determined by looking downstream.

Fish and Game Council contacts

Nelson-Marlborough: 66–74 Champion Street, Stoke,
   phone (03) 544 6382.
North Canterbury: 3 Horatio Street, Christchurch 1,
   phone (03) 366 9191.
West Coast: Airport Drive, Hokitika, phone (03) 755 8546.
Central South Island: 32 Richard Pearse Drive, Temuka,
   phone (03) 615 8400.
Otago: 40 Hanover Street, Dunedin, phone (03) 477 9076.
Southland: 231 Dee Street, Invercargill, phone (03) 214 4510.

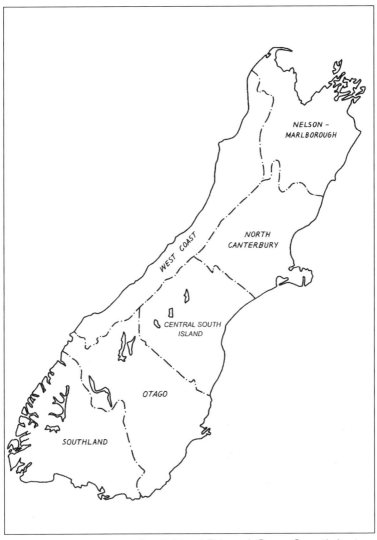

NELSON –
MARLBOROUGH

WEST COAST

NORTH
CANTERBURY

CENTRAL SOUTH
ISLAND

OTAGO

SOUTHLAND

South Island Fish and Game Council districts

Nelson-Marlborough Fish and Game Council region

This extensive region reaches from Kahurangi Point on the west coast to Springs Junction in the south and across to the Conway River mouth on the east coast. The region encompasses Golden Bay in the northwest, the Marlborough Sounds in the northeast, the Murchison district in the south, the fertile plains of Nelson, and the Blenheim wine-producing area in the Wairau River Valley. South of the Wairau Valley lies the arid, rugged, mountainous Molesworth country. Landforms and climatic variations are vastly different throughout the region, and these differences are reflected by the diversity of the rivers and streams.

From an angling perspective, there are five major river systems. In the south, the Buller River and its tributaries drain lakes Rotoroa and Rotoiti and the Nelson Lakes National Park. Across the fertile Nelson Plains and draining the Arthur Range lies the Motueka River and its tributaries. To the northeast flows the Pelorus River and its tributaries, draining the Richmond Range and the Marlborough Sounds, while the Wairau River flows from the mountainous interior of the region through Blenheim to the east coast. The southeastern boundary is delineated by the Clarence River and its numerous branches, some of which drain the remote, inaccessible Inland Kaikoura Range.

Trout and quinnat (chinook or king) salmon were first liberated in the Marlborough district in about 1876 by the Marlborough Acclimatisation Society. While trout have thrived, the salmon have not done well, although there is still a small spawning run up the Wairau and Clarence rivers in the autumn.

Unless specified, the season opens on 1 October and closes on 30 April. The bag limit is four trout of any size in most main rivers and lakes that are open all year round. In the upper reaches of most

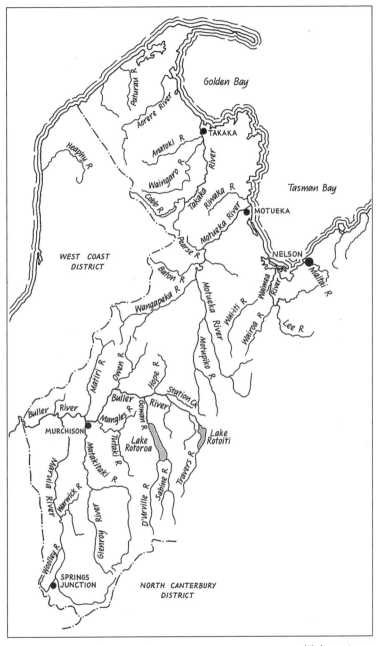

Nelson rivers

rivers, the bag limit is two trout. In the headwaters and in smaller streams, the bag limit is two trout but only one may exceed 50 cm in length.

Paturau River

Location Drains the heavily bush-clad Wakamarama Range and enters the sea at Paturau, south of Cape Farewell on the west coast.
Access Take the gravel road south from Puponga. This crosses the river near its mouth, south of Whanganui Inlet.
Season 1 October–30 April

The Paturau is a small to medium-sized shingly river that holds small numbers of brown trout. The few fish that I have seen were around the 1 kg mark, although larger sea-run fish may enter the river. The lower reaches are tidal, the middle reaches wind across partially cleared farm land, while the upper reaches are bush-clad. Fish can be spotted although the water becomes heavily tannin-stained in a fresh and takes time to clear.

There is good camping at the river mouth, but it is isolated and only worth exploring if you are visiting this scenic part of the west coast.

The Anatori River, further south at the road end, offers clear enticing-looking water but, as with the Paturau, fish numbers are low.

Aorere River

Location Drains the Tasman Mountains, Wakamarama, Gouland, Slate and Haupiri Ranges, flows northeast and enters Golden Bay at Collingwood.
Access From SH 60 to Collingwood, roads follow upriver to Rockville, Bainham and Brown Hut at the start of the Heaphy Track.
Season Above the road bridge at Rockville, 1 October–30 April. Below this bridge, the river is open for fishing all year round.
Restrictions Bag limit is two trout above the Rockville bridge and four trout below the bridge.

Jun Yamamoto and Patti Madsen discuss tactics on the upper Aorere River

This medium-sized to large river holds a good stock of brown trout averaging around 1.5 kg. Although fishing can be patchy at times, drift dives revealed 50 trout per kilometre of river at Devils Boot. The headwaters and upper reaches flow through dense native bush, while the middle and lower reaches wind across cleared farmland. There are some very deep holes and the water becomes tannin-stained after rain. Crossings can be difficult and care should be taken, but the large granite boulders provide secure footing. Rainfall is very high in the headwaters, with 3700 mm falling annually at Bainham.

Spinning accounts for most fish taken in the middle and lower reaches, but for the active bush-bashing angler the best water lies upstream from Brown Hut at the road end. In this upper section, in the Kahurangi National Park, trout can be spotted. It is best to ford the river at Brown Hut as there are cliffs a short distance upstream on the true left bank. A rough bush track runs down the true right bank, making the return trip reasonable. There are two days' fishing above Brown Hut to beyond Shakespeare Flat for the active 'boots and shorts' type angler.

Fly fishing can be rewarding in the middle reaches but it is difficult to sight fish. Better results can be obtained fishing to rising fish on warm summer evenings. The lower reaches hold sea-run and resident fish, which are best tempted by spinning.

There are a few trout in the remote, heavily peat-stained Heaphy River, but this is only of interest to trampers walking the Heaphy Track.

Cobb River

Location The Cobb River drains Lake Cobb and the Lockett and Peel ranges, flows southeast, and enters the Cobb Reservoir. This was formed when the river was dammed for hydro-electric power. Below the reservoir, the Cobb River joins the Takaka River at the Cobb powerhouse.

Access Turn off at Upper Takaka and follow up the Takaka River valley on the Cobb Dam road. This road is narrow and difficult, and great care should be taken. Beyond the Cobb powerhouse the road climbs up through native bush until a Department of Conservation information centre is reached on the top. After descending, the road follows the southeastern shore of the reservoir to Myttons carpark and the Trilobite Hut at the head of the reservoir. Basic camping is available and the Trilobite Hut can be used with a DoC permit.

Restrictions Fly fishing only is permitted upstream from the first gorge above the Cobb Reservoir. Bag limit is two fish, only one of which may exceed 50 cm in length. Catch and release is recommended for this headwater stream.

The most enjoyable fly fishing is in the river above Trilobite Hut. A trampers' track follows up the true right bank, and although it soon leaves the river it is useful to walk back on at the end of the day's fishing. The river is small, easily forded and has well-defined clear pools and runs. Both brown and rainbow trout up to 2.5 kg can be spotted, but they become spooky towards the end of summer. The river winds across tussock flats and through patches of beech bush. There is a day's fishing upstream from the carpark before the river becomes too small.

There are only a few fish in the Cobb River upstream from the Cobb powerhouse and access is very difficult.

Upper Cobb River in back country Nelson

Cobb Reservoir

Location and access See the Cobb River, previous page.
Season Open all year.
Restrictions Live bait fishing and boat fishing permitted. Bag limit is four trout.

This rather shallow hydro lake contains brown and rainbow trout averaging around 1 kg. It is best fished with a spinner, either trolling from a dinghy or threadlining from the shore. In bright conditions, cruising fish can be spotted and stalked with a fly, especially at the top end of the lake. There is often an evening rise to midges on calm summer evenings.

There are boat launching facilities, but towing a large boat over the Cobb Dam road is hazardous.

Takaka River

Location and access Drains the Arthur Range and joins the Cobb River at the powerhouse, then flows 8 km through a steep, bush-clad gorge, with the Cobb Dam road following the gorge, although sometimes well above the river. Emerging from the gorge, the river flows more placidly across farmland in a northerly direction to Takaka and enters Golden Bay north of this township. The road from Takaka to Upper Takaka (SH 60) generally follows the river, with a few side roads such as Uruwhenua Road offering good access. **Season and restrictions** Above the Waingaro confluence, 1 October –30 April; the bag limit is two fish. Below this confluence, there is an open season and the bag limit is four sportsfish.

The most exciting fishing lies in the gorge upstream from the Cobb Dam road bridge and although fish numbers are low, browns and an occasional rainbow up to 2.5 kg can be taken. There are well-defined, stable rocky pools and runs for 8 km upstream to the powerhouse and the Cobb River confluence. Both banks are bush-covered and a considerable amount of scrambling is required, but the river can be forded at the tail of most pools. Although the water is tea coloured, fish can be spotted with sunlight but it pays to fish the deeper sections blind. There is good water at Drummonds and Apple-tree flats, but the river is not worth exploring above the Cobb powerhouse.

The willow-lined middle reaches hold some good fish and access is much easier than in the top section. Pools are deep and slow flowing but fish can still be stalked during the day in bright sunlight. An evening caddis rise occurs under favourable conditions and lure fishing after dark accounts for some good fish. In summer, a willow grub imitation can be deadly.

A few sea-run browns and an occasional salmon enter the lower reaches. Spinning is the best method for enticing these fish. The river can be subject to flow fluctuations from the Cobb hydro-electric power station.

Both the promising-looking Waingaro and Anatoki tributaries, joining the true left bank of the Takaka River upstream from Takaka, hold few trout and are not highly recommended. Even the headwaters of these streams hold few fish.

Riwaka River

Location The north branch emerges from an impressive, deep, dark blue spring on the Takaka Hill south of Riwaka township. After joining up with the south branch, the main stream flows east through farmland and enters Tasman Bay just north of Motueka.
Access The scenic Riwaka River Valley road leaves SH 60 at the foot of Takaka Hill and follows up the true left bank of the main river and up both branches. It is a short scramble to the stream.
Restrictions Artificial bait and fly only. Bag limit is two trout, only one of which may be longer than 50 cm.

This small, clear, shingly stream is overhung by willows and other vegetation in some stretches but is generally a delight to fish. Drift dives near the Moss Bush picnic area have found good numbers of takeable brown trout in the 0.5–1.2 kg range. Wading is safe although the algae-covered stones are slippery. Fish are not easy to spot on the brownish riverbed, so many runs should be fished blind. In late summer willow grub is a good choice to use, but any small nymph or dry fly should entice a take.

 Motueka River and tributaries

Motueka River

Location Drains the Richmond Range to the east, the Hope and Lookout ranges to the south, and the Arthur Range to the west.

Flows generally north from Motupiko, through Ngatimoti to the Tasman Sea just north of Motueka.

Access The river is well serviced with roads on both sides of the river from the gorge and Golden Downs Forest, to its mouth near Motueka some 60 km away. SH 61 follows the river upstream on the east bank from Motueka to SH 6 at Kohatu, while on the west bank West Bank Road follows upstream from SH 60 to the Baton River confluence. Near Tapawera, the Lower Wangapeka Road follows downstream to the Wangapeka River confluence. Valley Road follows the river upstream from Kohatu through Golden Downs Forest to the gorge above Janson Bridge. Numerous angler accesses have been clearly marked on all these roads by the Nelson-Marlborough Fish and Game Council. Please ask permission before crossing private farmland.

Season Above the Ngatimoti Bridge, 1 October–30 April. Below this bridge, the river is open all year.

Restrictions Bag limit above the Wangapeka confluence is two trout, only one of which may exceed 50 cm. Below this confluence, the limit is four trout.

Despite being very popular and heavily fished, this moderate-sized river, only an hour's drive from Nelson, holds an abundance of brown trout averaging around 1 kg, with fish up to 3 kg occasionally taken. Although fish stocks may vary from season to season, 275 trout per kilometre of river have been counted at Woodstock. Both resident and sea-run trout are present, with the larger fish favouring the river upstream from the Wangapeka confluence. The lower and middle reaches offer long glides and riffles flowing over a gravel bed. There are some deep holes and rocky shelves, especially under the willows, which provide excellent stable trout habitat. Many of the larger fish wait until evening before emerging from these sheltered depths to feed. The river can flood but the water is normally sufficiently clear to enable some daytime sight fishing. However, many riffles and runs should be fished blind, such is the extent of the fish population. Wading is safe and crossings can be made in selected spots in the middle and upper reaches. On bright, sunny days fishing can be very testing, although small, well-presented dry flies and nymph imitations of both mayflies and caddis on a long fine tippet should prove successful. A willow grub imitation can be very useful later in summer. In the evening, caddis (sedge) fishing can be very exciting with a soft-hackled wet fly fished across and down on a floating line. Use a stronger tippet at night, as some of the takes can be fierce. This type of fishing is great for a beginner as rewards are easier to obtain than during the day.

The spin angler should try a small Veltic, a gold or silver Toby or a Meps, and fish the deeper runs beneath the willows. Spinning is best after a fresh and becomes more difficult in low water summer conditions.

Motupiko River

Location Rises near Tophouse, drains the St Arnaud Range and flows north to join the Motueka River at Kohatu.
Access SH 6 follows this river upstream from Kohatu, but a short walk across private farmland is sometimes necessary to reach the river. There is public access at Quinneys Bush Reserve, Long Gully (4 km from Kohatu off SH 6), Korere bridge and the Rainy River road bridge.
Restrictions Artificial bait and fly only. Bag limit is two trout, only one of which may be longer than 50 cm.

This is a spawning tributary of the Motueka River. It is similar in character to the parent river but much smaller. Best fished early in the season before fish drop back, as water flows reduce in long hot summers. In the 1998 drought, the river virtually ran dry. The first 5 km above the confluence hold the most fish, and these can be sighted and stalked. As the season progresses the fish become very spooky, and when frightened they bolt for the deeper runs against the cliffs. Stocks are not high, and catch and release is recommended.

Wangapeka River

Location Drains the Marino Mountains and Lookout Range of the Kahurangi National Park, flows generally northeast and enters the Motueka River 7 km downstream from Tapawera.

Access The lower reaches can be accessed by taking the Lower Wangapeka Road from Tapawera, which follows down the true left bank of the Motueka River to the confluence. From this confluence, the road turns south and follows up the Wangapeka River, eventually crossing it at Cylinder Bridge. There are many anglers' accesses off this road until the road ends. The middle and upper reaches are accessed from the Upper Wangapeka Road, where there are a number of marked anglers' access signs. It is possible to drive to Rolling River by four-wheel-drive, but this is all private farmland and permission must be obtained. The Kahurangi National Park begins above Rolling River and tramper-anglers can continue exploring upstream for many miles from the Wangapeka Track.

Restrictions Bag limit is two fish, only one of which may exceed 50 cm.

This is a popular small to medium-sized rock and stone type river whose headwaters lie in stable, bush-covered hills. The trout numbers are not high in the headwaters but the quality of the angling experience more than compensates for this. Fish up to 2.5 kg have been landed, and as the water is very clear, sight fishing is the preferred method.

The middle and lower reaches, which hold a greater fish population, flow through cleared farmland and bracken-covered hills. Most fish can be spotted and stalked in bright, sunny conditions. The banks are stable and there is a succession of pools and runs. However, the river discolours readily in a fresh. Best early in the season before resident fish become too wary or recovered spawners drop back downstream to the parent river.

Baton River

Location Drains the Arthur Range and flows northeast before joining the west bank of the Motueka River south of Woodstock.

Access Cross the Motueka River at Baton Bridge and turn south onto the Baton Valley road, which follows up the true left bank. There are great picnic spots in this valley but ask permission before crossing private farmland.

Restrictions Bag limit is two fish, only one of which may exceed 50 cm.

This delightful small stream with a rock and stone riverbed rises from rugged hills covered with native bush. The water quality is good, making sight fishing reasonably easy, but the fish become spooky as the season progresses and some drop back downstream when the river warms in summer. The removal of a concrete ford in 1999 should improve fish stocks. Best early in the season.

Pearse River

Location Drains the Arthur Range near Flora Saddle, flows south-east to enter the west bank of the Motueka River north of Woodstock.
Access Turn north after crossing the Motueka River at Baton Bridge and follow West Bank Road until it crosses the lower Pearse near its confluence with the Motueka. Pearse Valley Road follows upstream on the true left bank.
Restrictions Bag limit is two fish, only one of which may exceed 50 cm.

This is another small, clear spawning tributary where sight fishing can be very rewarding, especially early in the season. Tends to dry in long, hot summers.

Other Motueka tributaries holding a few fish, especially early in the season, include the Dove River at Woodstock and the Tadmor River near Tapawera.

Waimea River

Location The Wairoa and Wai-iti tributaries drain the Gordon Range south of Wakefield and join to form the Waimea River near Brightwater.
Access SH 60 crosses the lower tidal reaches near Appleby and gives access to a camping reserve, while SH 6 crosses at Brightwater some 7 km upstream. Blackbyre Road follows the

river's east bank from SH 60 to SH 6. Clover and Haycocks roads lead to Max's Bush picnic reserve in the upper reaches.

Season Both the Waimea River and its largest tributary the Wairoa River are open all year below the Lee River confluence. Above this confluence, 1 October–30 April.

Restrictions Bag limit is four fish.

The most enjoyable fly fishing water lies between SH 6 bridge and the weir at Max's Bush. Here the water is clear and the river quite boisterous in parts.

The middle reaches are slower flowing, with long willow-lined glides and shallow, shingly runs. Despite the riverbed being rather unstable, there are reasonable numbers of brown trout in the 0.5–0.75 kg range. Fish are difficult to spot.

The lower reaches are tidal but the occasional sea-run brown can be caught on spinning gear or a dark streamer fly fished through the deeper glides at night.

Both the Wairoa and Lee tributaries hold a few fish, especially early in the season. Roads follow up both tributaries from Brightwater.

The Maitai River, which drains the Bryant Range and flows west through Nelson city, holds small brown trout and is great for junior anglers. Exotic forestry activity in the headwaters has had a detrimental effect on the river. The Maitai Valley Road provides good access to the middle and upper reaches. It is open all year only below the Lower Nile Street Bridge.

The Wakapuaka River (Happy Valley), which is crossed by SH 6 at Hira on the Nelson side of the Whangamoa Saddle, also holds small trout and is quite heavily fished by local anglers. Access from Cable Bay road.

The Whangamoa River, on the eastern side of the Whangamoa Saddle in the same area, also holds small brown trout but is overgrown and hard to fish.

Pelorus River

Location Drains the Richmond and Bryant ranges to its main tributary, the Rai. Flows north from the Mt Richmond State Forest Park, then east through Canvastown and enters Pelorus Sound near Havelock.

Access *Upper reaches* Take Mangatapu Road, which leaves SH 6 near Pelorus Bridge and follows upstream for 14 km to a carpark at Larges Clearing. There are a number of access points off this road. From the carpark, a DoC track leads into the Mt Richmond State Forest Park. Captains Hut is a four-hour tramp from the carpark, and Midday Hut a six-hour tramp. There is little fishing beyond this point.

Middle and lower reaches SH 6 follows the river upstream from Havelock to Pelorus Bridge. There are numerous marked anglers' access points. At Daltons Bridge, Kaiuma Road leads downstream on the north bank. If in doubt, always check for permission at local farms.

Season and restrictions Above the Rai confluence, 1 October–30 April. Only two fish may be taken, with only one exceeding 50 cm. Below the Rai confluence, there is an open season with a bag limit of four fish.

The headwaters of the Pelorus River in the Mt Richmond Park hold only a few good-sized browns, which are easy to spot in this small rock and stone type wilderness river.

Fish numbers are much greater below the Rai confluence where the river swells, changes character and becomes quite large. There are long glides, deep runs beneath willows and shallow, shingly riffles. Good stocks of trout are present, with 70 percent of these being browns and 30 percent rainbow. Fish average from 0.75 to 1.5 kg, although an occasional trout weighing over 3 kg is landed. The river is safe to wade and even at night crossings can be made without too much trouble. An active evening rise is common in summer. During the day small caddis and mayfly nymphs and dries will take fish; at night try a soft hackle wet fly or a deer hair sedge fished across and downstream.

Surprisingly, the lower tidal reaches a few kilometres below Canvastown hold some large fish, but these are best tempted with a spinner. However, there are also many small rainbows in this stretch of water.

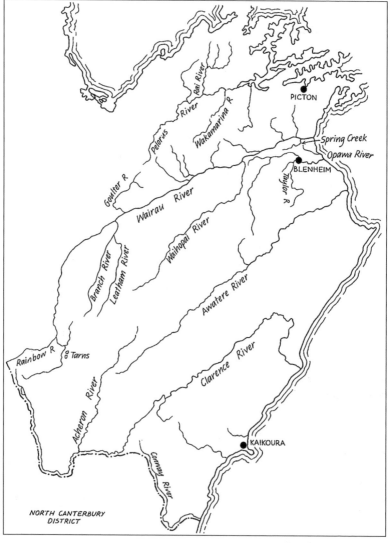

Marlborough rivers

Other smaller tributaries of the Pelorus that hold a few fish, especially early in the season, include the Tinline River upstream from Pelorus Bridge and the Wakamarina River at Canvastown.

Rai River

Location Along with its three feeder streams, the Rai River drains the Marlborough Sounds catchment and enters the Pelorus River at Pelorus Bridge.

Access SH 75 runs parallel to the river in the Rai Valley for 10 km above the falls, and this road and its branches offer easy access to the river. There is anglers' access at Rai Falls, Bulford Bridge, Raidale Farm Road, Ford Stream Bridge, Brown Stream Reserve, Opouri Valley Bridge, Tunakino Valley Bridge and Opouri Valley Road.

Restrictions Bag limit is four fish, but in the Ronga, Opouri and Tunakino feeder streams the bag limit is two trout, only one of which may exceed 50 cm.

This medium-sized tributary of the Pelorus holds good stocks of rainbow and brown trout (200 fish/km of river above the falls). The stream flows across farmland, and in bright conditions fish can be sighted and stalked. It is a challenging stream to fish because of long, clear, slow-flowing glides and bank obstructions of trees and scrub. Trout spook easily and scatter in all directions after a clumsy cast. Wading is generally unnecessary although the river can be readily forded at selected sites. The riverbed is gravel and mud. It discolours readily after rain, and the water becomes tea coloured from the bush lining the feeder streams.

The Ronga and Opouri streams also offer interesting fly fishing, especially early in the season, although willow infestation is a problem on some stretches. All three tributaries form the main river at Carluke. Permission is required to cross private land. In long, hot summers, low water flows and dairy effluent can result in eutrophication. Fish tend to drop back to the main river in these conditions.

Both the Alfred and Brown stream tributaries in Rai Valley hold a few trout in the lower reaches early in the season.

Wairau River

Location From its source in the Raglan, Spencer and St Arnaud ranges, the large Wairau River flows northeast for 150 km down the Wairau Valley before discharging into Cloudy Bay near Blenheim.

Access

Headwaters

- From the south on the Hanmer Springs hydro road.
- From the north on Rainbow Station Road, which links with the hydro road. Permission and a key must be obtained from Rainbow Station if you intend fishing beyond Six Mile Creek, as there is a locked gate (phone (03) 5211 838).

Pristine waters for sight fishing in the upper Wairau River

- The Rainbow Skifield Road, which joins the Rainbow Station Road, also offers access as far as Six Mile Creek. This road is only open to the public from December to February. A four-wheel-drive vehicle is an advantage on this road as it can be rough in parts after winter snows and there are fords to be crossed.

Upper and middle reaches There are numerous marked anglers' access points off SH 63, and off North Bank Road running up the true left bank from the Renwick Bridge on SH 6. This section of river is generally easy to access.

Lower reaches Roads run down both banks of the river between the SH 1 bridge and the Renwick bridge on SH 6. There are many marked anglers' access points, which make reaching the river relatively simple, especially from the ends of short side roads. Downstream from the SH 1 bridge the river splits into the diversion and the main channel. Both are easy to access from roads running down their north banks from SH 1.

Season Above Wash Bridge on SH 63, 1 October–30 April. Below this bridge and including the diversion, the river is open to angling all year.

Restrictions Above Wash Bridge, the bag limit is two trout, only one of which may exceed 50 cm. Artificial bait and fly only. Below the bridge, the bag limit is four sportsfish of which only two may be salmon. It is illegal to fish for salmon above Wash Bridge.

The Wairau River offers a variety of angling. In the headwaters, the river is a boisterous, clear, rock and stone type river suitable for sight fly fishing in summer. There is excellent water for 15 km above the locked gate at Six Mile Creek. Trout cannot always be spotted, so do not walk past likely looking water without throwing the odd cast. There are some deep slots where fish can hide. Stocks are not high but brown trout over 4.5 kg are not uncommon in these parts.

In the upper reaches downstream from Six Mile Creek, there is some delightful water almost as far down as Wash Bridge. The river is quite large and crossings should be undertaken with care. In high summer fly fishing to large sighted browns can be very exciting in some of the bouldery runs, but fishing pressure has increased over the past few years and previously unsophisticated trout now become more wary as the season progresses. There are plenty of sheltered campsites but take sandfly repellent. Native beech bush and mountains create a splendid scenic backdrop to this upper section of the valley.

The middle reaches downstream from Wash Bridge become braided and rather unstable. The riverbed is very wide, shingly and spread out but there is some good holding water, generally where the river runs against the bank or under willows. As the braids change from year to year, some early season exploration is required to find this likely looking water. Once the river clears from snowmelt, the water quality and clarity is excellent. Although most fish are caught on spinners in this section, there is some worthwhile fly fishing.

In the lower reaches below Renwick the braids coalesce into a single channel, but the water is deep and heavy. Spinning accounts for most fish, although night lure fishing can be productive both in the river itself and in the diversion. Early in the season, a whitebait lure fished across and down on a sinking line can be effective.

This large river holds both resident and sea-run browns, with a small run of quinnat salmon appearing in February and March. Some large browns are landed in the lower reaches and salmon up to 8 kg have been caught.

Rainbow River

Location Drains the southern end of the St Arnaud Range, flows northeast and enters the west bank of the upper reaches of the Wairau River.

Access As for the Wairau River headwaters. A four-wheel-drive vehicle may be used to follow up the shingly Rainbow River bed, but as this area is isolated, getting bogged would really present problems including a very long walk for help. The Rainbow Station landowners would not be pleased!

Restrictions Bag limit of two fish, with only one trout exceeding 50 cm.

This is the main headwater tributary, and it is rather unstable and prone to flooding. The lower reaches just upstream from the confluence tend to hold the most fish. Further upstream it is a long walk between good stable holding water, but the effort can be worthwhile early in the season when a few large browns are present.

Begley Creek some 10 km up the valley may also hold the odd fish, but the side creeks are spawning streams for the Wairau River and catch and release should be practised. Fish drop back downstream in low water, summer conditions.

Goulter River

Location Drains Lake Chalice and the Richmond Range, flows south and then east to join the true left bank of the Wairau River opposite the Branch hydro-electric station.
Access Take North Bank Road from the Renwick Bridge on SH 6. It is 50 km to Patriarch Station and another 12 km on a rough four-wheel-drive track to the carpark above the Goulter River at the end of the road. If it rains heavily, I suggest getting out quickly before a nasty side creek becomes impassable. It is possible to access the Goulter from the Branch Hydro Road after wading across the large Wairau River, but this guarantees a very long walk home!
Restrictions Bag limit of two fish, with only one trout exceeding 50 cm.

If you are prepared to walk, excellent sight fishing for good-sized brown trout can be obtained from this scenic, bush-lined river. It is a small to medium-sized, stable, rock and stone, clear water river with well-developed deep pools. Fish are easy to spot and river crossings are generally simple. Unfortunately this river has been subjected to heavy angling pressure over recent years, with guides even flying their clients in by helicopter to the upper reaches. Trout become extremely wary as the season progresses and long, fine tippets, small flies and accurate casts are essential if one is to hook a fish. There is a good population of resident trout and at times a few sea-run browns up to 4 kg in weight. The best fishing can be obtained above Crozier Stream. A cut track follows upstream on the true left bank, and it is two and a half hours' walk to the Mid Goulter Hut. There are a few fish beyond this hut. The track makes returning at day's end easier, although some anglers may prefer to take a 'short cut' via the riverbed.

Lake Chalice holds native fish only.

Branch River and its tributary, the Leatham

Location The headwaters of these two rivers drain the Raglan Range and saddle, with the Severn River headwaters in the Molesworth country to the south. Both flow north to join the Wairau near the Branch hydro-electric station, some 70 km up the Wairau Valley on SH 63 from Blenheim.

Access SH 63 crosses both the lower Branch River and the diverted water outlet from Argyle Pond. Roads run up both the canal and the lower Branch. Permission is required from the Department of Conservation in Blenheim (phone (03) 572 9100) to fish the upper Branch. Permission to fish the upper Leatham can be obtained from Leatham Station.

Both these rather unstable high country rivers drain barren tussock country, although the Leatham has some patches of native bush in its headwaters. Fish numbers are low, with a lot of walking required between fish. Recently, the Branch has not been worth the effort. However, the lower reaches of the Branch are worth a look early in the season before low water summer flows mark the return of fish to the main river.

Argyle Pond and hydro canals

Location and access This small hydro lake, formed by diverting water from the Branch River, is easily accessed from a side road, the Branch Hydro Canal Road, off SH 63 as described above.

Season and restrictions There is an open season on this small lake and the canals; the bag limit is two trout.

The pond has been stocked with both rainbow and brown trout, which average between 1 and 2 kg. Although the aesthetics are not the best, reasonable fish can be caught around the edges by all legal methods.

Waihopai River

Location Saddles with the Acheron River, flows generally north and enters the Wairau River just west of Renwick.
Access SH 63 west of Renwick crosses the lower reaches. Condors Forest Road follows down the east bank to its Wairau confluence. This is a walking track only. The Waihopai Valley Road leaves SH 63 just west of Renwick.

This small stream holds only a few fish but it can be worth exploring early in the season before trout drift back downstream to the Wairau.

Spring Creek

Location Rises from springs northwest of Blenheim near Rapaura, flows northeast, and enters the Wairau just north of SH 1 near the township of Spring Creek.
Access This is difficult as the creek flows through private residential property and farmland. However, east of SH 1, Stop Bank Road leads to a reserve and one can walk to the mouth. SH 1 crosses upstream from the mouth, and access is also available from O'Dwyers and Rapaura roads west of Spring Creek township. Please ask permission from landowners before fishing.
Restrictions Artificial bait and fly only; bag limit is two fish, only one of which may exceed 50 cm in length.

This narrow, deep, clear, weedy spring creek is a favourite with some anglers. Good-sized brown trout offer a real challenge. Although there are 25 large browns per kilometre of river, they are hard to catch, often hiding beneath banks of weed and only emerging in late evening to feed. Weed and snags also tip the odds in favour of the fish so a landing net is very useful. The creek has grassy and willow-lined banks and generally remains clear after rain.
 During the day cast small, weighted nymphs on a long, fine

tippet, or small mayfly and caddis dry flies to sighted fish. For serious anglers, a black lure swung deep through some of the holes in late evening can be effective provided you explore the terrain before nightfall. Trout over 4 kg have been landed.

Opawa River

Location and access Rises in the vicinity of Renwick, flows east through the outskirts of Blenheim before joining the Wairau River near its mouth. SH 1 crosses the river north of Blenheim, while Thomsons Ford and Hammerichs roads lead to the river further upstream.
Season Open all year below SH 1. Upstream from SH 1, 1 October–30 April.
Restrictions Bag limit is two fish.

This is also a weedy spring creek, where browns can be stalked between weed beds. Although popular with local junior anglers, there is some challenging fly fishing for those anglers prepared to fish in the suburbs.

A tributary of the Opawa River, Taylor River, rising south of Blenheim, also offers junior anglers some reasonable fishing close to Blenheim. It is open all year below the New Renwick Road bridge.

Other smaller tributaries of the Wairau River that hold a few fish, especially early in the season, include the Onamalutu River, Bartletts Creek and Top Valley Stream, which are all accessed from North Bank Road and enter the true left bank of the Wairau.

Awatere River

Location and access Drains the Inland Kaikoura Range, flows generally northeast to reach the sea near Seddon. The Awatere Valley Road follows upstream on the north bank from the notorious road/rail bridge on SH 1.
Season Open all year.

This unstable, flood-prone, snow-fed river looks most uninviting to fish. It rarely runs clear except in midsummer and rapidly discolours with rain. However, a scattering of very resilient brown trout inhabit some of the deeper, more stable pools, especially in the headwaters. It is generally best suited to spin fishing.

The Tarns at Tarndale

Location These tarns lie east of the Wairau River headwaters on Tarndale Station, an outstation of Molesworth.

Access From the south on the Hanmer hydro road, or from the north on the Rainbow Station Road (see access to the Wairau headwaters). A four-wheel-drive vehicle is an advantage on this road but there is no vehicle access to the tarns as a locked gate leading to a hut blocks progress. Sedgemere Lake is only five minutes' walk from the end of the vehicle track; Island Lake, Fish Lake and Bowscale Tarn are each about a 50-minute walk. One could fish Sedgemere, Fish and Bowscale in one day of solid walking.

Restrictions Bag limit is two trout.

Most of these tarns, which lie in exposed, swampy, tussock country, hold brown trout averaging 1–2 kg. In bright, sunny conditions trout can be spotted round the lake edges and stalked with a dry fly or nymph. However, in windy, overcast conditions this type of fishing becomes impossible and blind lure fishing or spinning is the best option.

Sedgemere Lake covers 1 ha but the northern shore is rush-infested and hence impossible to fish, while the other shores are swampy.

Bowscale Tarn covers 2 ha and the hill on the northern side of the lake makes spotting easier. However, you can be spotted by trout when perched up on the side of the hill! There is good shoreline access right round Bowscale, and a sheltered spot to eat lunch in the pines at the western end.

Island Lake covers 1.5 ha and is very shallow, but good sport can be obtained when fish are rising to caddis or midge pupae, or chasing bullies. Trout tend to be small in this lake. The lake outlet drains into the Alma River.

Fish Lake holds a few larger fish, which seem to feed around banks of weed just out of casting range.

Although these lakes are very exposed, the scenery is magnificent and on a warm summer's day the experience can be memorable.

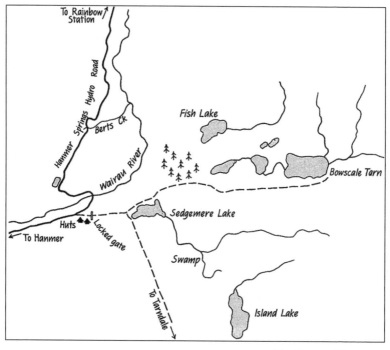

The Tarns of Tarndale

Nelson Lakes National Park

The park covers 100,470 ha of rugged mountains and unspoilt native bush, and contains two major lakes and a number of ex-citing rivers. There are sufficient snowfalls in winter to provide skiing on Mt Robert, but summer temperatures warm the lakes for swimming and water sports.

Visitors to the park should first visit the park headquarters at

St Arnaud for maps, hut permits and general information. There are motel and camping facilities at both lakes, and a trout fishing lodge at Lake Rotoroa. Insect repellent for sandflies is strongly recommended.

Lake Rotoiti

Location and access From Nelson, turn off SH 6 at Kawatiri Junction onto SH 63. It is 25 km to the lake, which can also be reached from the Wairau Valley and Tophouse.
Season Open for fishing all year round.
Restrictions Bag limit is four trout. Trolling is prohibited within 100 m of all stream inlets and outlets. Downriggers are legal.
Boat launching facilities At St Arnaud on the northern shore.

This scenic mountain lake is fed by melting snow water from the Travers River at the head of the lake and drained by the Buller River at the outlet. The lake, which is surrounded by bush, covers 1100 ha, is 9 km long and lies at an altitude of 600 m. It contains brown trout averaging around 1–1.5 kg and, apart from selected spots, is best fished from a boat. Methods include harling a streamer fly on a floating or sinking line, trolling a spinner or even using a downrigger. Popular streamer patterns include Yellow Dorothy, Parsons' Glory, Rabbit patterns, Mrs Simpson and Muddler Minnow. Popular spinners are Toby and Cobra varieties. Fly casting is generally restricted to a boat, except at the mouth of the Travers River and at the outlet. The odd cruising fish can be spotted under the beech trees and these will be receptive to a Coch-y-bondhu providing you can make the cast. In the evening there is often a vigorous caddis rise at the outlet, so try a soft hackle wet fly on a floating line.

Travers River

Location and access Drains Mt Travers (2338 m) and surrounding peaks, and flows in a northerly direction down a very scenic valley to enter the head or southern end of Lake Rotoiti. There are well-marked tramping tracks through the bush round both sides of the

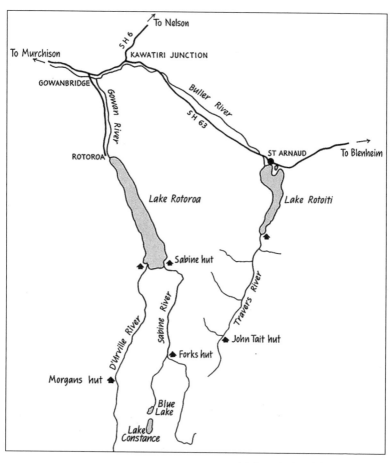

Nelson Lakes National Park

lake, but the journey may take three to four hours. This time can be considerably shortened by hiring a water taxi to the Lakehead or Coldwater huts at the head of the lake.

Restrictions Artificial bait or fly only; bag limit is two trout, only one of which may exceed 50 cm in length.

This valley is worth visiting for the scenery alone, as the river winds across wide tussock flats edged with beech bush and over-looked by towering mountains. The river has a reasonably stable shingle bed and holds browns averaging 1.2 kg. These can be spotted and stalked in very clear, blue water all the way up the valley as far as the John Tait Hut. They become more and more spooky as the season progresses, and accurate casting, careful stalking and a drag-free presentation is required. The valley is also popular with trampers.

Try Coch-y-bondhu, Royal Wulff, Humpy, Irresistible and Black Gnat dry flies, and Hare and Copper, Half Back and Stonefly nymphs. If the trout are very spooky and no one is fishing ahead of you, drop the fly size down or increase the length of your tippet. Although this river is restocked from the lake, catch and release is recommended. On a calm, warm, sunny summer's day when the trout are feeding, the Travers is a river to dream about — especially in the middle of winter!

Lake Rotoroa

Location and access Turn off SH 6 at Gowan Bridge, 5 km south of Kawatiri Junction. It is 10 km to the lake.
Season Open all year.
Restrictions Bag limit is four trout. Trolling is not permitted within 100 m of stream inlets or outlets.

At 20 km long and 2 km wide, this lake is both longer and larger than Lake Rotoiti. Surrounded by virgin native bush and mountain ranges, it is also very scenic. At the top or southern end, the Sabine and D'Urville rivers enter, while the outlet marks the beginning of the Gowan River, a major tributary of the Buller. There is a motel, a fishing lodge, a camping ground and a ranger station where information can be obtained about the lake and its environment. The sandflies are vicious, so take insect repellent.

As with Lake Rotoiti, fishing is best from a boat, either harling or trolling, but this lake also contains a few rainbow trout. Casting under the overhanging beech trees with a green beetle imitation can be fun at times. Trout average 1.3 kg. For the shoreline angler, the hot spots are the Sabine and D'Urville deltas and the outlet. The latter is best fished late in the evening when trout feed on caddis.

There is a marked track to the lake head along the eastern

shore, but as this takes six hours most anglers visiting this region take the water taxi.

Sabine River

Location Drains the Spencer Mountains, Lake Constance (via an underground stream) and the Blue Lake, flows northwest and enters Lake Rotoroa east of the D'Urville mouth.
Access By water taxi to the head of the lake, or a six-hour tramp round the lake shore. A marked track follows upriver on the true left bank; it is a four- to five-hour tramp to the Sabine Forks Hut. Permits and permission to use the Parks Board huts should be obtained from the ranger station.
Restrictions Artificial bait and fly only; bag limit two fish, only one of which may exceed 50 cm in length.

This clear, rock and stone, wilderness type river holds brown and rainbow trout with an occasional fish up to 3 kg. There are fish right up to the Sabine Forks, but few upstream above that point. Sight fishing is possible on some sections but do not neglect fishing some of the faster, deeper runs where fish are hard to spot. The lower, unfishable gorge usually holds some large fish that are well accustomed to tantalising anglers. The river clears rapidly after rain.

Lake Constance and the Blue Lake are worth visiting for the scenery, but don't take a trout rod as they are barren of fish.

D'Urville River

Location and access The D'Urville mouth can be reached by following the lake shore round from the wharf at Sabine Hut. A marked trampers' track follows upriver.
Restrictions Same as for the Sabine River.

The D'Urville flows down an attractive bush-covered valley parallel to but west of the Sabine. This river holds mainly brown trout, which can normally be spotted under bright conditions. In long, hot summers the river flow can diminish to the point where some fish return to the lake. It is best fished early in the season. There is

12 km of fishable water to well above Morgans Hut. As with the Sabine, stalking, presentation and size of the fly are more important than the pattern. These fish are normally not selective unless fished over recently.

 Buller River and tributaries

Buller River (upper reaches)

Location Drains Lake Rotoiti, flows west to Kawatiri Junction then turns and flows south to Murchison. Below the inaccessible Upper Buller Gorge at Lyell, the river enters the West Coast Fish and Game Council region.

Access SH 6 follows the river upstream from Murchison to Kawatiri Junction; SH 63 follows on up the river to Lake Rotoiti. There are numerous (28) marked anglers' access points on both these roads. Some of these are the outlet at the Nelson Lakes National Park camping ground, the end of Teetotal Road on the true right bank, Upper Buller Bridge, Speargrass Creek, Homestead Creek, Howard River confluence, Baigents Road, Windy Point, Kawatiri Junction, Washout Creek, Gowan Bridge, Granity Creek, Raits Bridge, Owen Domain, Matiri Valley Road, Murchison Motor Camp, Matakitaki Bridge and Hinehaka Road. A walk is often required to reach the river. Between the Mangles and Owen rivers access is through private farms, but permission is seldom refused. There are camping grounds and campsites at Lake Rotoiti, Kawatiri Junction, Owen Domain and Murchison.

Season and restrictions Above Gowan Bridge, 1 October–30 April; the bag limit is two fish. Below Gowan Bridge, the river is open all year; the bag limit is four fish.

Above the Gowan confluence, the Buller is a moderate-sized river and can be crossed at selected fords with care. Below this confluence, the Buller swells into a large river and unless water flows are very low, crossings can be hazardous. Although the algae-covered stones provide good trout habitat, they can be very slippery. The Buller is a highly regarded, self-sustaining brown trout fishery that holds good stocks of fish averaging 1.5 kg (33 large and 172 medium-sized fish per km). As the Buller drains Lake Rotoiti, it remains clear and fishable above the Howard confluence even after persistent rain.

The outlet offers good sedge fishing at night. Downstream to Kawatiri Junction there is excellent water, with some sight fishing possible along the edges of runs. However, the more boisterous water should also be covered as many fish shelter behind rocks and are very difficult to spot.

The Buller is not an easy river to fish and requires a degree of fitness to manage the fast runs and turbulent pocket water. Long casting and drag-free drifts increase your chances of success. Well-weighted bead head or stonefly type nymphs and buoyant, highly visible deer hair dry flies are a good choice for this water. The banks are grass covered, with the occasional clump of beech trees or patch of manuka scrub.

Below the Gowan confluence where the river is large, there is still plenty of scope for fly fishing as most trout feed in less than a metre of water and along the edges of currents and runs. It is worth having a reel holding 100 m of backing as there are some big fish in this river. Once they lie side-on against the current it is very difficult to follow them downstream in some sections.

Around Murchison the river is very wide, deep and slower flowing. During the day spinning is the best method, but on warm summer evenings trout move out of the deep water to feed on caddis. A soft hackle wet fly or a deer hair sedge can be most effective. Listen for the splashy rise-forms. Below Murchison there is very heavy water but trout are taken on flies as well as spinners. Winter fishing by hardy anglers using a sinking line and a Woolly Bugger accounts for some fish.

Three small tributaries of the upper Buller are worth a look early in the season. Speargrass Creek and the Howard River enter the true left bank and are crossed by SH 63. Howard Valley Road follows the Howard upstream. Station Creek enters the true right bank. Leave SH 63 and cross the river at Harleys Bridge; this small side road crosses Station Creek.

Location Drains Lake Rotoroa and flows northwest for 11 km before joining the Buller just above Gowan Bridge.

Access There are marked anglers' access points at the Gowan River outlet bridge downstream on both banks, at a fisherman's cottage off Gowan Valley Road, from Gowan Valley Road itself and from both ends of East Bank Road. The riverbanks are very overgrown with willows, blackberry, bracken and manuka scrub, and access to some sections is very difficult. There is a good camping ground on East Bank Road.

Restrictions Bag limit of two fish, with only one trout exceeding 50 cm.

Unless the lake level is low, the Gowan is a very boisterous, swift and overgrown river that is difficult to fish. Crossings can be extremely treacherous and should not be attempted unless the river is very low. The algae-covered rocks and stones are as slippery as ice. If a large hooked fish decides to run downstream, its chances of

The boisterous Gowan River

escaping are good as very often the angler is unable to follow. Trout size has diminished in recent years but drift dives have found reassuringly high numbers of fish, especially just downstream from the outlet (350 fish/km). The majority of fish are brown trout although there are some rainbow present. Similar methods to those described for the upper Buller should be used, although sight fishing is hardly an option. Heavy, well-sunk nymphs on a long drift or buoyant, easily seen dry flies are effective. At dusk, providing you have found a suitable pool during the day, caddis imitations work well.

Like the upper Buller, the Gowan remains fishable after rain even though it becomes more difficult to fish with a higher rate of flow. A landing net is useful.

Owen River

Location Flows generally south from the Lookout Range and Mt Owen to join the Buller at Owen River Junction and the Owen River Hotel on SH 6.

Access A gravel road follows up the Owen Valley from the bridge on SH 6. The Nelson-Marlborough Fish and Game Council has clearly marked anglers' access points along this road. Beyond Brewery Creek, permission to fish further upstream must be obtained from the first farm across the creek. In some parts, access to the river is impeded by blackberry, scrub, bracken and willows.

Restrictions Bag limit of two fish, with only one trout exceeding 50 cm.

The Owen is a small, gentle stream that is delightful to fish, but excessive angling pressure in recent years has made the trout much more wary. Although the water is lightly tannin-stained and overhung by native bush in some sections, fish can be spotted and stalked. An accurate, gentle presentation with the first cast is all-important. The river is stable, with well-developed pools and runs. Wading and crossing presents no obstacles, although the stony riverbed can be slippery. The gorge is normally easy to negotiate. The river holds a good stock of brown trout averaging 1.5 kg, with fish up to 2.5 kg not uncommon. Because of the intense angling pressure, the fishing is best early in the season. By midsummer, after trout have been repeatedly fished over, they seek shelter in a hide during the day and often only emerge at night to feed.

Mangles River

Location Rises in the bush-clad Braeburn Range. The Tiraumea, Tutaki and Te Wiriki tributaries join at Tutaki to form the Mangles, while the Blackwater joins further downstream. This small to medium-sized river then flows west through a gorge and enters the Buller River at Longford, a few kilometres north of Murchison on SH 6.

Access The Tutaki Valley Road leaves SH 6 at Longford, 5 km north of Murchison, and follows the river upstream to Tutaki. Gravel roads then follow up both branches. There are many well-marked anglers' access points off this road that can be used, but permission is required to use other routes through private farmland. The river flows deep in an overgrown gorge for the lower 10 km, but above the gorge access is much easier, across farmland.

Restrictions Bag limit of two fish, with only one trout exceeding 50 cm.

This popular, small to medium-sized river holds a good stock of brown trout (130 fish/km in the gorge) that average 1 kg, although the occasional fish weighing 2.5 kg is caught. The gorge is only fishable in low water conditions and anglers need to be fit to tackle this section. Boots, shorts and sandfly repellent are required as the pools can be very deep and the rocks large and slippery. Native bush, scrub and blackberry make the going tough in places. Trout are very difficult to spot in the gorge as the water is greenish in colour and turbulent in some stretches. Trout respond to well-weighted nymphs and mayfly dry flies. It pays to carry a landing net.

Above the gorge the river is much more placid and friendly, but in recent years increasing angler pressure has made the trout more wary as the season progresses. There are stable pools and riffles, and trout can be sight fished on a sunny day. The stream has a stable gravel bed — ideal habitat for mayfly and caddis. There are patches of beech and scrub but the banks are mainly grassy, allowing unimpeded casting. The stream is easy to wade and cross in this section, although the stones are slippery.

Two tributaries, the Tutaki and Te Wiriki (Braeburn) rivers, also hold fish and are well worth a look, especially early in the season.

Fish respond to small dry flies and nymphs of the caddis and mayfly variety, but the first cast must be accurate and delicate as fish spook off into their hides very rapidly when disturbed. There can be a good evening rise in summer, and I have vivid memories of good-sized trout actively feeding on emergers. I stopped fishing at around 10 p.m., totally defeated and frustrated after failing to find the specific emerger imitation.

Matiri River

Location The north branch drains the Matiri Range and Lake Matiri, and joins the west branch at the road end. The main river then flows south to enter the Buller River just south of Murchison.
Access The Matiri Valley Road leaves SH 6 at the Longford Bridge and follows the river upstream. There are anglers' access points from the East Matiri Road, at the Matiri Bridge and from the Matiri Valley Road itself. Beyond the last farm (ask permission), a four-wheel-drive track ends at the Department of Conservation carpark near the confluence of the north and west branches. The Lake Matiri tramping track follows up the north branch on the true right bank.
Restrictions Bag limit two fish, only one trout exceeding 50 cm.

The middle and lower reaches of this small to medium-sized river are slow flowing and clear, with long deep glides connected by short gravel riffles. Trout cruise these glides like a lake, so stalking and intercepting a cruiser can be very difficult without spooking it. The best water lies in the 1–2 km downstream from the confluence of the north and west branches. The occasional fish can be spotted in ideal conditions but the water is lightly tannin-stained. There are some enticing pools and runs in this section.

The west branch holds only a few fish in the region of the swingbridge before it rises steeply into a cataract. The north branch

Stalking a brown in the upper Matiri River

offers a day's fishing to agile anglers used to fishing deep, short, swirling pocket water between large, slippery boulders. The fish population in this section is good but the catch rate is limited by the difficult water. Fish cannot be spotted in the greenish-brown water unless they rise. It is imperative to carry a landing net.

There are no trout in Lake Matiri or the upper Matiri River flowing into the lake.

Matakitaki River

Location Drains the Spenser Mountains and generally flows north-west to its confluence with the Buller River just south of Murchison.

Access *Upper reaches* From the Mangles–Tutaki Valley road through Tutaki to the road end at Matakitaki Station. A tramping track follows up the true right bank to Downie Hut.

Middle reaches From Murchison and SH 6, follow the road to Matakitaki, Upper Matakitaki and the Glenroy Valley road. At times the river lies close to the road; other times it is some distance away. Please ask permission to cross farmland.

Lower reaches From the Matakitaki bridge on SH 6.

Seasons and restrictions Below SH 6, the river is open all year and the bag limit is four fish. Above SH 6, 1 October–30 April; the bag limit is two fish. Above the Glenroy confluence, the bag limit is two fish, only one of which may exceed 50 cm in length.

Upstream from Upper Matakitaki, this medium-sized river is unstable, braided, shingly and flood-prone. Despite the poor trout habitat there are fish in the more stable pools, especially where there is a permanent bank. However, a lot of walking is required between pools. There are a few deep, stable holes above Downie Hut but this is two to three hours' walk from the road end.

The middle reaches are the most popular as the river is much more confined and stable. The bed is rock and stone, and the banks are partially cleared farmland. There are some gorgy sections but these can be negotiated, especially in low water flows. Some fish on the edges can be spotted but many lie under the shelter of rocky ledges, deep slots and turbulent runs. After rain, the river takes some days to clear and will often run silt-laden for days at a time. There is a good stock of brown trout averaging 1.4 kg, although larger fish are present.

The lower reaches can frequently be silt-laden from a west bank tributary entering just upstream from SH 6; although the river is a bit of a rusher in this section, it is worth fishing. The river is rapidly restocked from the Buller.

A few side creeks such as Six Mile, Station and Nardoo are worth a look early in the season.

Glenroy River

Location and access Drains the Spenser Mountains. Accessed from the Matakitaki Valley and Glenroy Valley roads and by walking.

This small Matakitaki tributary flows down a long, partially beech-clad valley. The river is unstable, shingly and fast flowing. Stable water can be difficult to find and the river can carry snow-melt until Christmas. The lower reaches have recently been gold-mined. There are a few good fish present, especially if the river runs clear for a few days, but a long walk may be necessary.

Deepdale River

Location The inaccessible Deepdale River drains the Brunner and Victoria ranges, and runs parallel to but west of the Maruia River valley. The river flows north and empties into the Buller River near Newton Flat.

Access *Lower reaches* By carefully crossing the Buller River by boat. *Middle and upper reaches* By tramping west from SH 65 at Glengarry from Peacock's farm (permission required). This is a difficult, four- to six-hour tramp through untracked, virgin native bush, and only experienced trampers carrying a compass should attempt it. The ridges do not follow the river valleys and can be very confusing. Most overseas anglers fly in by helicopter with a guide.

The Deepdale is a small, stable, rock and stone type back country stream with bush-clad banks. There are some very deep holes, and because of the water's exceptional clarity it can be deceptively deep. Crossings can be made at the tail of most pools and fish are easy to spot. The river holds browns averaging 2.5 kg, with an occasional fish up to 4.5 kg. The valley is not easy to negotiate and there are some gorgy sections. Only reasonably fit anglers should fish this river, and only anglers who are very experienced in bushcraft should attempt to tramp in. Campsites are scarce.

 *Maruia River and tributaries*

Maruia River

Location Rises in the Spenser Mountains, and flows south through Cannibal Gorge to meet SH 7 near Maruia Springs in the Lewis Pass. It then follows SH 7 west to Springs Junction before turning northwest and following SH 65 and the Shenandoah Road. Finally, the Maruia River discharges into the Buller River 10 km southwest of Murchison.

Access There are numerous access points from SH 65 and from side roads including West Bank, Boundary and Creighton roads.

Season and restrictions Below the Maruia Falls, the river is open all year and the bag limit is four trout. Above the Maruia Falls, 1 October–30 April; the bag limit is two trout.

This moderate-sized river is popular and highly recommended as it holds good stocks of medium to large fish in clear mountain water. (Drift dive figures reveal 100 fish/km at Paenga.) The most fished section of river lies between Springs Junction and the Maruia Falls where the banks are lined with native bush, manuka scrub and partially cleared farmland. In this section the river is reasonably stable and generally occupies one channel, whereas above Springs Junction it becomes braided, shingly and unstable.

In the headwaters, including the Alfred River tributary, there are only a few rainbows. Access is from the Lake Daniells track.

Downstream from Springs Junction the majority of trout are browns, but there is the odd rainbow. Fish average around 1.3 kg, and can be readily spotted and stalked. The most productive section of river lies in the gorge west of Mt Rutland where the road leaves the river between Ruffe Creek and the Warwick Stream confluence. However, it takes a very long day's walk to fish this section.

Below the Maruia Falls there are only browns, and the water is heavier and more difficult to fish with a fly. However, there are still some good stretches that are worth exploring.

There are campsites at Maruia Falls, Springs Junction and at other locations throughout the valley, and most farmers are very helpful when approached. The sandflies can be tough!

Warwick and Rappahannock streams

Location and access Both these streams are crossed by SH 65 between Burnbrae and Warwick Junction. Permission must be obtained from the local farms before fishing.

These are two small, clear spawning tributaries of the Maruia River. Both hold a few good fish early in the season, which can be spotted and stalked with a small nymph. Catch and release is encouraged.

Woolley River

Location Rises from the remote bush-clad Victoria Range and flows north to join the Maruia River.
Access West Bank Road crosses both the Maruia and Woolley rivers 2 km south of Maruia.

Another small, clear-water spawning tributary of the Maruia, best fished early in the season before trout drop back downstream to the main river. The upper reaches flow through native bush but hold few fish. The lower reaches both above and below the bridge generally hold a few fish. These become very shy after being fished over but they are still a challenge. Can remain clear after rain when the Maruia discolours.

Rahu River

Location Also drains the Victoria Range. Flows east and then north before entering the Maruia River just north of Springs Junction.
Access Travelling north from Springs Junction on SH 65, take the first side road on your left. This crosses the Rahu at a bridge.

The last Maruia tributary is another small, clear spawning stream, which holds a few browns early in the season. Fish are easy to spot in sunny conditions but are also easy to spook. There is a couple of hours' fishing upstream from the bridge.

Lake Daniells

Location and access Look for the sign on SH 7 a few kilometres east of Springs Junction. An easy, scenic, two-hour tramp on a well-marked track through native bush is required to reach the

Manson-Nicholls Memorial Hut. The hut has 40 bunks and provides unsophisticated accommodation.

Restrictions Bag limit is two trout, only one of which may exceed 50 cm in length.

This natural lake, surrounded by native bush, contains a good population of rainbow trout but is worth visiting for the scenery alone. Fish average 1–2 kg, although there are larger fish present. Depending on the lake level, shoreline wading is possible along the eastern side but the west side is steep and overhung with bush. In summer, trout can be spotted cruising the drop-off and will accept dry flies, nymphs, bully imitations and spinners. Take plenty of insect repellent.

Lake Tennyson

Location Lies in a cold basin in the headwaters of the Clarence River beneath the Spenser Mountains.

Access Take the Hanmer hydro road over Jacks Pass to the Clarence Valley. Turn left at the junction and follow the Clarence upriver, eventually reaching the outlet of Lake Tennyson.

Restrictions Bag limit is four fish.

There's easy walking on the shingle shore and tussock flats right round this high country lake and camping is permitted. However, beware the nor'west storms that can funnel down the lake and carry your tent away! There is very little shelter at the outlet.

The lake holds a small stock of brown trout in the 1–2 kg range, and in good conditions these can be spotted cruising the shore and drop-off. The lakebed seems rather devoid of weed and the trout are not always in good condition.

Any well-presented fly should take fish provided they are visible and feeding. The Clarence delta at the top of the lake is the hot spot. The outlet stream holds many small fish. In winter the surrounding mountains are snow-covered and the area becomes inhospitable and bleak.

Clarence River

Location Drains the Spenser Mountains, flows through Lake Tennyson then southeast down the Clarence Valley to just north of Hanmer. Having received the Acheron tributary, the river turns northeast and flows through a series of deep gorges in rugged, inaccessible country between the Inland and Seaward Kaikoura mountains, finally entering the Pacific Ocean 40 km north of Kaikoura.

Access *Upper reaches* The Hanmer hydro road reaches the Clarence River over Jacks Pass. This follows the river upstream beyond Lake Tennyson and downstream to the Acheron River confluence.

Middle reaches These are very isolated and hardly worth accessing from a fishing perspective. Rafting is the easiest method in summer.

Lower reaches SH 1 crosses above the mouth 40 km north of Kaikoura. A gravel road follows upstream to Bluff Station, where the river can be reached with a four-wheel-drive.

Season Above the Acheron confluence, 1 October–30 April. Below the Acheron, the river is open for fishing all year.

Restrictions Bag limit is two sportsfish. Only two salmon may be taken and only from below the Styx River confluence near the St James farm buildings.

The best water lies across the tussock flats off the Hanmer hydro road from the Acheron confluence to Lake Tennyson. This valley is exposed and often windy, but on calm, warm, sunny days in summer the river is popular for fishing and picnicking. Trout numbers are not high but browns up to 2.5 kg can be sight fished. Schools of smaller fish are also present and these spook each other when cast over. There are attractive pools and runs across a rock and stone riverbed and access is easy. Crossings are not difficult in normal summer conditions.

Below the Acheron confluence there is walking access only and the river becomes much larger. However, in summer there is good sight fishing for a further 10 km downstream. By March there are often a few salmon present in the deeper holes.

71

The remote middle reaches run silt-laden for much of the year, although it is worth carrying a rod if rafting the river in low water midsummer conditions.

The lower reaches are flood-prone, silt-laden and unstable, but a few salmon and trout are caught on spinning gear.

Leader Dale

Location Drains the Boddington Range on Molesworth Station, flows southwest and enters the true left bank of the Clarence 4 km upstream from St James Station.
Access From the Hanmer hydro road by wading across the Clarence River.
Restrictions Bag limit is two fish, only one of which may exceed 50 cm in length. Artificial bait and fly only.

This small, clear, freestone spawning tributary of the Clarence holds a few fish early in the season. When flows diminish in summer, the trout drop back to the main river.

Acheron River

Location The headwaters lie northwest of the Molesworth Station homestead, on Muller Station. The main river flows south through Molesworth to join the Clarence at the historic Acheron Guesthouse north of Hanmer.
Access The Molesworth road follows the river upstream on the true right bank to the Severn River confluence. Here it leaves the river for a few kilometres at Isolated Saddle, rejoining it at Isolated Flat. This road eventually crosses the headwaters. Vehicle access is only possible when Molesworth Station is open to the public. This is usually in January and part of February. Otherwise, the river can be reached on foot.
Restrictions Salmon fishing is not permitted above the Severn River confluence.

This medium-sized tributary carries as much water as the Clarence River itself where they merge. The water can often be slightly silt-laden and this rapidly increases after rain. The Acheron is hard going and anglers need to be reasonably fit. It is difficult to cross except in low water summer conditions, and there is a succession of steep, rocky gorges to negotiate. Briar rose adds a further impediment to progress in this barren valley. In ideal conditions some trout can be spotted, but the runs and pools are often very deep; these should not be neglected and passed by without a cast or two. The river holds brown trout averaging around 2 kg, with a few in the 3 kg range.

There are three or four days' fishing to the Severn confluence. Above this junction the river becomes unstable and braided, although it still holds a few good fish.

Alma River

Location and access Drains the Crimea Range and Island Lake at Tarndale, flows northeast to join the Severn River at Red Gate Hut on Molesworth Station. Permission is required from Molesworth to fish this stream. A four-wheel-drive track follows upriver from Red Gate to Tarndale.

Restrictions Bag limit is two fish, only one of which may exceed 50 cm in length. Artificial bait and fly only.

The Alma is a pleasant, small, clear stream to fish providing the weather is settled. This valley lies in exposed tussock country and is often windy. Trout can be sight fished in bright conditions, but on dull days many will be missed and spooked. The river takes two or three days to clear after heavy rain.

From the Severn confluence, there are two full days of fishing upstream before the river divides and braids out some distance from Tarndale homestead.

Severn River

Location and access Drains the Raglan Range on Molesworth Station, flows south, joins the Alma at Red Gate Hut and enters the Acheron a further 4 km downstream. Permission to fish this river should be obtained from Molesworth Station.

Restrictions Bag limit is two fish, only one of which may exceed 50 cm in length. Artificial bait and fly only.

The best water in this small river lies between the Acheron and Alma confluences. Browns averaging 2 kg can be stalked in clear water providing the nor'wester is not blowing hard downstream. Above Red Gate Hut the river braids out and holds few fish, although there is the odd fish in the gorge well upstream.

Saxton River

Location and access Saddles with the Leatham and Waihopai rivers, flows south and joins the Acheron below Wards Pass. The Molesworth road crosses the lower reaches. Permission should be obtained from Molesworth Station before fishing.
Restrictions Bag limit is two fish, only one of which may exceed 50 cm in length. Artificial bait and fly only.

This is an isolated, flood-prone stream that only holds a few fish in the gorge. These are the only stable pools.

The only other Clarence tributary that holds trout and is reasonably accessible is the Dillon River, which enters the Clarence's true left bank a couple of hours' walk downstream from the Acheron confluence.

Conway River

Location and access Rises in the Seaward Kaikoura Range, flows southeast and enters the sea east of Hundalee. Access is available from SH 1 at Hundalee, although the gravel road to Ferniehurst leads to better water.
Season and restrictions This river is open all year and the bag limit is two fish.

The Conway is not highly recommended, as it is flood-prone and may dry in long, hot summers. It holds a few small trout in some of the more stable pools, and sea-run browns enter the river late in the season to spawn.

To complete the Nelson-Marlborough region, Middle Creek 5 km north of the township of Kaikoura and Lyell Creek in the town itself both hold a few small trout.

West Coast Fish and Game Council region

This region stretches from Kahurangi Point north of the Heaphy River in the north to Awarua Point at Big Bay in the south. Geographically, this area comprises most of the Kahurangi National Park and a long narrow strip of coastal land west of the Southern Alps/Ka Tiritiri O Te Moana. The headwaters of most large rivers lie in rugged, inaccessible, bush- and snow-covered mountains, and many of the rivers south of Harihari are snow- and glacier-fed. These rivers have a short steep course to the sea, and with an annual rainfall between 2000 mm on the coast and 6400 mm in the alps, flash floods are common. Most of these larger, unstable rivers carry snow-melt and silt in spring and provide an undesirable trout habitat. When clear, however, sea-run browns enter many of the rivers, and winter fishing can be worthwhile. In addition, there are many spring- and rain-fed streams and creeks with stable beds that provide an excellent environment for trout. Most of these remain clear after rain, or at least clear rapidly. The lower reaches of many of the rivers are swampy and difficult to reach without a boat, but most lagoons, estuaries, and flax-lined creeks hold an enormous resource of estuarine-living or sea-run brown trout that feed on whitebait. Because of the difficulties of access this resource is virtually untapped, but there is some great fishing in spring and early summer for anglers possessing local knowledge. Despite the high rainfall and flash floods, there are excellent lakes and rivers to fish on the Coast, and one could spend a lifetime exploring and fishing without covering all the water. On a sunny, clear summer's day there is no better place to be — providing you have plenty of insect repellent!

Those who have spent time exploring West Coast waters maintain this region offers the best brown trout fishing in New Zealand.

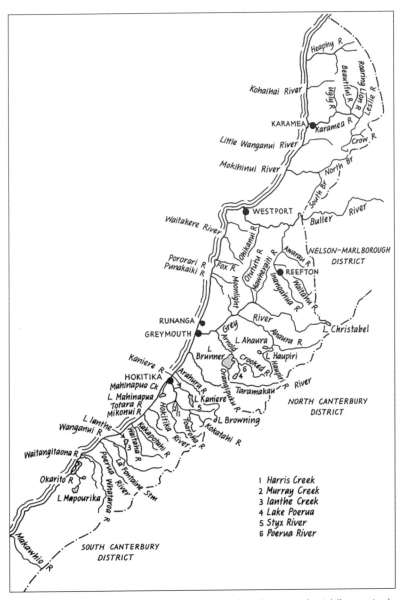

West Coast district (northern and middle section)

The scenery is breathtaking, and the variety of fishing water unlimited. As spring tends to be wet, with a succession of westerly winds, the most settled period in which to fish this region is from mid-January through to the end of March. For the sake of your sanity, wear long trousers and take sandfly and mosquito repellent.

Brown trout are the predominant species, with rainbow trout present in only the Taramakau, Arahura and Hokitika river systems. Quinnat salmon run up the Hokitika, Taramakau, Arahura, Paringa and Cascade rivers. Lake Mapourika holds resident salmon, and sea-run fish enter the lake from the Okarito River from December to March and spawn in McDonalds Creek. Salmon also enter Lake Paringa from the Paringa and Hall rivers and spawn in the Windbag Stream. Lake Moeraki also hosts a small run, which spawns in the Moeraki (Blue) River.

Unless otherwise stated, the season for trout opens on 1 October and closes on 30 April. The bag limit is four sportsfish, of which one may be a salmon and two may be rainbow trout.

Kahurangi National Park

This extensive block of remote, undeveloped country lies in the northwest corner of the South Island. The park covers 405,786 ha and contains some of the oldest and most complex rock formations on the West Coast. The country rises from near sea level to peaks over 1700 m, and is prone to the vagaries of northwest storms. Snow covers the tops in winter. Generally the land is heavily bush-clad, with few cut tramping tracks. Land formations have also been affected by the Murchison (1929) and Inangahua (1968) earthquakes. These have contributed to the ruggedness of the country, creating a number of small lakes from landslides. Several large rivers rise from these mountain ranges: in the north the Heaphy, Aorere and Cobb rivers; in the centre the Karamea and its many tributaries; in the south the Little Wanganui, Mokihinui, Matiri and Wangapeka rivers. The Aorere, Cobb, Matiri and Wangapeka are described in the Nelson-Marlborough Region.

It is strongly recommended that all who venture into the park carry detailed maps and have an understanding of survival and tramping skills. Within the confines of the park lies the Tasman Wilderness Area, in which helicopter access is prohibited. This area includes the headwaters of the Aorere River, the Roaring Lion, Beautiful and Ugly rivers, and the Karamea River between the Roaring Lion–Karamea and Ugly–Karamea confluences. Landings are permitted at the Roaring Lion and Greys huts.

While most rivers hold brown trout, only those considered worth visiting are described here. Unless specified, the season opens 1 October and closes 30 April. The bag limit is two trout.

The Kohaihai River at the road end north of Karamea is a tea-stained, bush-lined stream that holds a few browns. The Oparara River north of Karamea at Calderville is similar, but is more famous for its limestone caves.

 Karamea River and tributaries

Karamea River

Location The main river rises in the Allen Range, where it saddles with the Little Wanganui and Wangapeka rivers. In the first part of its course the river flows north through heavily bush-clad hills, but at the Leslie River junction (Big Bend) it turns west, eventually reaching the Tasman Sea at Karamea township.

Access *Headwaters* From the Wangapeka Track, a two-day tramp to Luna Hut.

Upper reaches
- By tramping downstream from Luna Hut.
- From the Graham Valley near Ngatimoti: a two-day tramp over the Mt Arthur tableland and down the Leslie Valley.
- From the Baton Valley: a long day's tramp over the Baton Saddle to the Leslie Valley and Big Bend.
- From the Cobb Valley via Lake Peel and Balloon Hut on the Mt Arthur tableland: a two- or three-day tramp to Big Bend.

Middle reaches By tramping downstream from Big Bend to the Roaring Lion Hut (5 hours) or upstream from Karamea and the Greys Hut (2–3 days). Both routes are difficult.

Lower reaches 11 km of the lower reaches can be accessed through private farmland from Arapito or Umere roads. Upstream from here, a track follows the north bank of the river for one and a half hours, then trampers must walk the riverbed for another three hours to Greys Hut (6 bunks). This route is difficult unless the river is low. It is another day's tramp upriver to the mouth of the Ugly River.

Many overseas anglers fly in by helicopter from Nelson or Karamea, while others tackle the river by raft (grade 4).

Season Open all year below a cableway at the mouth of the lower gorge. Above this point, 1 October–30 April.

Restrictions Bag limit above the cableway is two fish; below the cableway, four fish.

This is by far the largest river in the park. The main river and its many tributaries offer wonderful wilderness brown trout fishing equal to the best in New Zealand. From Luna Hut all the way to Karamea the main river provides an endless stock of self-sustaining fish averaging 2 kg.

The headwaters and upper reaches above the Leslie confluence flow rapidly over a rock and stone bed, and offer great nymph and dry fly fishing to the agile boots-and-shorts angler (40 large fish/km above the Crow Hut). Some fish can be spotted but the water is lightly tannin-stained and fish lying in the deeper slots can easily be missed. The river can be forded at selected sites provided care is taken, but by the time it reaches the Leslie River junction the river is moderate in size and the pools are larger, deeper and slower flowing (50 large fish/km).

Near the Roaring Lion confluence lie the Earthquake Lakes, formed during the Murchison earthquake, and these are well stocked with both trout and eels. Spinning is especially effective as the lakes are too wide to be covered by a fly rod. Watch for fish cruising the edges, however. Below the Roaring Lion the country becomes very remote, the river gorgy and the angling pressure minimal. There is still great water, however.

The lower reaches at Karamea are large, slower flowing, and better suited to spinning, although trout can still be taken on a fly, especially at dusk during the evening rise. Drift dives at Arapito reveal good stocks of mainly medium-sized trout (100 fish/km).

All reasonable-sized tributaries contain trout but only the six most important ones are described here.

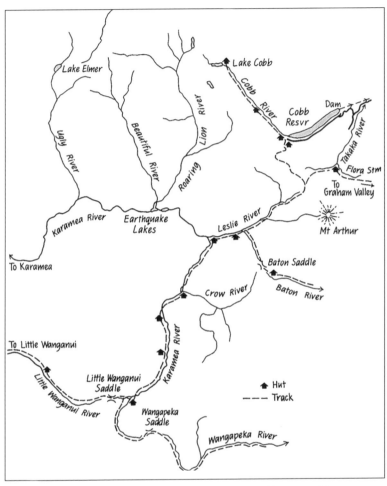

Karamea River system

Crow River

The Crow Hut at the Karamea-Crow junction offers 'back country accommodation' and a base for fishing this small to medium-sized, remote, clear-water tributary. The river flows west and holds good numbers of fish that are easily spotted on a sunny day. The fish are generally not sophisticated feeders and will accept a large variety of carefully presented dries and nymphs. Wear overtrousers and long sleeves for protection against the sandflies. There are two days of fishing upstream from the Karamea confluence, but in some sections the going is not easy. The riverbed boulders are large and slippery, there are gorgy sections and the bush needs to be entered in order to negotiate some stretches of river. Some pools are very deep. Bag limit is two trout.

Leslie River

This is the most accessible tributary, with the Karamea Bend Hut being the best base. The Leslie Hut has recently burned down. The river is small and easily waded and crossed, but there are some deep holes. Like all these tributaries, the Leslie is bush-lined, with clear water and a rock and stone riverbed. There is a good day's fishing upstream from the mouth. Bag limit is two trout.

Roaring Lion River

Access
- A hard five- to six-hour tramp downriver from Big Bend to the Roaring Lion Hut.
- From the Cobb Valley either via Kimbell Spur or from Chaffey Hut via Chaffey Stream and Breakfast Creek (7–9 hours).
- From the Ugly or Aorere headwaters via Aorere Saddle.
Note: These routes are for experienced trampers only.
- By helicopter.
Restrictions Bag limit is two trout.

This is a marvellous medium-sized, remote river that flows south from its source through heavily bush-clad mountains. It offers similar conditions to the Crow and Leslie, but the river is larger and fords are tricky in the lower reaches, some being more than waist deep. There are trophy fish in this river, although helicopter pressure from overseas anglers has made the fish more wary. Good fishing is available up as far as Breakfast Creek, a long day's tramp from the Roaring Lion Hut near the mouth.

This small tributary can be reached easily across from the Roaring Lion Hut, providing the Roaring Lion is fordable. Only the lower 1–2 km are worth fishing, before the river rises steeply and becomes very rough going. There are a few good pools in the lower reaches. Bag limit is two trout.

Ugly River

Access This is the most remote tributary, and only experienced trampers should attempt to reach the river — either upriver from Karamea, downriver from the Roaring Lion Hut or via the saddle between the Roaring Lion and Ugly headwaters.
Restrictions Bag limit is two trout.

This river is slightly smaller than the Roaring Lion, and flows south from its source at Lake Elmer. The east branch joins a few kilometres below the lake. It holds good stocks of brown trout, which can be sight fished, with the best water lying between McNabb and Domett creeks. The river floods easily but also clears rapidly. It holds the odd trophy fish in the headwaters.

The Cawthron Institute conducted research on trout behaviour in 1999 on this river. They found that spooked trout took at least 24 hours to reappear from their hide, whereas fish that had been caught and released remained hidden for up to three days. Trout were also aware of the fly they had previously taken, and were resistant to accepting that pattern a second time.

Lake Elmer, formed by the Murchison earthquake, holds trout but they were not in good condition when I last visited.

The sixth and last tributary of significance downstream is the Kakapo River, but this holds a few fish in the lower pools only.

Little Wanganui River

Location Drains the Scarlett and Allen ranges south of the Karamea River system, flows generally west and enters the Tasman

Sea at Little Wanganui township, some 15 km south of Karamea.

Access *Lower reaches* From SH 67. A side road, the Little Wanganui Road, follows up the true right bank to the start of the Wangapeka Track to Nelson.

Middle reaches From the Wangapeka Track. The Little Wanganui Hut, which sleeps 18, is three hours' tramp upstream and is a good base for fishing. The track is marked and generally follows the true left or south bank.

Season Open all year downstream from SH 67 bridge. Above this bridge, 1 October–30 April.

Restrictions Bag limit is two trout.

The lower reaches are shingly and rather unstable, but sea-run browns enter the river chasing whitebait and can provide good sport. The middle reaches are more stable and although stocks are not high there is reasonable sight fishing in the vicinity of the Little Wanganui Hut for tramper-anglers walking the Wangapeka Track.

Mokihinui River

Location This river drains a very large catchment of rugged bush country, including the Radiant, Allen, Matiri and Lyell ranges. The north and south branches flow north and south respectively to The Forks. The main river then flows west to enter the sea at Mokihinui, some 40 km north of Westport.

Access *Lower reaches* SH 67 and the Mokihinui–Seddonville road provide access to 11 km of the lower reaches. Beyond Seddonville, a four-wheel-drive is advised.

Middle reaches By tramping upstream on a track at the end of the Mokihinui–Seddonville Road and following the south bank of the river. This track has been washed out and some areas have become very treacherous, especially where it crosses slips.

Upper reaches The Forks Hut (6 bunks) is a seven- to eight-hour tramp from the road end, and many anglers and hunters now use a helicopter for access. Sinclair Hut (4 bunks) on the north branch is only 30 minutes' walk across the river flats from Forks Hut. There is also a hut on the Johnson River.

On the south branch, Goat Creek Hut, opposite Hennessy

Creek, is three hours' tramp from the forks and sleeps four. An update on the condition of these huts should be obtained from the Department of Conservation before embarking on a trip to this remote watershed. If in any doubt, carry a tent.

By tramping over Kiwi Saddle into the Johnson tributary from the Wangapeka Track.

Season Open all year below a cableway near Welcome Creek. Above the cableway, 1 October–30 April.

Restrictions Bag limit for the main river and tributaries above the cableway is two trout; below the cableway, four trout.

This is a superb, remote brown trout fishery that almost rivals its northern neighbour, the Karamea, although it is somewhat smaller.

In the upper reaches and tributaries there are long stretches of clear, rock and stone type mountain water, with fish averaging 2 kg (30 large trout/km in the north and south branches). It is pointless just fishing the water in these upper reaches as most feeding fish can be seen easily. This scenic river and its tributaries flow down valleys of beech bush and tussock flats. All major tributaries hold fish, with the Johnson, Allen, Hemphill, Larrikin and Hennessy creeks being especially recommended. The river can flood in dramatic fashion after heavy rain and at times the flats at the forks can resemble a lake. The upper reaches clear rapidly after rain.

The middle reaches are more difficult to access and the river becomes much larger. However, there are still plenty of trout to entice the fit and active angler.

The lower reaches offer sea-run fish, especially during the whitebait season in the spring. These can be caught on spinners or a smelt fly.

 *Buller River (below Lyell) and tributaries*

Buller River

(See Nelson-Marlborough region for the Upper Buller.)
Location From Murchison, the river soon passes through the Upper Buller Gorge, then flows more sedately through Inangahua.

Below Inangahua the river flows through the Lower Buller Gorge before discharging into the Tasman Sea at Westport.

Access SH 6 follows the river from Murchison to Westport. Some gorgy stretches are difficult to negotiate but there is anglers' access at Windy Point, Titotoa, Hawkes Crag, Stitts Bluff, Whitecliffs and at the confluences of the Ohikanui, Blackwater and Inangahua rivers. From the true right bank at Westport, access is available from the bridge, the domain and Reedy's Road.

Season Open all year downstream from Lyell.

Restrictions Bag limit is four sportsfish.

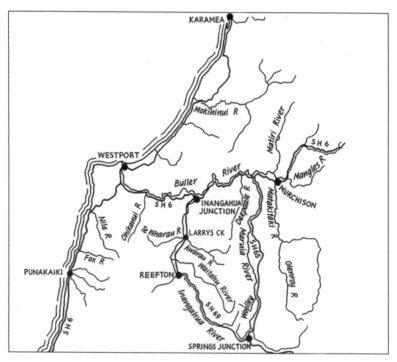

Lower Buller and tributaries

While the upper reaches above Murchison are manageable from a fly fishing point of view, the river below Lyell becomes very large, deep and heavy. Most fish are taken on spinners and live bait, but there are some stretches that yield fish to the fly. Although trout are generally smaller than in the upper reaches, there is a large stock of trout and the river is not heavily fished. The water is tannin-stained, making sight fishing difficult, but on warm summer evenings trout will rise to caddis and mayflies. Good sea-run browns are taken on spinners near the mouth when whitebait are running.

Inangahua River

Location and access Rises near Rahu Saddle and flows north through Reefton to enter the Buller at Inangahua. SH 7 follows the upper reaches to Reefton, while SH 69 continues to Inangahua. From SH 69, try Brazils, O'Grady, Golf Links and Perseverance roads and Landing bridge.
Restrictions Bag limit is four fish.

This large, tannin-stained tributary flows for more than 60 km over a rock and stone bed through native bush and cleared farmland. The river is lined with bush, blackberry, willows and scrub. Fish along the edges of runs can be spotted in bright conditions, but all likely looking water should be fished. In the past, open-cast coalmining operations have polluted the river below Garvey Creek and in 1995 goldmining repeated the damage. Despite these insults, the river holds good stocks of sizeable brown trout (30 large fish/km at Inangahua Landing). The most productive water lies between Cronadun and Inangahua Landing but there is still good fishing upstream from Reefton at Blacks Point and Crushington.

Waitahu River

Location This major tributary of the Inangahua River drains the Victoria Range, flows northwest and enters the Inangahua 5 km northwest of Reefton.
Access From Gannons Road off SH 69, which leads to and crosses the river. Rough four-wheel-drive tracks lead upstream on both banks but it is safer to walk unless you have specialised equipment. I suggest leaving your vehicle at the settling ponds on the true left bank. A marked track leads upstream on the true right bank as far as the Montgomerie River confluence. It is a two-hour walk. The

Montgomerie Hut offers basic back country accommodation up the Montgomerie tributary.

This is a small to medium-sized, clear-water, scenic, bush-lined stream that holds browns averaging 2 kg, with a few larger fish in the deeper holes. Fish numbers are not high but the quality of the angling experience on a sunny day is not to be missed. The trout become more wary as the season progresses and fish rapidly spook off to their hide with any wayward or clumsy cast into the gin-clear water. Fishing improves away from the road, with both the upper reaches of the main river and the Montgomerie River well worth exploring.

Fishing runs out on the main river at the Shaw Stream confluence, but there is another full day's fishing on the Montgomerie. The river is normally easy to wade and cross at selected sites, with the granite boulders offering secure footing. The nor'wester blows upstream.

Te Wharau River (Stony)

Location Drains the bush-covered ranges northwest of Reefton, flows east and enters the west bank of the Inangahua River just upstream from Larry's Creek.
Access From SH 69, the lower reaches can be reached from a small side road by crossing the Inangahua River on a swingbridge. Walk up the true left bank of the Inangahua to the mouth of Te Wharau River.
Restrictions Bag limit is four trout.

Te Wharau is a small, clear-water, bush-lined stream flowing over a granite boulder and shingle bed. The pools are well defined and the fish easy to spot on a fine day. The bouldery riverbed is hard going on the walk back, and there is at least two days' fishing upstream from the mouth to the upper forks. The browns are beautifully marked.

Awarau River (Larry's Creek)

Location Flows through heavily bush-covered hills parallel to but north of the Waitahu River, to join the Inangahua River 14 km northwest of Reefton.

Access *Lower reaches* Crossed by SH 69. You can walk downstream from this bridge or access the river from a picnic area.

Middle and upper reaches Turn right onto a forestry road up the true right bank. A track follows further upstream from the road end.

This medium-sized river has a reputation for trophy brown trout but they are not easy to entice. They become more selective and difficult after being repeatedly fished over as the season progresses. Although the water is very clear, some of the pools are large and very deep. The fish most commonly accept carefully presented heavily weighted small nymphs, but it can be difficult to get these down deep enough for the fish to be interested. Awarau River is indeed a challenge but the rewards are well worth the effort. There are two to three days' fishing upstream from the bridge. Beyond the Caledonian Pool lies a gorge that can be waded through in low water conditions. An alternative route to the more open upper reaches is via an old miners' track. Fishing ends at the junction of Farmers and Silcocks creeks.

Ohikanui River

Location The headwaters saddle with the Rough just east of the Paparoa Range. The river flows generally north to join the Buller 32 km east of Westport.

Access SH 6 crosses just upstream from the mouth. There is no marked route up this river but a rough track follows upstream from the bridge on the true left bank. Only active, fit anglers should attempt this river, as there are no huts, tracks or roads in this valley.

Restrictions Bag limit is two fish.

This remote, bush-lined, rough, bouldery, clear river offers great sight fishing for the fit angler who is unafraid to camp out. The best fishing lies well upstream where crystal-clear greenish pools and runs hold a good population of medium and large brown trout. Wear overtrousers and take insect repellent for the sandflies.

Overseas anglers fish the upper reaches after flying in by helicopter, but there is plenty of good water to fish.

Rivers between Greymouth and Westport

SH 6 crosses a number of small to medium-sized rivers which hold brown trout. Most arise from rugged, steep, heavily bush-clad hills and have a short course to the sea. Not many hold large numbers of resident fish but sea-run trout enter these rivers, especially in the spring and early summer when they are chasing whitebait. For this reason, fish stocks can be unreliable. Unless specified, the season for all these rivers is 1 October–30 April. They include:

Ten Mile Creek An unstable rock face from mining has made this river dangerous to explore at present. There is some excellent clear water, but fish stocks are unreliable. This stream is now open all year for fishing.

Punakaiki River at Punakaiki A clear, freestone river worth a look in the lower reaches. Open all year below SH 6.

Pororari River The water is lightly tannin-stained. Open all year.

The Fox River

Fox River at Tiromoana Fish are easy to spot in the clear water but only seem to inhabit the lower reaches despite excellent, stable water upstream.

Waitakere (Nile) River at Charleston Tea-coloured water holding a few trout in the lower reaches only. It is open all season downstream from the Awakere confluence.

Other rivers in the Westport area that hold trout include the Okari, Orowaiti and Whareatea, and the Waimangaroa and Ngakawau rivers north of the town.

 *Grey River and tributaries*

Grey River

Location This large river and its tributaries drain the country from the Main Divide to the coast and from Reefton in the north to Lake Brunner in the south. The main river follows a southwesterly course and discharges into the Tasman Sea at Greymouth.

Season Above the Clarke confluence, 1 October–30 April. Below this confluence, the river is open all year.

Restrictions Bag limit is four fish but catch and release should be practised above Gentle Annie Gorge.

Upper reaches

Access
- From Palmer Road, which is not signposted and can be easily missed. The road leaves SH 7 on a sharp bend 4 km from Springs Junction, and runs south through bush and farmland to the Robinson River confluence. The Brown Grey is the first tributary on your right, followed by the Blue Grey draining Lake Christabel on your left at the first farm. Landowner permission should be obtained before fishing.
- From Hukarere (Snowy River turn-off) 2 km north of Ikamatea on SH 7, to Hukawai, the Alexander River confluence and Forest Home Pastoral Holdings (McVicars). It is a 27.5-km drive on a dark, narrow bush road to the road end. Permission

must be obtained from the farm. A rough four-wheel-drive farm track follows up the true right bank but it is easy to get bogged after rain. It is a 13-km walk from the road end upstream to Palmer Road at Robinson River.

- From Waipuna and Golf Links roads off SH 7, 6 km north of Totara Flat and south of Ikamatua. Waipuna Road leads up the true left bank to the Clarke River confluence and bridge. Permission is required from Ferguson farm. If you reach the quarry, you have gone too far.

The headwaters and upper reaches are a superb brown trout fishery. There is a seemingly inexhaustible supply of trout and a wide variety of water to fish.

The best water in the area lies in the Big Grey below the Blue and Brown Grey confluence at Palmer Flat. The river often flows some distance from the road and permission should first be obtained before crossing private farmland. The water is normally crystal clear, enabling sight fishing in the turbulent, bouldery runs. As the gradient lessens down the valley, deeper slower flowing pools and more gentle runs replace the boisterous water of the upper section. At the Robinson River confluence, the river is even more placid with well marked pools and shingly riffles and bouldery runs. This section of river, from the Robinson River upstream to the Blue and Brown Grey confluence is an outstanding brown trout fishery. Fish average 1.8 kg and stocks are good. The Robinson tributary is also well worth a look as far upstream as the second footbridge.

It is only a 13 km walk downstream from the Robinson River confluence to the end of the farm track at McVicars (Forest Home Pastoral Holdings) but the river's character changes dramatically. Although much wider, and more flood-prone and unstable, there are long glides, shingly riffles, braids and well formed pools flowing over an alluvial gravel bed. There are grassy banks, patches of manuka scrub and long sand and stone beaches. The best water is often a deep side braid running against a permanent bank. There are numerous backwaters on this section of river and almost every one holds a large cruising trout. The stones of the riverbed are washed clean of algae so crossing is easy on most stretches.

Below the farm (McVicars) the river enters the Gentle Annie

gorge. This can be fished through in low water but the going is rough due to some enormous boulders brought down by the Murchison earthquake. Below the Alexander River confluence, a second gorge with steep banks, deep water and overgrowing scrub and bush makes the river difficult to explore and fish. Eventually the river emerges downstream at the Clarke River confluence.

Waipuna Road provides easy access to long stretches of the river below the Clarke River confluence. The river is large here and crossings are hazardous due to algae covering the boulders and stones. Cleared grazing land, manuka scrub and patches of bush line the banks. There are long, smooth shingly glides and some more interesting bouldery, turbulent runs. Fish tend to be smaller but stocks are greater with 240 mainly medium-sized trout per kilometre of river. There are plenty of angling opportunities in this section with around 20 km of river to fish, easy access, unrestricted casting and a good stock of trout. Unless fish are feeding along the edges of runs and pools, they are not easy to spot. Fish seem to move about in this section of river and while some pools hold a lot of fish, others can be barren. It is generally more productive to fish the bouldery runs and pocket water rather than the deep, slow-flowing pools.

Middle and lower reaches

Access SH 7 follows the true left bank from Ikamatua to Greymouth. Atarau Road follows the true right bank for some distance. Access is not difficult, although a considerable walk across private farmland is required in some locations as both roads often run some distance away from the river. Access points include Totara Flat, Ahaura, Blackball, Matai, Stillwater Bridge, Taylorville and Omoto Racecourse.

The river is now very large and receives numerous tributaries on its way to the sea. The water is heavy, tannin-stained and very deep in parts. Spinning and live bait fishing accounts for most trout caught. However, before Christmas fly fishing can be worthwhile, especially in the evenings when there is often an evening rise. Because of its enormous catchment in an area of heavy rainfall, some frightening floods occur in this section of river. It can take a week to clear after heavy rain before becoming fishable.

Location and access From Palmer Road, as for upper Grey.
Restrictions Bag limit is two fish.

Both these rivers hold a few good fish. The Brown Grey is moderately tannin-stained but trout can be spotted in both rivers on a bright day. Both flow through bush and cleared farmland. Trout cannot reach Lake Christabel from the Blue Grey River, but a recent reliable report suggests they have been liberated into the lake.

Robinson River

Location and access From the end of Palmer Road. This valley is tracked and there are two huts up the valley.
Restrictions Bag limit is two fish.

The most productive water lies between the Grey confluence upstream as far as the second footbridge. Trout are easy to spot in clear water.

Alexander River

Location and access From McVicars Road to Forest Home Pastoral Holdings.
Restrictions Bag limit is two fish.

Only the lower reaches hold an occasional trout, and it is hardly worth the effort considering good fishing is available in the upper Grey close by.

Clarke River

Location Drains the rugged, remote bush-clad ranges between the upper Grey and the Ahaura rivers, flows north and enters the Grey River at the end of Waipuna Road.
Access From the end of Waipuna Road, as described for the upper Grey River.
Restrictions Bag limit is two fish.

This small, tea-coloured tributary usually holds a few fish in the lower reaches near the bridge. Floods have devastated the river above the bridge where it is braided and unstable. Further upstream there is a gorge that can only be negotiated with difficulty in low water, but above the gorge there is more stable water holding some very large browns. Only experienced tramper-anglers should tackle the upper reaches.

Mawheraiti River (Little Grey)

Location Rises near Reefton and follows SH 7 to Ikamatua where it joins the Grey.
Access Take the metalled road that leaves SH 7 opposite the Mawheraiti Hotel, south from Mawheraiti township. This leads to good water on the true right bank. SH 7 crosses the river twice, but further downstream a long walk across farmland and the railway from the main road is required to reach the river. Atarau Road crosses the lower reaches near Ikamatua.
Restrictions Bag limit is four fish.

A medium-sized, tea-coloured stream, the Mawheraiti holds a good stock of brown trout averaging just over 1 kg (60 trout/km). Fish are hard to spot, but in view of the favourable drift dive figures it is worth fishing all likely looking water.

There is good water both below and above the Atarau Road bridge, with fish rising eagerly beneath the willows on a fine summer's evening. Discharges from local dairy farms are not helping this river.

Rough River (Otututu)

Location Rises from the eastern side of the Paparoa Range and flows for 30 km southwest to eventually join the Grey River near Ikamatua.
Access *Lower reaches* From Atarau Road, which crosses the river not far from Ikamatua.
Middle reaches From Atarau Road, take Mirfins Road on the true left bank to a sawmill. The sawmill gates close at the end of each

working day and at weekends. Anglers can walk upstream across partially cleared farmland and fish to Mirfin Creek.

Upper reaches By tramping through untracked bush upstream from Mirfin Creek or flying in by helicopter. The valley has no tracks or huts.

Restrictions Bag limit is two fish.

The Rough is very popular with overseas anglers and their guides, who usually 'chopper' into the remote, bush-clad upper reaches between Mirfin and Gordon creeks. However, there is plenty of excellent water downstream from Mirfin Creek. The water is very clear and a light greenish colour, flowing over granite boulders, rock and shingle. Trout can be spotted but many will be missed as they often lie beneath white water or in deep slots in the rock. There are good stocks of browns averaging around 2 kg, and these become very spooky later in the season after being fished over. The river can be forded at the tail of most pools as the granite boulders are not slippery.

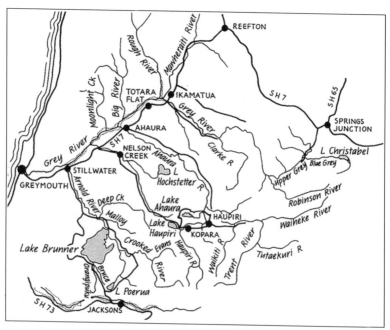

Grey River system

Big River (Slaty Creek)

Location Flows south, generally parallel to but west of Rough River, and enters the Grey at the farming settlement of Slaty Creek.
Access Atarau Road crosses the lower reaches. The upper and middle reaches can be accessed through private farmland off Logburn Road. There is a sandfly-ridden campsite at Pfaff's Clearing.
Restrictions Bag limit is two fish.

The lower reaches are shingly and braided but still hold the odd fish. In the gorgy middle reaches there are some good, deep, stable pools holding fish but these are not easy to hook in this type of water. They often lie facing downstream in a backwash and spot you well in advance of casting. Drag also becomes a problem. However, they are a challenge. Above Pfaff's Clearing the river divides. There are only a few fish up the main river, but the Pike River (true right) is worth exploring early in the season. If the proposed mine up this tributary goes ahead, the fishing may well deteriorate. There is a bush track down the true left bank to walk back on at the end of fishing.

Moonlight River

Location Flows parallel to but west of the Big River and enters the Grey near the settlement of Atarau.
Access Moonlight Valley Road follows the stream.
Restrictions Bag limit is two fish.

Like the Big River, the headwaters of the Moonlight rise from rugged bush-clad hills, but the river is smaller and the fish numbers considerably fewer than the Big. Amateur and commercial gold prospectors still work this river and the river flats. According to gold prospectors, there are very few fish in the upper reaches.

Ahaura River

Location The Trent and Waiheke rivers join to form the Ahaura, with the Waikiti, Nancy and Haupiri tributaries entering a few kilometres further downstream. The river flows west to enter the Grey River at Ahaura on SH 7.

Access *Upper reaches* From SH 7 turn off at Ngahere to Nelson Creek and Kopara. Continue on to the settlement of Haupiri. From here it is wise to seek permission and directions from the local farmer (Bill Perry, phone (03) 738 0221) before fishing the upper reaches.
Middle reaches From the Ahaura–Kopara Road (Watterson Road).
Restrictions Bag limit is two fish.

The most productive fishing in this medium-sized, freestone river lies below the Nancy and Haupiri confluences but access is difficult and best achieved by raft. The upper reaches are clear and swift, although the colour changes when the tea-coloured Haupiri River joins it. The river is flood-prone, shingly and unstable, but there are a number of relatively stable sections against banks holding fish (33 large fish/km). Most fish can be spotted and stalked, although a lot of riverbed walking is required to cover the upper reaches.

Trent River

Location Rises north of Harper Pass, flows north to join the Waiheke River and form the Ahaura.
Access From the road end at Haupiri settlement (permission required from Bill Perry, phone (03) 738 0221), by tramping up the Ahaura and then up the Trent River. The derelict Trent Hut at the Tutaekuri confluence is three to four hours' tramp upstream. The hut does provide shelter, however, which is often necessary in this region of high rainfall.

This remote tributary holds a few good brown trout, especially in the area close to Trent Hut. Fish can be stalked in clear water and are generally in good condition. Further upstream the flood-prone river braids out and is not worth exploring.

The Waiheke River also holds a few good fish in the lower reaches only, but a lot of walking is also required to fish this area.

The Tutaekuri River is small, unstable and a rusher. The Nancy is not worth exploring, and the Waikiti River holds only a few fish in the lower 2 km before an impassable gorge blocks progress.

Haupiri River

Location Two branches form the main river. One, a clear-water snow- and rain-fed river, rises near the Harper Pass and flows northwest down a picturesque mountain valley. The other, a heavily tannin-stained tributary, drains Lake Haupiri. The tributaries meet just upstream from the road bridge at the settlement of Kopara to form the main river. This then flows east to join the Ahaura River near the Haupiri farm settlement.

Access Take the Nelson Creek–Kopara road to Haupiri School. The road crosses the river 1 km past Lake Haupiri, before reaching the school. The private Wallace Road follows up the clear-water tributary but permission is required from Gloria Vale Farm Community (phone (03) 738 0224). Alternatively, there is riverbed access from the tributary confluence. Access to the main river, which flows behind the school, can be obtained by walking downstream or across private farmland.

Restrictions Bag limit is two fish.

In the clear-water tributary there is 10 km of sight fishing for good-sized brown trout all the way to the hot springs. The first 2 km of river have been modified by stopbanks but above the farm there are well-formed, stable pools. This is boots-and-shorts type fishing, with plenty of walking required. The river is easily crossed at the tail of most pools, and the banks of grass overhung by bush and scrub provide plenty of terrestrial insects for fish. A farm track helps with the walk back.

The heavily tannin-stained tributary draining Lake Haupiri is not worth fishing, but below the confluence of the two streams there is excellent water holding very high stocks (200 fish/km). There is easy access to this section of water from the road bridge, with the confluence lying a few hundred metres upstream. Downstream from the road bridge there is excellent water holding plenty of fish, although sight fishing becomes difficult because of the water colour.

Nelson Creek, which enters the Grey River at Ngahere, is at times polluted from gold mining but holds a few brown trout, especially in the lower reaches.

Arnold River

Location Drains Lake Brunner at Moana, flows north to Stillwater on SH 7, where it enters the Grey River.

Access There are a number of anglers' access points off Arnold Valley Road, some of which are signposted. These include the Moana footbridge at the outlet, Kotuku, Arnold River Bridge near Aratika, from Aratika, below the Arnold Dam, Arnold Creek, Old Arnold Road and Kokiri Bridge near the freezing works.

Season and restrictions Open all year. Bag limit is four sportsfish.

Story tellers!

This medium-sized, tea-coloured river has been modified by a hydro-electric dam that has been built at Kaimata, 13 km down-river from Lake Brunner. The water that backs up for 4 km behind the dam is known as Lake Ullstrom. The Arnold River has a very high population of mainly brown trout that average 1–2 kg (240 fish/km at Kotuku and 75 fish/km at Kokiri). As the river drains Lake Brunner it is very stable and remains fishable after rain, especially above Malloy and Deep creeks, although access becomes more difficult when the river is high. The banks are covered with patches of bush and willows, although there are open stretches with gravel beaches, especially when the river is low. Trout can rarely be spotted in the brownish water and the algae-covered stones are slippery for wading. The insect life is prolific and at times the fish can become rather selective. There is usually an active evening rise to caddis, when a soft hackle wet fly, an Elk Hair Caddis or a Goddard Caddis can be most effective. During the day, fish the edges and riffles blind with a small, weighted nymph and an attractor-type dry fly as an indicator. In November and December, a green beetle imitation works well.

Lake Ullstrom is a series of interconnected willow-lined lagoons that are very difficult to access except by dinghy or float tube. They contain a good fish population.

Two small tea-coloured streams flowing through farmland, Deep Creek and Malloy Creek, join the Arnold at Kotuku north of Moana. The Arnold Valley Road crosses both creeks near the Kotuku Rail Station. Both hold brown trout and are worth exploring, especially early in the season. As with the Arnold, you will need to fish the water, as although some fish can be sighted on a bright day many remain unseen in the tea-coloured water. There is good road access, but permission should be obtained to cross private farmland.

The Grey Valley lakes and adjacent rivers

Although there are a number of lakes in the Grey catchment, only five can be recommended for fishing. These are lakes Brunner, Poerua, Haupiri, Hochstetter and Lady Lake. The water in all these lakes is tannin-stained from rainwater leaching through the surrounding native bush, which makes spotting fish difficult except on bright, sunny days.

Lake Brunner

Location At Moana, 25 km southeast of Greymouth.
Access There is limited road access from Moana, Iveagh Bay and from Mitchells at the southern end, but much of the shoreline can only be reached by boat.
Season and restrictions Open all year; the bag limit is four trout.
Boat launching At Moana, Iveagh Bay and Mitchells.

At 10 km across, this is the largest lake in the area. Much of the shoreline is bush-covered, especially on the western side. The lake holds a large population of of brown trout averaging just over 1 kg, and a local tourist promotion maintains that most of these die of old age.

Spotting cruising fish is difficult, although a sandy flat near Mitchells and the Crooked and Hohonu deltas can be sight fished. Most blind fly fishing is carried out using a slow-sinking line and a damsel nymph or bully imitation such as Hamill's Killer, Woolly Bugger or Mrs Simpson. Casting nymphs over weed beds from a boat is also popular, especially near the Bruce River mouth where the trout population is very high.

Trolling a spinner accounts for most of the fish taken, with popular stretches being between Te Kinga Hill and Clematis Bay, and near the outlet of the lake. Fish can be caught from the drop-off anywhere in Lake Brunner, with popular spinners being Toby, Cobra and Tasmanian Devil variations.

Crooked River

Location Drains the Alexander Range, flows northeast and enters the eastern side of Lake Brunner south of Howitt Point.
Access *Lower reaches* 11 km south of Moana, turn off on the road to Iveagh Bay. This road crosses the river. The delta is best accessed by boat.

Middle reaches Between Te Kinga and Rotomanu the road crosses the river. There is easy access both upstream and downstream.

The Bell Hill–Inchbonnie Road crosses at the Crooked River Reserve, just below a short gorge.

Upper reaches A rough private farm track follows the true left bank upstream to the Evans River confluence. Permission is required from the landowner.

Restrictions Bag limit is two trout.

This medium-sized, clear-water river rises from rugged, inaccessible bush-clad mountains. Because of its stability the river rarely discolours after rain, although it becomes more difficult to fish. Frequent floods have cleaned the rock and stone riverbed and made wading and crossing reasonably safe at selected spots. There are well-defined deep pools and runs, and although the trout population can be unreliable the quality of the sight fishing compensates for this.

The upper reaches are partially bush-clad, whereas the middle and lower reaches flow across farmland. Trout cannot negotiate the gorge upstream from the Evans River confluence, and although the Evans is a spawning tributary it is an unstable rusher and its fish stocks are very low for most of the year. The middle reaches of the Crooked offer interesting dry fly and nymph fishing to sighted trout.

Bruce Creek

Location Drains swampy country near the southern end of Lake Poerua, skirts the base of Mt Te Kinga, and together with the Orangipuku River empties into Swan Bay.

Access From the road junction at Inchbonnie, continue towards Mitchells on the Kumara–Inchbonnie Road. Take the northernmost side road on your right leading in the direction of Mt Te Kinga. This road reaches the river at an old farm bridge. If you cross the Orangipuku Bridge you have gone too far. It is wise to obtain permission from the landowner, even though this is usually just a formality.

Restrictions Bag limit is two trout.

This slightly tea-coloured spring creek winds its way placidly through partially cleared farmland. The upper and lower reaches are difficult to access because of bush and swamp, but the middle reaches offer a full day's fishing. Cross the bridge, walk downstream on the true right bank and fish back upstream. Some fish feeding the edges can be spotted but many will be missed unless the water itself is fished. Fish stocks are good, there are some very deep holes, and this stable creek remains fishable after rain. The riverbed is weedy, offering a great food supply and shelter for trout. Most fish are caught on a weighted size 14 Pheasant Tail type nymph, but some trout will rise to a mayfly imitation dry fly during the day.

A few hundred metres above the bridge, the creek divides into three tributaries. The middle tributary is worth following until it becomes overgrown. Fish are easier to spot on the sandy creekbed but are also a real challenge to catch.

On favourable evenings there can be a vigorous evening rise, and trout emerge from weed beds to actively feed. However, they can be very selective and frustrating in these conditions.

Orangipuku River

Location Rises close to the Taramakau River valley, follows the base of the Hohonu Range, joins Bruce Creek just above Lake Brunner and empties into Swan Bay.
Access The road to Mitchells (Kumara–Inchbonnie Road) crosses the lower reaches. A farm track follows down the true right bank almost to the mouth.
Restrictions Bag limit is two fish.

Only the 2 km stretch downstream from the bridge and a few hundred metres of water above the bridge are worth fishing. The upper reaches are very overgrown with gorse and scrub. This is a small, clear-water, rain-fed stream where trout can be spotted easily. The river is shingly, and as the upper reaches flow across partially cleared farmland, it rapidly becomes unfishable after heavy rain. The banks are lined with willow, native bush, blackberry and gorse, but this offers cover to anglers spotting fish. Trout numbers can be extremely variable, with fish seemingly moving into and out of the river from the lake at will. Fishing is often better late in the season when a spawning run enters the stream. Stealth in stalking and an accurate, gentle presentation are crucial. If another angler is already fishing this stream, it is wise to find an alternative river.

Eastern Hohonu River

Location Drains the Hohonu Range east of Lake Brunner, flows north then east before entering the lake just north of Bain Bay on the western shore.
Access *To the mouth and lower reaches*
- By boat to the mouth.
- By walking from Mitchells on the Bain Bay walking track.

Middle reaches From Arnold Valley Road near Aratika, via Aratika Tree Farm (permission required).
Upper reaches By walking downstream from the bridge where the Kumara–Inchbonnie Road crosses.
Restrictions Bag limit is four trout.

The lower reaches of this small to medium-sized river are slow-flowing and log-jammed. The middle reaches are much more boisterous, and worth exploring by fit anglers who are not afraid to bush bash. The water is clear and trout can be sight fished. Stocks are not high, however. The mouth is best fished from a boat.

Lake Poerua

Location Lies south of Lake Brunner and just north of the Inchbonnie settlement.
Access From the Inchbonnie–Rotomanu Road at Te Kinga Reserve, where there are facilities for launching small boats.
Restrictions Bag limit is four fish.

This small, tea-coloured lake holds good numbers of brown trout averaging 1.8 kg. The western side is bush-covered and inaccessible from the shore. There is limited shoreline access north of Te Kinga Reserve and, for hardy, determined anglers, across the swamp at the southern end. A small boat is a definite advantage as fish can be spotted cruising over mud and sand, and cast to in a number of locations round the lake. The narrows are a popular spot for trolling and harling. Dead trees and snags can be a problem at the southern end as hooked fish make a beeline for their hide. Cruising fish will accept a small nymph cast well in front of their path.

Poerua River

Location Drains the northern end of Lake Poerua, skirts the bush-clad Mt Te Kinga, then flows north for 7 km before entering the Crooked River in the vicinity of Lake Whitestone. The river parallels the railway line on its western side.
Access *Upper and middle reaches* From the Inchbonnie–Rotomanu Road take Station Road to the Rotomanu Rail Station then Hodgkinson Road.
Lower reaches From Te Kinga–Iveagh Bay Road.
Restrictions Bag limit is four trout.

A weigh net reveals the truth

This small, willow-lined, tea-coloured stream flows across farmland, and is lined in part by native bush on its true left bank. It holds a small population of brown trout, averaging 1 kg, which are not easy to spot. The stream is easy to cross but the brown stones are very slippery. The lower reaches upstream from the Crooked River confluence hold the most fish.

Lake Haupiri

Location and access Lies 42 km from Greymouth and east of Moana. The Nelson Creek–Kopara Road follows the northern shore.
Restrictions Bag limit is four trout.
Boat launching There are facilities for launching small boats from the road towards the eastern end of the lake.

This attractive wildlife reserve, which is surrounded by bush and farmland, is best fished from a boat either trolling a spinner or fly casting from stream mouths. Brown trout stocks are good in the small, heavily tannin-stained lake, although it is not easy to sight fish.

Lake Hochstetter

Location and access Lies 9 km southeast of Nelson Creek on the Nelson Creek–Bell Hill Road. Turn left onto a metalled forestry road, and after 10 km turn left again onto Lake Hochstetter Road.
Restrictions Bag limit is four trout.
Boat launching For small boats, from a small side track.

This small, scenic, bush-lined lake has heavily tannin-stained water. Shoreline access is very limited, and as fish are difficult to spot most trout are caught trolling a spinner or harling a fly.

Lady Lake

Location and access Lies adjacent to the Bell Hill Road 20 km from Moana.
Restrictions Bag limit is four trout.

Boat launching Small boats can be launched with some difficulty from Bell Hill Road.

The last of the Grey Valley lakes is small, tea-coloured and surrounded by bush and swamp with limited shoreline access. When the lake is low there are a couple of beaches to fish off, but generally it is best fished from a boat. The outlet stream is also impossible to fish from the shore due to swamp, rushes, flax and scrub.

Taramakau River

Location Rises near the Harper Pass, flows generally west and meets SH 73 and the Otira River at Aickens. Eventually, the river empties into the Tasman Sea west of Kumara Junction.
Access SH 73 runs parallel to the river for much of its course.
Season and restrictions Open all year below the Stanley Gooseman Bridge at Jacksons. Above this bridge, 1 October–30 April. Bag limit is four sportsfish, of which only one may be a salmon and two rainbow trout.

This large, unstable, shingly, flood-prone river does not provide good trout habitat. However, despite these unfavourable features, the river does hold some small rainbows in the upper reaches and a few good brown trout in the more stable holes near Kumara. The river has improved since dredging operations ceased in 1981 but it may still take four to five days to clear after rain. Drift dives near Kumara where the river is more stable reveal 40 browns/km of river. Because the river is prone to change course after a flood, local knowledge or, alternatively, a lot of exploring, is required to find the good stable pools. Over recent years a small run of quinnat salmon has appeared in the river during February and March. Spinning accounts for most fish caught.

The Taipo River enters the Taramakau 10 km west of Jacksons and is crossed by SH 73 close to its confluence. Because it is even more flood-prone and unstable than the Taramakau, it holds only a few resilient brown trout. There is some attractive, albeit generally unproductive, water upstream from the gorge.

Location and access These small spring creeks rise separately in the Hohonu Range and flow parallel to but north of the Taramakau River across the farming settlement of Taramakau. They can be accessed across private farmland from the end of Nicholas Road. Permission is required.

Restrictions Bag limit is four trout, but catch and release is recommended.

These two small spring creeks join about 2 km before they empty into the Taramakau River. There is good spring creek type fishing below their confluence, although willows obstruct casting in the lower reaches. Above the confluence, Clear Stream does not hold many fish. However, Nicholas Stream (the right branch walking upstream) has another 3 km of testing water. The creeks are weedy and very clear unless cows get into the water. Fish can be spotted easily, and just as easily spooked. Wear dull clothing, walk slowly upstream behind vegetation if possible, and look very carefully. The first cast is all-important and must be accurate and gently presented. Browns in this creek take mayfly and caddis imitations in the smaller sizes. Watch for fish feeding on emergers! It pays to carry a landing net.

Salmon from the Taramakau River spawn in these streams in the autumn.

Arahura River

Location Rises from the Newton Range and mountains east of Lake Kaniere, flows northwest and discharges into the sea 6 km north of Hokitika.

Access *Lower reaches* From SH 6, where a frightening combined road and rail bridge crosses the river.

Middle reaches From Arahura Valley and Humphreys Gully roads.

Upper reaches From Milltown Road via Lake Kaniere and tramping upstream.

Season and restrictions 1 October–30 April above Landsburgh Bridge. Open all year below this bridge. Bag limit is four sportsfish.

This moderately large river emerges from rugged bush-covered country to flow over farmland. Gold dredging ceased in 1960 but the river has long been a source of greenstone and has considerable significance for Maori.

The upper reaches above the Milltown Bridge are manageable for fly anglers, and sight fishing in moderately large water is possible up as far as Newton Creek. The water is clear and the river has a rock and stone bed. However, it floods easily and may take four or five days to clear.

The middle and lower reaches are best fished with a spinner as the water is large, deep and slower flowing. Holds a reasonable stock of browns, with sea-run fish entering the lower reaches early in the season when whitebait are running.

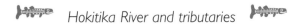 Hokitika River and tributaries

Hokitika River

Location Rises from the western slopes of the Southern Alps, flows northwest to Hokitika where it enters the Tasman Sea.
Access *Lower reaches* SH 6 crosses near the mouth in Hokitika.
Middle reaches There is good road access at Kokatahi and from roads in the region of Kowhiterangi.
Upper reaches Kokatahi Road leads to the Hokitika Gorge.
Season Open all year below the swingbridge in the lower gorge. Above this swingbridge, 1 October–30 April.
Restrictions Bag limit is four sportsfish, of which only one may be a salmon and only two may be rainbow trout.

This is a very large, flood-prone, unstable, shingly river, especially in the middle and lower reaches. However, a small population of medium-sized brown trout and sea-run fish enter the river chasing whitebait early in the season. Most fish are taken on spinners.

In the middle reaches, the river is unattractive and hardly worth a look. It is too large and too unstable.

The upper reaches can be accessed by tramping from the road end, but the river often contains glacial flour. However, there are a few rainbows in this upper section.

From January to April, a run of quinnat (king or chinook) salmon enters the river, providing excitement for salmon anglers.

Whitcombe River

Location and access Drains the Main Divide of the Southern Alps, flows north through a remote valley before joining the Hokitika River. It is a two-hour tramp on a bush track from the end of Kokatahi Road to the river. There are Department of Conservation huts in the valley that are good to use as a base, but up-to-date

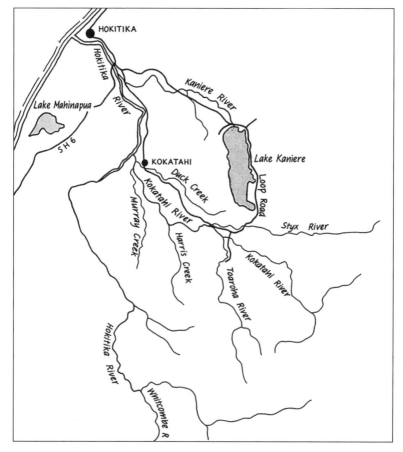

Hokitika River system

information on their state should be obtained from DoC before embarking on the tramp.

Restrictions Bag limit is four sportsfish, only one of which may be a salmon.

Fly tying in the camper on a rainy day

From a fly fishing viewpoint, the remote Whitcombe River tributary holds considerable interest as it contains a healthy population of rainbow trout. The Whitcombe is a medium-sized river that usually contains glacial flour, so trout are very difficult to spot. Rather, the likely looking water in this river should be fished blind with heavily weighted nymphs and an indicator or a large, buoyant terrestrial imitation dry fly. The rainbows are generally in good condition and fight well in the strong current. It is often not easy to follow a lively fish downstream. Remember, this is high rainfall country and the sandflies are fierce. A few of the larger side streams such as the Cropp and Price rivers hold fish in their lower reaches and are also worth exploring for the tramper-angler.

Kaniere River

Location Drains the northern end of Lake Kaniere, flows northwest and enters the Hokitika River close to the SH 6 bridge.

Access From Lake Kaniere Road by scrambling down through scrub and bush in some places.
Season Open all year.
Restrictions Bag limit is four sportsfish, but only one of these may be a salmon.

This small to medium-sized stream is heavily tannin-stained and has been modified for hydro-electric power. The upper reaches are heavily bush-clad, but there is fishable water below the power station. However, it is fast flowing and not highly valued. The river holds brown trout, with a few salmon entering from January to April. Best fished with a spinner.

Kokatahi River

Location Rises from bush-clad foothills inland from Hokitika, flows northwest and joins the Hokitika River at Kokatahi.
Access From Upper Kokatahi and Lake Kaniere Loop roads.
Season Below the Styx River confluence it is open all year. Above the confluence, 1 October–30 April.
Restrictions Bag limit is four sportsfish, of which only one may be a salmon.

This medium-sized river is similar to its parent river in being unstable and flood-prone. However, for anglers who are prepared to walk, there is more stable water upstream from the Kaniere Loop Road bridge. Here, fish can be sight fished, and although stocks are not great the scenery, isolation and angling experience makes a long day worthwhile.

Styx River

Location Flows in a westerly direction just south of Lake Kaniere to join the Kokatahi River a few kilometres below the Upper Kokatahi Road bridge.
Access From Upper Kokatahi and Lake Kaniere Loop roads.
Restrictions Bag limit is four sportsfish, but only one of these may be a salmon.

A small, clear-water, freestone type stream that holds a few brown trout. The best water can be accessed by tramping upriver from the road. There is 8 km of scenic, bush-clad river to explore, although fish numbers are not high.

Toaroha River

Location Joins the Kokatahi River upstream from Styx confluence.
Access From a side road off the Upper Kokatahi Road just south of the Styx River.
Restrictions Bag limit is four sportsfish, but only one of these may be a salmon.

A small freestone stream that holds low numbers of small brown trout. The upper, bush-clad reaches above the gorge are worth exploring early in the season for the active angler.

Duck, Harris and Murray creeks

Location The last of the Hokitika tributaries to be described are three spring creeks in the Kokatahi farming district southeast of Hokitika. They all flow into the Kokatahi River.
Access
• Duck Creek from Upper Kokatahi Road.
• Harris Creek from Cropp and Ford roads.
• Murray Creek also from Ford Road.
Permission must be obtained from the local farmers before fishing these creeks.
Restrictions Bag limit is two trout.

Despite being adversely affected by dairy-farming operations, these creeks hold brown trout and are worth a look, especially on a bright day. Fish spotted in the weedy creeks must be approached with care. As with most spring creeks, use small mayfly or caddis imitations and long fine tippets. When hooked, trout make a dive for the weed beds, so it pays to carry a landing net. The creeks remain fishable after moderate rain.

Lake Kaniere

Location and access Lies southeast of Hokitika and can be reached from Kaniere Valley Road.
Season Open all year.
Restrictions Bag limit is four sportsfish.

This very attractive bush-lined lake holds brown trout and perch in tea-coloured water. There is limited shoreline fishing at Sunny Bay, Hans Bay and at the mouth of Geologists Creek. Most fish are caught by trolling from boats.

Lake Mahinapua

Location and access Turn off SH 6 at the Mahinapua Hotel, 12 km south of Hokitika.
Season Open all year.
Boat launching At Shanghai Bay, off Ruatapu Road on the western shore.

As shoreline access in this lake is limited to Shanghai Bay and part of the walkway, most of the fishing is done from a boat, either trolling a spinner or jigging. Like Lake Kaniere, the tea-coloured water holds perch and small brown trout but fish cannot normally be spotted. Dense weed beds make shoreline spin fishing difficult.

Mahinapua Creek

Location Drains Lake Mahinapua, flows north and enters the south side of the Hokitika River near its mouth.
Access Turn right off SH 6 onto Golf Links Road and right again at the Mahinapua Creek bridge.
Season Open all year.

This tannin-stained creek is difficult to fish in most places as it is overgrown with flax. However, sea-run browns chasing whitebait are caught on spinners early in the season, near the mouth.

Totara River

Location From its rainforest headwaters, this small river flows west to enter the sea just north of Ross.

Access *Lower reaches* From SH 6, which crosses the river.

Middle reaches From Totara Valley Road, which leaves SH 6 north of Ross.

Season Below SH 6, open all year. Above SH 6, open 1 October–30 April.

This small, bouldery, tea-coloured river holds small resident brown trout, with sea-run fish entering the estuary early in the season. It is best fished from Totara Valley Road, although a scramble down through bush is required to reach the river.

Mikonui River

Location From its remote, mountainous headwaters in the Southern Alps, this medium-sized river flows generally northwest to enter the sea just south of Ross.

Access *Lower reaches* From SH 6 and a rough metalled track to the mouth.

Middle reaches Walk upstream from SH 6 bridge.

Upper reaches From the end of Totara Valley Road at Gribben Flat. This is a long, tortuous, one-way metalled road that could become impassable after heavy rain. Best accessed with a four-wheel-drive. Permission should be sought from the landowners.

Season Open all year below SH 6. Above SH 6, open 1 October–30 April.

The Mikonui is a clear-water, freestone river, flood-prone and unstable in its middle reaches, yet it holds some healthy brown trout. The lower reaches see good numbers of sea-run browns early in the season when the whitebait are running. These can be caught on spinners or smelt flies. The deep holes near SH 6 hold a few fish, but as access is easy they get a lot of attention from passing anglers.

The upper and middle reaches hold a few good fish in the more stable runs and pools but a lot of walking is required between fish.

The riverbed is wide and shingly, and the more stable water running against a bank is often overhung by bush. It is not worth fishing above the Tuke River confluence. The Tuke itself soon enters a very difficult gorge and, rather surprisingly, there are very few fish in these deep holes. The north branch (Mikonui) has a good spawning run late in the season but holds few resident trout.

Ellis Creek

Location and access Ellis Creek, a tributary of the Waitaha River, winds across cleared farmland to join the main river just upstream on the north side of the Waitaha Bridge on SH 6. The confluence can be reached from this bridge, while Waitaha Valley Road crosses further upstream.
Restrictions Bag limit is four trout, but catch and release is recommended.

This small, tea-coloured, rain-fed creek is worth exploring from the mouth and upstream for 1 km above the Waitaha Valley bridge. Trout are difficult to spot except on bright sunny days, and fish stocks are too unreliable for the creek to be successfully fished blind. Dairy farming has affected the creek. The banks are grass, with patches of native bush and a few willows, while the stream bed is shingle and mud.

The Waitaha River is a large, flood-prone, shingly river, which being snow- and glacially fed carries silt for much of the year. When clear there are a few brown trout in some of the more stable holes, and sea-run fish enter the estuary early in the season. Open all year below SH 6.

Lake Ianthe

Location and access SH 6 skirts the eastern shore south of Ross.
Season Open all year.
Restrictions Bag limit is four sportsfish.
Boat launching Off SH 6 near the southern end of the lake.

This small, shallow, scenic lake holds a good stock of brown trout. Because of the limited shoreline access it is best fished from a boat or float-tube. The lake is surrounded by bush. Trolling can be difficult near the shore because of the shallow weed beds, but fly casting from a boat can be very profitable. Try lightly weighted damsel nymphs and Woolly Buggers retrieved slowly between weed beds.

The outlet creek at the southern end is also open all year. At times this holds good cruising fish, but it can be reduced to a muddy drain when the flooded, silt-laden Wanganui River flows back up the creek towards the lake.

The flood-prone Wanganui River holds a few trout but, being a typical unstable, snow-fed West Coast river, it is not worth spending time fishing it. The estuary, however, is worth exploring for sea-run browns early in the season, and an occasional salmon in February and March. It is open all year below SH 6. Take Wanganui Flat Road from Harihari to the estuary.

La Fontaine Stream

Location Drains a swamp south of Harihari, flows north across farmland for 16 km and enters the Wanganui River north of Harihari.
Access Turn down Wanganui Flat Road from Harihari. A number of side roads on your left lead to the stream. Take Petersons Road for access to the upper reaches and look for marked anglers' access points off La Fontaine Road. Many sections of the stream can be reached across private farmland, provided you obtain permission first.
Restrictions Bag limit is four trout.

This small, spring-fed stream is highly regarded by fly fishers. The lower reaches are willow-choked in parts, the middle reaches have flax, willows and patches of bush along the banks, while the upper reaches are reasonably clear, although the stream can be weedy. Although fish spotting is difficult because of the brown stones and lightly tea-coloured water, there are sufficient numbers of brown trout averaging around 1.2 kg to make blind fishing worthwhile. If trout are rising then so much the letter, but there are some fine pools and attractive riffles to fish. At times trout can be selective so it pays to match the hatch and use a long fine tippet. Mayflies and caddis form the majority of the food, but terrestrials such as the green manuka beetle, grasshoppers and cicadas also contribute. Soft hackle wets and emergers have their place, as have small Pheasant Tail, Green Caddis and Hare's Ear nymphs, Parachute Adams, Sparkle Dun, Dad's Favourite and Coch-y-bondhu dry flies.

Berry's Creek

Location This creek also drains the Wanganui River flats north of Harihari before emptying into the Wanganui River.
Access Take Wanganui Flat Road from Harihari, but instead of turning left onto La Fontaine Road, carry straight on to where the road crosses the creek and ends at a stopbank on the Wanganui River. Drive down this stopbank as far as possible before walking left across to the creek. Please ask permission at the last farm before fishing (Mr Berry).
Restrictions Bag limit of four fish, which is ridiculous in my opinion. I strongly suggest catch and release.

This small, clear spring creek can provide a full day's fishing for sighted brown trout averaging 1.3 kg. The banks are swampy and overgrown in places, but there is plenty of unobstructed water to fish. As with most spring creeks, fish are easier to see on a bright day, but the background foliage does help on this stream. Use similar flies to those suggested for La Fontaine, wear dull green or brown clothing, walk very slowly and carefully, and make the first cast pay. There are few fish upstream from the road bridge.

The Poerua River south of Harihari, off Petersons Road, is shingly and unstable. It holds a few sea-run browns and an occasional salmon in the lower reaches but is not highly recommended. Open all season below SH 6.

Whataroa River

Location Drains the glaciers and snowfields of the Main Divide, flows northwest at first through remote bush-clad mountains, then across farmland before entering the Tasman Sea north of Whataroa.

Access Crossed by SH 6 north of Whataroa township.

Season Open all year.

This very large, unstable, flood-prone river does not appear to offer a stable environment for trout. For most of the year it carries snow-melt and glacial flour. However, in low water winter conditions, brown trout can be caught on spinning gear in the holes adjacent to the SH 6 bridge. These may be spawning sea-runners rather than resident fish, but at times the river holds a good stock of these fish. For tramper-anglers, the Perth tributary in the upper reaches is worth spin fishing.

Waitangitaona River

Location Drains swampy country around Whataroa, skirts the northern boundary of Okarito State Forest and enters the sea just north of the Okarito Lagoon.

Access From Whataroa, take Whataroa Flat Road past the old sawmilling settlement of Rotokino to the White Heron Sanctuary Tours boat launching ramp. This road crosses the river and offers 6 km of reasonable access both below and above the road bridge.

Restrictions Bag limit is four fish.

In about 1965 a major flood altered the course of this river and directed the unstable, silt-laden upper waters into Lake Wahapo. The lower reaches remained as a medium-sized spring creek. Fishing subsequently improved, as the stable lower river now seldom discolours, whereas after rain the upper river sends silt into Lake Wahapo.

The lower river meanders its way west across swampy farmland and provides excellent sight fishing for large brown trout averaging 2 kg. Fish stocks are generally good but sea-run fish enter the river before Christmas, boosting numbers. As the bank vegetation is generally low, a sheen on the water makes spotting fish very difficult except on bright, sunny days. The trout are very spooky, and unless you can spot them some distance ahead, your chances of tempting them are remote. It pays to fish with a friend and take turns spotting. The banks are generally clear although there are clumps of toetoe, a few willows and the odd patch of bush. Wading and crossing under normal conditions is safe on a gravel and sand bed. There are some very deep holes that hold fish over 4 kg, but these are impossible to tempt during the day. A mouse imitation at night may be the answer! Anglers fishing the lower reaches can expect to be disturbed by a jetboat, but the trout appear to have become used to this. Most fish are taken on well-weighted nymphs such as Perla, Stonefly and Hare and Copper. However, in summer, trout can be stalked along the bank edges with a dry fly such as Black Gnat, Elk Hair Caddis and Royal Wulff. Use a long tippet as lining the fish will scatter them in all directions.

Lake Wahapo

Location and access SH 6 follows the southern shore of this lake a few kilometres south of Whataroa.
Season Open all year.

Although this small lake holds brown trout, the water quality has been ruined by the upper Waitangitaona River changing its course and dumping silt into the lake. Shoreline access is difficult. Best fished from a boat.

Lake Mapourika

Location Lies 10 km north of Franz Josef on SH 6.
Access SH 6 follows the eastern shore.
Season Open all year for trout. For salmon, 1 October–31 March.
Restrictions Bag limit is four sportsfish, but only one of these may be a salmon. Minimum length of fish is 25 cm. McDonalds Creek is closed to fishing.
Boat launching Facilities are at the southern end of the lake.

This is an excellent medium-sized lake, which holds good numbers of brown trout averaging 1.6 kg and a small population of resident quinnat salmon, first released into the lake in 1932. From December to March a run of quinnat salmon enters the lake from the sea via the Okarito Lagoon and Okarito River. Whereas the resident salmon average 1–2 kg, the sea-run salmon average 5 kg with some reaching 8 kg in weight. Despite the tea-coloured lake water and the shoreline bush, cruising trout can be spotted on sunny days especially when the lake level is low. However, shoreline fishing is restricted to an area between the mouth of McDonalds Creek and the Okarito River outlet, and at the mouth of Red Jacks Creek.

Trout seem most receptive to bully imitations such as Mrs Simpson, Hamill's Killer and Woolly Bugger lures. Fly casting under the bush from a boat with a green beetle is worthwhile in summer. Most salmon are caught deep trolling a spinner, with top spots being near the outlet, Jetty Bay and around the mouth of Red Jacks Creek.

The Okarito River holds fish, but is generally swift, tea-coloured and overgrown with bush. The road to Okarito crosses the river near The Forks and SH 6 follows the river upstream for some distance. You need to be desperate to spend time fishing this river.

Okarito Lagoon holds sea-run browns and salmon at times.

Karangarua River

Location and access Drains the Main Divide in the region of Aoraki/Mt Cook, flows northwest through bush-clad country and enters the Tasman Sea north of Makawhio Point. The mouth and estuary can be reached by walking for two hours north along the beach from Hunts Beach.

Season Open all year below SH 6. Above SH 6, open 1 October–30 April.

This typically large, unstable, snow- and glacier-fed river becomes clear and fishable during low water flows in winter. It is best suited to spin fishing, although some side braids and spring creeks near the mouth can be explored with a fly. The estuary holds good numbers of sea-run browns during the whitebait season.

The Copeland River tributary in the headwaters is more stable and holds some good brown trout, but this river is a five-hour tramp upstream on the Copeland Track.

The Manakaiaua River near Hunt's Beach sometimes holds a few sea-run browns but stocks are unreliable.

Jacobs River (Makawhio)

Location Drains the Main Divide, flows generally northwest and enters the sea at Makawhio Point just north of Bruce Bay.
Access *Lower reaches* SH 6 crosses the river at the settlement of Jacobs River, near the school. There is access both above and below the main road bridge.
Middle reaches A private farm track follows up the true left bank for some distance. It is necessary to obtain permission from the landowner to use this track as the gate is locked.
Upper reaches By tramping upstream or by helicopter.
Season Open all year below SH 6 bridge. Above SH 6 bridge, 1 October–30 April.
Restrictions Bag limit is four fish.

The upper reaches flow through remote bush-clad mountains, and only anglers experienced in bushcraft should attempt to access them. This medium-sized, rock and stone type river offers good sight fishing and stalking for a good population of wild brown trout averaging 1.5 kg.

The middle reaches emerge from the hills and flow much more sedately across cleared farmland. There are long, smooth glides and the clear water makes fish very easy to spot. However, they see you a mile away and are easily spooked. It is a real test to deceive fish in these conditions. Careful stalking, a long fine tippet and an accurate first cast will help.

Large sea-run browns enter the lower reaches from September to December chasing whitebait, and these provide good sport to spin anglers and fly fishers using smelt fly patterns.

The unstable Mahitahi River at Bruce Bay also offers sea-run browns in the lower reaches at the same time of year. Open all year below SH 6.

Paringa River

Location Drains the Strachan Range and other remote bush-clad mountains, flows northwest and reaches SH 6 just north of Lake Paringa.

Access From SH 6 by walking upstream, or downstream 5 km to the Hall River confluence and the mouth. There is a rough access track to the mouth for whitebaiting.

Season Open all year below SH 6. Above SH 6, open 1 October–30 April. Season for salmon is 1 October–30 April.

Restrictions Bag limit is four sportsfish, only one may be a salmon.

Despite carrying snow-melt and glacial flour, this medium-sized, flood-prone, shingly river does hold a few good brown trout, mainly downstream below the SH 6 bridge. Only in low water conditions can fish be spotted, and tannin-stained water entering from the Hall River does not help water clarity further downstream.

Sea-run brown trout chase whitebait into the lower reaches in the spring, while a small run of salmon enters the river from January to March. Although there is a salmon farm at the SH 6 bridge, these fish are best fished for below the Hall River confluence.

The tea-coloured Hall River, which drains Lake Paringa, holds brown trout but a long walk down the Paringa riverbed is required and the river is overgrown with bush.

Lake Paringa

Location and access SH 6 runs along the southeastern shore of this small lake between Bruce Bay and Haast. There are basic camping facilities and a motel.

Season Open all year for trout fishing but the salmon season is 1 October–31 March.

Restrictions Bag limit is four sportsfish, only one of which may be a salmon. Minimum length of all fish taken is 25 cm.

Boat launching Facilities are available.

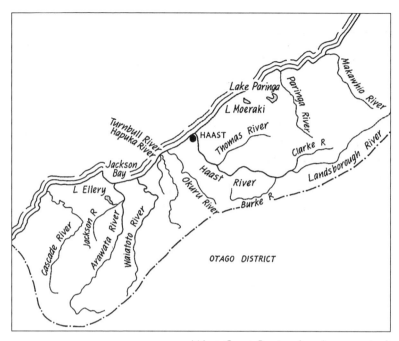

West Coast Region (southern section)

This tea-coloured lake is surrounded by bush and swamp, making shoreline angling virtually impossible. Boat fishing by trolling a spinner is the favourite method, although stream mouth fly fishing, after boat access, is possible in low water conditions. Casting a Coch-y-bondhu dry fly from a boat along the bush margins can be effective. The mouth of Collie Creek in the south arm is a favourite spot.

Sea-run salmon can be caught from January to March by deep trolling a spinner.

Windbag Creek is worth exploring for bush-bashing anglers, as it does hold a few brown trout in attractive-looking water. These can be sight fished, although some of the holes are dark and deep. SH 6 follows up the creek for some distance just south of Lake Paringa before finally crossing it. The season for trout is 1 October–30 April; for salmon 1 October–31 March. However, I cannot imagine trying to play a salmon in this small, overgrown creek.

Location and access Lies closer to the sea than Lake Paringa, and 15 km further south on SH 6. There is access from the main road although a small boat is a decided advantage.

Season Open all year for trout, 1 October–31 March for salmon.

Restrictions Bag limit is four sportsfish, only one of which may be a salmon. Minimum length for all fish is 25 cm.

Boat launching A small boat can be launched near the outlet.

This small, lightly tea-coloured lake holds good numbers of browns averaging 1.5 kg, although in the past trout up to 4 kg have been caught. Shoreline fishing is restricted to the eastern shore and to the Moeraki (Blue) River delta.

Fish can be seen cruising on a bright day. However, most fishing is done from a boat by trolling a spinner as the shoreline is swampy and very difficult to negotiate. Casting an attractor pattern such as a Green Humpy over the weed beds along the southern shore is worth trying.

A small run of salmon enters the lake from the outlet stream from January to March, and these can be caught by deep trolling a spinner.

Moeraki (Blue) River

Location Drains the Main Divide, flows northwest and enters the southern end of Lake Moeraki.

Access *Upper and middle reaches* The old Paringa–Haast cattle track leaves SH 6, 7 km south of Lake Paringa. It is well-signposted and crosses the middle reaches 5 km from SH 6. The upper reaches can be accessed by tramping upstream in remote country from this crossing, or by helicopter.

Lower reaches These are easily seen and accessed from SH 6.

Season Above SH 6, open 1 October–30 April. Open all year below SH 6. The salmon season closes on 31 March.

Restrictions Bag limit is four sportsfish, only one of which may be a salmon.

This river is reasonably stable, although like all West Coast rivers it can rise alarmingly after heavy rain. Sight fishing is easy in the clear water although fish stocks are not great in the lower reaches. The mouth is a top spot for cruising trout. The middle and upper reaches offer good back country fishing, but remember to take insect repellent.

The Waita River further south, which is crossed by SH 6 soon after it reaches the coast, also holds a few browns especially in the estuary when whitebait are running. It is lightly tea-stained from the Maori River tributary.

 Haast River and tributaries

Haast River

Location This large snow- and glacially fed river drains an enormous catchment of the Southern Alps. It flows west for much of its course and enters the sea near Haast township.
Access SH 6 crosses the lower reaches and follows the river upstream for many kilometres towards the Haast Pass. Access is not difficult from this main highway.
Season Open all year below Pleasant Flat Bridge. Elsewhere, 1 October–30 April.

The upper reaches between the Wills and Burke tributaries are gorgy, boisterous and difficult. Near the Burke confluence the river becomes manageable, in that it can be waded and crossed at selected sites. It is a clear, rock and stone type river with bush lining the banks. Trout stocks are not high, however.

The middle and lower reaches become very large below the Landsborough confluence and the river often carries glacial flour and snow-melt. There are some very deep holes but not many trout; spinning is the best method of tempting them.

Some large sea-run browns are occasionally caught at the mouth on spinning gear.

Location Flows southwest through remote, high-rainfall, bush-clad, mountainous country to join the true right bank of the Haast River 12 km upriver from Haast settlement, opposite the Thomas Bluff.

Access

- By fording the Haast River or crossing by boat and tramping into the valley. The Thomas Hut (6 bunks) is 6 km up the valley on the true left bank. The Haast River can be very dangerous to cross except in low water conditions, and even then great care should be taken. The track through the bush is difficult and overgrown.
- By struggling up the true right bank of the Haast River from the SH 6 bridge and tramping into the Thomas Valley. This is even more difficult.
- By helicopter.

Restrictions Bag limit is four trout.

Only experienced tramper-anglers should attempt to walk in to this remote valley. Floods can be frightening as there is old driftwood 5 m above the river at the Thomas Hut. The river is normally small and easy to cross, and sight fishing for good-sized brown trout in among snags and fallen trees can be a challenge. The best water lies two hours upstream from the hut, away from snags, where the occasional fish can reach 4 kg in weight. Downstream from the hut lies an impressive, rugged gorge that is not worth fishing. Towards the Haast confluence there are some large pools that hold trout. Sandfly and mosquito protection is essential for one's mental health, and it is necessary to keep the hut fire going all night to prevent a mosquito invasion down the chimney!

Location Joins the true right bank of the Landsborough River 5 km upstream from Clarke Bluff.

Access This can be hazardous as the Landsborough River must be forded. In low water, experienced tramper-anglers can cross below

Strutt Bluff. The Landsborough River must be treated with great respect.

Restrictions Bag limit is four trout.

Angling is best combined with tramping or deer stalking as the river is not worth the effort of fishing alone. The lower reaches are shingly, braided and unstable. In the region of Rabbit Flat, some 10 km upstream, there is more stable water but stocks are not great.

Landsborough River

This is the largest tributary of the Haast, at over 50 km in length, and it drains the glaciers and snowfields of the Main Divide. Rarely does the river not hold snow-melt and glacial flour. Trampers, hunters, mountaineers and rafters frequent this valley, and although this boisterous, flood-prone, unstable river holds a few fish it cannot be recommended as a fishery.

Burke River

Location This small to medium-sized river joins the true left bank of the Haast 10 km upstream from Clarke Bluff.
Access From SH 6, although the upper Haast River needs to be crossed. This is normally not difficult in low water. An overgrown tramping track follows upstream on the true left bank but access to the river is steep and difficult from this track.
Restrictions Bag limit is four trout.

Only the lower reaches hold a few brown trout as an impassable gorge prevents progress to the upper reaches. The lower reaches are deep, gorgy and exceptionally clear and difficult to fish. The water is an intense blue colour and any trout can be spotted very easily. They see you equally well and even a long, fine tippet cast over them will scare them into their hide.

The last tributary of the Haast River is the rugged Wills River at the Gates of Haast, but this is not worth fishing.

Rivers and lakes south of Haast

Season Downstream from the Haast–Jackson Bay Road the rivers are open for fishing all year. Above this road, 1 October–30 April.
Restrictions Bag limit is four trout.

Okuru River

Location Drains the Browning and Mark ranges south of the Haast River, flows northwest at first through bush-covered mountains, then across farmland, and enters a lagoon just west of the Haast Motor Camp.
Access *Upper reaches* By tramping upriver from the road end or by helicopter. Franklin Hut is a good base, but it is a very full day's tramp from the road end.
Middle and lower reaches Nolan's Road off the Haast–Cascade Road leads up the true left bank. The lagoon lies just west of the Haast Motor Camp.
Season Open all year below the Haast–Jackson Bay road.

The upper reaches of this medium-sized river offer good sight fishing in clear mountain water for browns averaging 2 kg.

There is good water upstream from Franklin Hut until the river enters the bush.

The middle reaches off Nolan Road are clear and willow-lined, with long glides and gravel runs. Reasonable numbers of brown trout can be spotted and stalked. Watch for snags, however, as most fish when hooked make a dash for their hide, usually beneath a fallen tree.

The lagoon holds estuarine-living trout and is best fished with a spinner.

Turnbull River

Location Rises from similar mountainous terrain to the Okuru River, flows parallel to but south of the Okuru, and discharges into the same estuary.
Access As there are no trout above the Venture Gorge power station only the middle and lower reaches are described. Roads

leave the Haast–Cascade Road and follow up both banks near the Haast Motor Camp.

Season Open all year below the Haast–Jackson Bay road.

This medium-sized river, which flows across farmland, holds a reaonable stock of brown trout. The banks are willow-lined in places and the pools are long and clear. There is good sight fishing on a stable, shingle riverbed, but the trout use sunken logs and debris to their advantage when hooked. There is good water across the paddocks near the Haast Gun Club.

Hapuka River

Location Drains swampland south of the Turnbull River, flows north and enters the same lagoon as the Okuru and Turnbull rivers.
Access Walk across the paddocks opposite the Okuru venison factory.
Season Open all year.

This small river differs from the Turnbull and Okuru rivers in that the water is heavily tannin-stained. The banks are swampy and flax-infested, making access very difficult. It is best fished with a spinner early in the season when the whitebait are running.

Waiatoto River

Location This large glacier- and snow-fed river rises from Mt Aspiring and flows north through remote unroaded and untracked country to enter the Tasman Sea 12 km south of Okuru.
Access *Upper and middle reaches* By tramping, jetboat or helicopter.
Lower reaches The Haast–Cascade Road crosses just upstream from the mouth. A small gravel side road leads down the true left bank as far as Hindley Creek.
Season Open all year below the Haast–Jackson Bay road.

Only the lower reaches are worth a look in spring and early summer when the whitebait are running or in winter when the river is low and clear. There are a few large estuarine-living and sea-run browns, which are best fished to with a spinner.

Hindley Creek also holds some good browns but access is difficult. Tramper-anglers visiting the upper reaches should carry a collapsible spinning rod and try Te Naihi at Axius Flats, the Drake at Drake Flats, and the upper reaches of the main river around Bonar Flats. However, there are many better rivers to fish on the West Coast than the Waiatoto.

Arawata River

Location Drains the Olivine Ice Plateau, flows north parallel to but south of the Waiatoto River, and enters the sea just north of Neils Beach.
Access As the upper and middle reaches are not worth fishing only the lower reaches are briefly considered here. The Haast–Cascade Road crosses the lower reaches and the mouth can be accessed by walking north from Neils Beach.
Season Open all year below the Haast–Jackson Bay road.

Like its neighbour the Waiatoto, the Arawata is a large, unstable, snow- and glacier-fed river that holds a few good sea-run fish in the lower reaches in spring and early summer. Rarely does the river run free of glacial flour, but when it clears it can be fished with a spinner.

Jackson River

Location Drains the McArthur Tops and Lake Ellery, flows generally north and joins the Arawata River near the main road bridge.
Access The Haast–Cascade Road follows up the true left bank and access is reasonably easy from this road.

Above the Ellery confluence the river is small and clear, and holds a few good browns in the more stable pools and runs. The native bush that overhangs parts of the river provides plenty of terrestrial food.

Below the Ellery confluence fish numbers are greater but the river becomes lightly tea-coloured.

Lake Ellery

Location Lies inland, south of Jackson Bay.
Access The Haast–Cascade Road crosses the outlet stream in the Jackson River Valley. From a carpark there is a 40-minute walk on a cut track up the true right bank of the outlet stream to the lake.
Season Open all year.
Restrictions Bag limit is four sportsfish, only one of which may be a salmon. The minimum length is 25 cm.

This small, peat-stained lake is surrounded by native bush, making shoreline access difficult. It is possible to navigate up the outlet stream to the lake in a rubber dinghy, and this would be an advantage. When the lake is low there is reasonable wading and fly fishing around the outlet. However, most visits to the lake are to observe the birdlife. The trout feed on freshwater mussels, and as yet I have not managed to tie an artificial mussel!

Martyr River

Location Drains the northern end of the remote Olivine Range, flows north and joins the Cascade River 3 km west of the old Martyr Homestead.
Access The lower end of the Haast–Cascade Road follows the true left bank for some distance downstream. Beyond the road end, access is across private farmland and permission should be obtained. It is an hour's walk to the Cascade-Martyr confluence.

There are no trout above Monkey Puzzle Gorge. Below the gorge the river is small, shingly and flood-prone, but the lower 2 km of river and the Cascade-Martyr river confluence are well worth fishing. Trout can be spotted and stalked.

Cascade River

Location Drains the Olivine Range and the Red Hills, flows north to The Bend near Smiths Ponds, then turns northwest to enter the sea 20 km south of Jackson Bay.

Access *Lower reaches* Walk across private farmland from the road end after obtaining permission from the small farmhouse that replaced the old Martyr Homestead. The river flows through difficult, swampy country.

Walk down through Nolan's cattle yards at the top of the hill before reaching the road end.

Middle and upper reaches Can only be accessed by tramping upriver through typical remote West Coast terrain. There are no tracks or huts above The Bend. Some anglers fly in by helicopter, which is not unreasonable considering the country.

Season Open all year.

Restrictions Bag limit is four trout.

The lower 18 km below the Martyr River confluence are tidal and swampy but support the largest whitebait population in New Zealand. There are plenty of trout in these lower reaches which, because of the difficult access, rarely get fished.

The middle and upper reaches flow through dense native bush and are typically rock and stone in character. Fish numbers are good in this clear-water section of river, although they vary a little from year to year. The river can be crossed at selected sites in normal conditions. There is no difficulty with sight fishing, and especially above the Cascade Gorge browns up to 3–4 kg can be stalked. Beware of flash floods in this remote country, and take plenty of insect repellent.

The inaccessible Gorge River between Cascade and Big Bay holds a few sea-run browns in the lower reaches but this is only of interest to trampers.

North Canterbury Fish and Game Council region

This large and varied region stretches from the Waiau River in the northeast to the Rakaia River in the southeast; from Lewis Pass in the northwest to the Rakaia headwaters in the southwest. The Southern Alps, which rise to over 2000 m, are the western boundary. To the east lie the fertile, intensively farmed Canterbury Plains.

Although the prevailing winds on the coast are easterly, inland the nor'wester dictates the weather pattern. The nor'wester collects moisture from the Tasman Sea and, as the airstream rises and cools, dumps most of this in the Alps and on the West Coast. The resulting strong, dry, warm wind then sweeps across the Canterbury Plains in a similar fashion to the 'chinook' in Montana, drying all before it.

An angler leaving Christchurch in a light easterly wind can find a strong nor'wester blowing in the high country. These strong winds are especially common in spring, and usually precede a centre of low pressure followed by a cold front. They bring heavy rain to the Alps and can cause flooding in large snow-fed rivers such as the Waiau, Hurunui, Waimakariri and Rakaia. Anglers may find it difficult to stand upright in a good blow, let alone cast a fly. However, high country trout do not seem to be affected by the nor'wester and often feed with great enthusiasm, much to the frustration of anglers carrying lightweight, soft rods. An easterly wind in the high country is generally not conducive to good fishing; trout do not seem to feed.

With hot, dry summers and nor'west weather, rain-fed streams and spring creeks on the Canterbury Plains often suffer low water conditions to the point where trout survival is jeopardised. This has been accentuated over the last few years by the introduction of dairy farming in place of traditional dry land farming. Irrigation has become essential, thereby depleting ground water and the source of some low country creeks. In the dry summer of 1999, the Irwell and Hawkins rivers dried completely and the Selwyn River ran very low.

Canterbury is blessed by having four large, snow-fed rivers — the Waiau, Hurunui, Waimakariri and Rakaia — which host a healthy quinnat salmon run from December to April. There are brown and rainbow trout throughout the region, a few macinaw in Lake Pearson, landlocked quinnat salmon in Lake Coleridge and the odd splake in Lake Letitia.

The North Canterbury Fish and Game Council region is divided into two zones: western and eastern. The eastern zone is the area

North Canterbury region

east of a line extending from white posts on the Rakaia River near the Coleridge Power Station, to the white post at Woodstock on the Waimakariri River, to the Oxford–Glentui Road bridge on the Ashley River, to the junction of the Hurunui River with its South Branch, to the junction of the Waiau and Hope rivers; and excluding Lake Rubicon.

The western zone is the area west of the eastern zone, and includes Lake Rubicon.

Season *Eastern zone* Unless otherwise stated, 1 October–30 April. *Western zone* Unless otherwise stated, for all rivers except those flowing into lakes and Broken River (note specific Rakaia River closures), 1 October–30 April. All rivers and streams flowing into western zone lakes, 1 December–31 March. The Wilberforce River and tributaries, including the diversion and canals, are included in this category.

For all western zone lakes, first Saturday in November–30 April. For the Rakaia River and tributaries for trout fishing, and for salmon fishing in all rivers in the western zone, 1 October–28 February.

Restrictions Bag limit is six sportsfish.
Trout Eastern zone, four; western zone, four in lakes Coleridge and Sumner, elsewhere two.
Salmon In Lake Coleridge, six; elsewhere two.

 *Waiau River and tributaries*

All tributaries lie in the western zone, with the season opening on 1 October and closing on 30 April. Bag limit is two trout, although catch and release is strongly recommended.

Waiau River

Location Rises in the Spenser Mountains, flows south until it joins the Hope River at Glenhope on SH 7. The river then turns northeast, parallels SH 7 almost to Culverden and finally reaches the sea north of Cheviot.

Access *Upper Waiau*
- By walking for 2–3 hours over Malings or Fowlers Pass from the Hanmer Hydro Road. Prior permission should be obtained from St James Station.
- By tramping St James Walkway for two days from Lewis Pass.
- By four-wheel-drive through Glenhope Station (permission required). The Station charges for access and use of its huts.

Middle and lower Waiau There is reasonable access from SH 7, the Rotherham–Waiau Road and Waiau township.

Mouth This is difficult without a jetboat. There is a gravel launching area opposite a quarry off the East Waiau Road in Spotswood.

Season Open all year below the Hope confluence. Above this confluence, 1 October–30 April. For salmon fishing, 1 October–28 February.

Restrictions Bag limit is two trout above the Hope confluence; below this point the limit is four sportsfish, but only two of these may be salmon. For salmon anglers, the river becomes difficult when the flow rate exceeds 90 cumecs.

The upper Waiau is difficult to access. The headwaters flow through bush-clad hills, but by Malings Pass the river runs through pasture and patches of manuka and matagouri scrub. Although medium-sized, the river can be crossed, and trout sight fished in clear, bright conditions. However, in nor'west rain the river rises rapidly and soon becomes impassable. The riverbed is shingle and rock, with a gorgy section above the Ada confluence. There are deep pools and long stable runs with grassy banks, and although the trout population is not high, most are well worth catching, with always the chance of a trophy fish.

There are three full days' fishing from the Hope confluence to Malings Pass, but few fish above this location. Like most high country brown trout, the fish are not super-selective provided they are carefully stalked and the first cast is accurate.

Catch and release is suggested in this section to preserve the gene pool. Once spawning salmon enter the river in mid-March, brown-trout fishing becomes very difficult as spooked salmon race up and down the river frightening all the other fish.

The middle reaches above Hanmer hold some good fish but are difficult to cover with a fly except in low water summer conditions. Below Hanmer the river is best fished with a spinner, as it becomes large, unstable and braided. A moderate quinnat salmon run appears from January to March and most fishing in this stretch of water is devoted to salmon.

There is a large lagoon at the mouth, although the mouth changes with storms. Salmon can be caught both in the surf and in the lagoon, along with an occasional sea-run brown trout.

Lewis River

Location and access Rises from the Lewis Pass and parallels SH 7. There is easy access from this highway.

This clear, medium-sized mountain river is rather steep, rough and unstable, with the fishing water limited to the lower reaches early in the season. There are not many pools to fish. The river flows through beech bush and tussock.

Nina River

Location Drains the Main Divide, flows east and joins the Lewis River near Palmer Lodge, the New Zealand Deerstalkers Association hut on SH 7.
Access Cross the Lewis River by the swingbridge opposite Palmer Lodge. A bush track leads to the Nina. The Nina-Lewis confluence can be reached by scrambling down the true right bank of the Lewis River for 1 km.
Restrictions Bag limit is two trout.

Fish stocks are low in this rock-and-stone type river and as access is reasonably easy, angling pressure ensures the trout become very wary as the season progresses. There are some very deep pools in the lower bush-clad section, and although there are usually a few good fish these are difficult to cover. Further upstream the river winds through some grassy clearings.

Location Rises east of the Lewis Pass and at first flows south through heavy bush parallel to but east of SH 7. It then turns west to join the Lewis and Nina rivers west of the Boyle settlement and SH 7. After the confluence it once more turns south and joins the Hope River near the Windy Point carpark.

Access *Upper reaches* A private four-wheel-drive track follows up the true left bank from the Boyle settlement but there is a locked gate on Glenhope Station. There is walking access to the river above this point.

Middle and lower reaches There is reasonable access from SH 7, which crosses the river near the Boyle settlement and follows the river downstream to the Hope confluence.

The upper reaches on Glenhope Station hold few fish and lots of walking is required. It is well worth doing some careful spotting on the rough, gorgy section above the Boyle settlement as there are a few good fish in the pockets between white water. However, the best water in this medium-sized, freestone river lies between Windy Point and the Boyle settlement. Here brown trout average 2.5 kg and can be spotted and stalked in clear mountain water. Stocks are not high but there are always a few good fish in this section of river, especially where the river has one stable bank. Nor'westers blow down the valley! The deep gorge upstream from the Hope River confluence holds only a few large fish, but is very difficult to access unless the river is very low. For success, stealth and accurate casting are mandatory on these back country browns.

Doubtful River

Location Saddles with the Waiheke River at Amuri Pass, flows east and joins the Boyle River on its true right bank, 5 km south of the Boyle settlement and SH 7 bridge.

Access First the Boyle River must be forded, which can be very tricky early in the season, especially after nor'west rain in the headwaters. Extreme care should be taken.

Restrictions Bag limit is two trout, but catch and release is recommended.

Brown trout stocks vary from year to year in this small, freestone high country river, and although fish numbers are never very high there is always the chance of a fish over 4 kg. The best water lies an hour's tramp upstream where the river is more stable. Doubtful Hut, 6 km upstream near the mouth of Devilskin Stream, offers basic overnight shelter and there are usually a few fish upstream from the hut.

A lot of riverbed walking is required to fish this river. The upper reaches become more attractive as the river winds through native bush and across tussock-covered flats.

Hope River

Location Saddles with the Tutaekuri River at Hope Pass, flows east and joins the Boyle River below Windy Point carpark.
Access From SH 7 at the Windy Point carpark on the Boyle River, a swingbridge just upstream from the carpark marks the start of the Hope River track. There is private access up the true right bank through Glynn Wye Station on a four-wheel-drive track.

Trout numbers are not high in this medium-sized high country river but a trophy is always possible for the energetic tramper-angler.

Fish should be sighted and stalked or else a lot of 'dead' water will be fished. There are two to three full days' fishing to well above the gorge near Kiwi Stream but a lot of walking is needed. DoC huts offer basic back country-style accommodation for those willing to tramp into the upper reaches. This river can flood in spectacular fashion after heavy nor'west rain. Like the majority of fish in high country rivers, the trout are generally not very selective. Of far more importance is spotting, stalking, accurate casting and avoiding drag. Trophy fish should be weighed, measured, photographed and returned to the river. Over recent years this river has been more heavily fished, especially by guides and their clients.

Kakapo Brook

This tributary joins the Hope River at Glynn Wye Station on SH 7. At times it holds a few fish, especially early in the season, but at other times it is barren. There are a number of good-looking pools in this small stream which promise more than they deliver.

Percival River

Location Drains the Hanmer Range, with the Rogerson and Chatterton tributaries joining just south of Hanmer township.
Access After turning off SH 7 to Hanmer and crossing the Waiau River, two gravel side roads on the left lead to the river. Anglers may have problems when fishing this stream as there are reputed to be riparian rights.

This small, shingly, willow-lined stream is best fished early and late in the season. Trout stocks are variable but there are usually a few small browns in the 1–1.2 kg range that can be spotted and stalked. Don't drink from the stream as giardia is present. I can personally attest to this!

Other rivers in the district — including the Hanmer, Mason, Lottery, Leader, Dog Brook, Counting Stream and Home Stream — may hold the odd fish early in the season but are generally not worth fishing. They are either unstable or dry in summer, in part due to dairy-farm irrigation.

Lake Guyon

Location Lies 2–3 km from the true left bank of the upper Waiau River, upstream from the Ada confluence.
Access
• By tramping for two to three hours from the Hanmer Hydro Road, either by Fowler or by Malings Pass. It is wise to obtain prior permission from St James Station.
• By walking for 40 minutes from the upper Waiau Valley.
Restrictions Bag limit is four trout.

This small, scenic, high country lake holds good numbers of brown trout averaging 1.3 kg. The lake is partially bush-clad but casting is generally unobstructed, especially at both ends of the lake. Trout cruise the shoreline and can easily be stalked on a bright day. In strong nor'west conditions, trout feed in the waves at the southern end of the lake and providing you can cast, fishing can be most rewarding. Carry a few small midge imitations and some damsel flies as well as the usual attractor-type dry flies. There is a good hut which is owned by the Department of Conservation but shared with St James Station.

Lake Sumner Forest Park

Lake Summer Forest Park covers 74,000 ha of mountains, forests, lakes and rivers. Permits are only required for hunting, but vehicle access beyond a locked gate at Loch Katrine requires permission from the Department of Conservation (phone (03) 371 3706).

There are 18 Parks Board huts scattered throughout the park; permits to use these, and a detailed map, should also be obtained from the Department of Conservation in Christchurch.

Access

- From the township of Hawarden in North Canterbury, take the gravel road to Lake Sumner. It is unwise to venture beyond Lake Taylor unless you are driving a four-wheel-drive vehicle. Even then, it is wise to carry chains as the track becomes very rutted and boggy after heavy rain. There is vehicle access to the upper Hurunui swingbridge at the head of Lake Sumner.
- From SH 7 (Lewis Pass Road) tramp up the Hope Valley.
- From the West Coast by tramping the Taramakau Valley and Harper Pass.
- There is private farm road access to Lake Sheppard and to the Lake Sumner outlet but a fee is charged by the Lakes Station. There is no charge for anglers walking the road.
- There is a rough private four-wheel-drive track to Lake Mason, up the south branch of the Hurunui River, and a DoC hut to use. An access fee is charged.

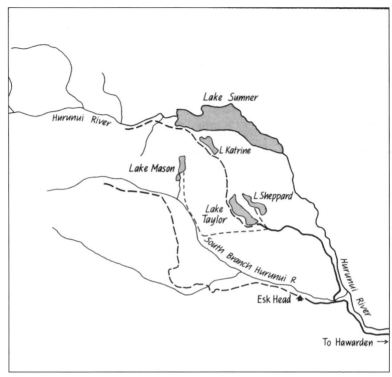

Lake Sumner Forest Park

Season From first Saturday in November–30 April. There is a winter extension for lakes Taylor, Katrine and Sumner 1 June– 30 September. For the upper Hurunui River, 1 December–31 March. **Restrictions** Bag limit is four trout from Lake Sumner. Elsewhere, two trout only.

Fishing from a mechanically powered boat is permitted in Lake Sumner. Fishing from a boat not mechanically powered is permitted in lakes Taylor, Katrine and Sumner. Lake Sheppard is restricted to fly fishing only.

All lakes contain brown trout, although rainbows have been introduced into Lake Sumner in the past. Quinnat salmon also enter Lake Sumner from the Hurunui River from February to April. **Lake Sumner** is by far the largest lake, with an area of 1364 ha. Most trout are caught by trolling from boats, although the catch rate is not high in this lake. Sight fishing for cruising fish is best around the Hurunui delta at the top of the lake.

Lake Taylor generally holds small browns averaging 1 kg, which can be stalked along the shore. The water is very clear and on a calm warm day it is a common sight to find fish rising all over the lake.

Lake Sheppard can also be sight fished along some shores, and the browns are larger than those in Taylor. Green manuka beetle, Royal Wulff, Black Gnat, cicada and damsel imitations all work well in this lake.

Loch Katrine is a small lake with private fishing huts along the southeastern shore. There is good shoreline fishing at the outlet at the northwestern end, although the creek is difficult to cross and boat access is more satisfactory. Damsels and midges make up a large proportion of trout food. Cruising trout can be spotted.

Lake Mason is really two lakes, of which the smaller southern lake is best for fly fishing. It is a relatively easy two-hour walk up the true left bank of Taylor Stream from the head of Lake Sumner and over the hill. Cicada fishing on a sunny, windy February day can be exciting in this shallow lake. In the evening there can be a very active caddis rise. Trout can be stalked along the shore during the day.

There is no shortage of water to fish in the park, which also includes the upper Hurunui River, described below, and the Hope River, described on page 141. It is a very pleasant family location for camping, boating, swimming and fishing, but take insect repellent and beware of nor'west storms.

 Hurunui River and tributaries

Hurunui River

Location The North Branch saddles with the Taramakau River at Harper Pass, drains the Nelson Tops and Crawford Range, and flows into and out of Lake Sumner. From the Lake Sumner outlet, the river flows east across partially cleared farmland to join the South Branch at Esk Head Station Road.

The South Branch drains the Crawford and Dampier ranges and flows northeast through Esk Head Station to the confluence. Below this junction the main river enters a steep, rocky gorge.

Below the Mandamus confluence the main river flows through farmland and exotic forest to reach SH 7 at Hurunui village on the edge of Balmoral Forest. SH 1 crosses the river at Greta Paddock. The river finally reaches the Pacific Ocean at Hurunui mouth, southeast of Cheviot.

Access

North Branch

Headwaters By four-wheel-drive vehicle on the Lake Taylor to Lake Sumner track. It is wise to carry chains as the road becomes boggy and severely rutted after rain. A permit is required from DoC in Christchurch to open the locked gate at Loch Katrine.

Upper reaches The Lake Sumner road follows the river for some distance from the top of the gorge to Sisters Stream, where there is a track to the Hurunui River and a swingbridge. There are a few vehicle tracks to campsites on the river, but in other sections a scramble down a steep bank is required to reach the river. As described under Lake Sumner Forest Park, there is a private farm road to the outlet at Lake Sumner, but the Lakes Station charges a fee to use this.

South Branch

Headwaters From Esk Head Station a rough four-wheel-drive farm track leads upstream to the Stony Hut. Permission is required from Esk Head Station.

Lower and middle reaches Can be accessed from the Esk Head road by walking and fishing upstream from North Branch confluence.

Main river

Immediately below the confluence of the two branches, access can be obtained from the Lake Sumner Road. However, the river soon gorges below where the river leaves the road and access through private farmland becomes very difficult. There is road access from Balmoral Road on the true left bank near the Mandamus confluence. SH 7 and SH 1 both cross the river. Ethelton Road follows up the true left bank from SH 1.

There is road access to Hurunui mouth from SH 1 just north of Domett.

Season

North Branch headwaters above Lake Sumner, 1 December–31 March.

Above the North and South Branch confluence (western zone), 1 October–30 April.

Elsewhere, there is an open season all year round.

Salmon season: in the western zone (above the confluence), 1 October–28 February; in the eastern zone, 1 October–30 April.

Restrictions Bag limit for trout in the western zone (above the branch confluence) is two trout and two salmon. In the eastern zone, the limit is four trout and two salmon.

In the North Branch headwaters above Lake Sumner there is a full day's fishing upstream from the four-wheel-drive track end at the swingbridge. There is also reasonable water downstream to the mouth at the lake. The river is moderate in size, clear, shingly and flood-prone, but holds some good-sized brown trout in the more stable water, which can be spotted and stalked on a bright day. The fish are easily spooked and will remain hidden for at least a day after being fished over. Catch and release in this section is recommended to conserve the gene pool. The river can be safely waded and crossed in normal conditions. The nor'wester often blows strongly downstream.

In the upper reaches of the North Branch, from the Lake Sumner outlet to the South Branch confluence, the river is large and clear and flows over a rock and gravel bed. The pools are very deep and often only the edges of the expansive runs can be covered with a fly. It is not an easy river to fish, as long casting is often required and the river is dangerous to cross and tricky to wade. The banks are covered with manuka scrub, bracken and grass, although the shoreline in most sections is stony. A few fish can be spotted on a bright day, but generally the river is fished blind with heavy stonefly nymphs or large attractor dry flies. This is not easy when the prevailing nor'wester is blowing directly downstream. Fish stocks are good, as drift dives reveal more than 50 large fish per kilometre of river. Because the river drains Lake Sumner, the water remains clear after a fresh although the fishing falls off when the river is high. If the flow rate in the main river is over 60 cumecs it is hardly worth fishing the upper reaches. There is a full day's fishing from the Sisters swingbridge upstream to the outlet.

The South Branch is smaller in size and offers good water in the lower section, especially early in the season before angling pressure makes trout very wary. The river is less stable than the North Branch and rapidly discolours after rain. There are few fish in the unstable gorgy section near the North Esk confluence, but high upstream near the Stony Hut there are 6 km of more stable water holding a few good-sized fish. These should be released if caught.

Below the confluence of the two branches, the section above the gorge holds some excellent trout but these can generally only be reached by active anglers in low water summer conditions. The gorge itself is virtually unfishable as the river is very large, deep and well-confined between steep rock walls.

From the Mandamus confluence to the mouth, the river is large, shingly, braided and unstable, but the better water still holds some good brown trout. These are best fished to with a spinner, although when the river is low and clear there are some fly fishing opportunities. A lot of exploring or local knowledge is required to successfully fish these reaches as the pools and runs can change with each flood.

At the mouth, there is good salmon fishing in the surf during a run and it is not uncommon to land sea-run brown trout on salmon gear.

Five tributaries are described, although none is highly recommended. They are best fished early in the season when water flows are consistent.

North Esk River

Location Saddles with the Waimakariri tributaries to the south, flows northeast and empties into the South Branch a few kilometres from Esk Head farmhouse.
Access Through Esk Head Station. Permission required.
Restrictions Bag limit is two trout.

Although this small river looks promising, it holds only a few brown trout and these generally lie in the gorgy lower reaches. It is reputed to have held rainbows in the past but I have not seen evidence of this. The lower and middle reaches flow through pasture, while the upper reaches drain beech bush.

Mandamus River

Location Drains the bush-clad Organ Range southwest of Hanmer, flows south and enters the Hurunui River just west of Balmoral Forest.

Access From SH 7 turn left onto Balmoral Road then Glens of Tekoa Road. The lower stretch of river can be fished upstream from the bridge but it is wise to seek permission from Glens of Tekoa Station before fishing the middle section.

Restrictions Although four trout can be legally taken from this small river, catch and release should be practised as fish stocks are low and fragile.

The headwaters of this small rock-and-stone type river are clothed in beech bush and manuka scrub, while the middle and lower reaches flow across pastoral land. There are a few stable pools holding fish but these tend to be well fished over as the season progresses.

The river is gorgy in parts, especially in the lower reaches, but easy to negotiate. Most fish are found below the Silver Brook confluence and these can be readily spotted and stalked. Salmon spawn in this stream late in the season. Take insect repellent when exploring the middle and upper reaches.

The Jollie Brook, Glenrae, Glencoe and Dove rivers, also west of Balmoral Forest, enter the true left bank of the Hurunui. They are all rather unstable, shingly, flood-prone and difficult to approach. A lot of walking is required for one or two trout.

Pahau River

Location and access Crossed by SH 7 just south of Culverden, and by the Culverden–Pahau Downs Road.

This small, shingly, willow-lined stream suffers from varying flow rates, which are not conducive to good trout habitat. Water draw-off and water discharge from irrigation ensures the stream holds only a few small brown trout.

Waitohi River

Location and access From Hurunui on SH 7, proceed to Horsley Downs. Medbury and Bakers roads lead to the river.

This small, shingly stream holds a few small brown trout in the lower reaches and is best early in the season as it tends to dry in long, hot summers.

Waikari River

Location and access Drains the Waikari basin and flows northeast through Scargill and Greta. Access through private land at Greta.

Only the mouth and lower section is worth a look early in the season, as this river also has a tendency to dry. A small, willow-lined stream with a mud and shingle bed.

The Kaiwara River near Ethelton holds a few trout in the lower section below the bridge, and the mouth is worth a look early in the season.

Other small North Canterbury streams that hold a few trout in their lower reaches are the Motunau and Waipara rivers. The willow-choked, sluggish Omihi east of Waipara also holds a few fish but has been polluted by farming operations.

Ashley River

Location Rises in the Puketeraki Range, flows through Lees Valley and Ashley Gorge, then turns northeast and flows across the plains just north of Rangiora to reach the sea at Waikuku Beach.
Access There is good access from roads on both sides of the river up as far as Ashley Gorge, just north of Oxford. The Lees Valley Road follows upstream high above the river on the true right bank, then

descends to cross the river at the top of the gorge.

Season Above the Oxford–Glentui Bridge (western zone), 1 October–30 April. Below this bridge, the river is open all year.

Restrictions Catch and release only above the Oxford–Glentui Bridge. Below the bridge, bag limit is four trout and two salmon.

The medium-sized Ashley River holds low numbers of brown trout. Being close to Christchurch, the river receives a lot of attention from anglers. There are sea-run browns at the mouth, but upstream as far as the gorge the river is rather unstable, braided and shingly and often dries in summer. Winter and early season are the best times to fish this stretch. The river is best fished when the flow rate is less than 15 cumecs.

Immediately above the gorge and in the gorge itself there are stable pools that hold a few good brown trout. These can be sight fished in optimum conditions but a good nor'wester makes fishing the gorge impossible. A few stray salmon spawn above the gorge in the upper reaches.

The Townshend, Whistler and Lillburn tributaries in Lees Valley are very unstable and provide poor trout habitat. The Okuku tributary at White Rock is rough, gorgy and hard going but at times it holds the odd good fish. The Waikuku spring creek near the mouth holds small numbers of browns but becomes weed-infested after Christmas.

 Waimakariri River and tributaries

Waimakariri River

Location Drains a large catchment of the Southern Alps in the region of Arthur's Pass. Flows generally east through mountainous terrain and emerges from the Waimakariri Gorge to spill over the Canterbury Plains in typically braided fashion. Enters the Pacific Ocean north of Christchurch at Kairaki.

Access *Upper reaches* SH 73 meets the river between Cass and Bealey before crossing to Arthur's Pass. The Mt White Station road leaves SH 73 soon after this highway meets the river, and crosses at the Mt White bridge. There is access both up- and downstream to beyond the Poulter River confluence from the Mt White road.

The Gorge Easiest access is by jetboat launched from the south bank at Waimakariri Gorge Bridge on SH 72.

Middle and lower reaches SH 1 crosses the river between Belfast and Kaiapoi. On the north bank, take the access track that starts under the old highway bridge and runs to Brown's Rock a few kilometres short of the Waimakariri Gorge Bridge. On the south bank there is access from Kowai Bush and from the Old West Coast Road and its small side roads (Weedons Ross, Willows Intake, Cooks, Courtnay and Kimberley), although a long walk across the riverbed may be required to reach the river. The McLeans Island stopbank, accessed from Dickeys Road, is a popular spot.

Mouth From Kairaki on the north side and Spencer Park on the south side. A popular salmon fishing spot is McIntosh's Rocks. These can be reached by taking the Kaiapoi–Kairaki road, Ferry Road and then walking over the stopbank.

Season In the western zone (above the white posts at Woodstock), 1 October–30 April. For salmon in the western zone, 1 October–28 February. In the eastern zone the river is open all year.

Restrictions In the western zone, the bag limit is two trout and two salmon. In the eastern zone, four trout and two salmon may be taken.

This is a very large, braided, snow- and glacier-fed river that is flood-prone and unstable. It becomes unfishable when the flow rate exceeds 100 cumecs. In the upper reaches, between the Poulter River and the Mt White bridge, a lot of exploring and walking is required at the beginning of each season to locate stable water with a permanent bank. When the river is low and clear a few good-sized brown trout can be spotted along the edges of runs and pools. The river is normally too large to cross but it can be safely waded. The prevailing nor'wester can make casting almost impossible at times. Late in the season, salmon also appear in the river. The lower few pools of the Bealey, the Cora Lynn swamp, Cass Hill Stream and Bullock Creek behind Lake Sarah occasionally hold the odd fish early in the season.

The Gorge is deep and swift and more suited to spinning. There are some brown trout present but access by jetboat is generally reserved for salmon fishing from January to April.

The middle reaches from the gorge to SH 1 are very braided and unstable. However, there are reasonable numbers of small rainbows present which will accept flies and spinners. Best fishing is at low water during the winter. The more stable and deeper pools hold salmon during a run.

The lower reaches below SH 1 and the mouth have been polluted in the past but are popular with salmon anglers. A few good-sized sea-run browns are also caught but usually by anglers fishing for salmon. Being so close to Christchurch, the Waimakariri River is the most heavily used recreational river in the South Island.

Poulter River

Location Drains the Dampier, Poulter and Savannah ranges and Lake Minchin, flows south and joins the Waimakariri River near Whale Hill.

Access The Mt White road crosses the lower reaches. A washed-out four-wheel-drive track follows up the true right bank for a short distance. Beyond the washout, it is all walking. It is a five-hour tramp upstream along the Poulter River flats to Casey Hut, or six to eight hours via Binser Saddle or Andrews Stream to the same hut.

Season 1 October–30 April for trout. 1 October–28 February for salmon.

Restrictions Bag limit is two trout and two salmon.

This medium-sized freestone river can flood readily with heavy rain. It drains a large catchment of bush-covered mountains. The two most productive and stable stretches of water lie an hour's walk upstream at Pete's Stream and opposite the Casey Hut at the Casey Stream confluence. Here, some good-sized brown trout can be spotted and stalked in clear pools and runs that have a permanent bank. The remainder of the river is hardly worth fishing, although late in the season a few large rainbow follow spawning salmon into the river to feast on salmon eggs. These can be taken on Glow Bugs and heavily weighted nymphs. However, once the salmon enter the river, the brown trout become easily spooked and are difficult to catch.

The East Branch holds few trout but there are a few rainbows in the Cox River, although access is extremely difficult.

Lake Minchin

Location and access Lies in the Poulter River headwaters three and a half hours' tramp upstream from Casey Hut. A trampers' track follows the eastern shore.
Restrictions Bag limit is two trout.

This small lake is mainly of interest to tramper-anglers. It is a very scenic mountain lake, partially bush-clad, and it holds a large stock of small rainbow trout. The hot spot is around the mouth of the inlet stream at the top end of the lake. Best early and late in the day, when trout rise to caddis. The outlet stream also holds small fish but is overgrown in most sections. Falls prevent trout moving up the outlet stream into the lake. Take insect repellent.

Esk River (south)

Location Drains the Dampier and Puketeraki ranges, flows south parallel to but east of the Poulter River, and enters the Waimakariri 5 km downstream from the Poulter River mouth.
Access With permission from Mt White Station, from the farm road following up the true right bank some distance from the river. A four-wheel-drive vehicle is essential and a scramble down a steep briar rose and matagouri-covered face is required to reach the river. It is possible to walk upstream from the mouth.
Restrictions Bag limit is two trout.

This is a small, shingly, unstable, flood-prone river that is not worth fishing in the lower reaches. However, in the vicinity of Nigger Stream there are more stable pools that hold some good-sized brown trout. In ideal conditions, when the river is low and clear and the nor'wester less than 20 km/hr, these trout can be sight fished. Nigger

Stream also holds a few brown and rainbow trout but access is difficult and the weather is seldom favourable for fly fishing.

Lake Letitia

Location and access Close to the Mt White Station homestead.
Season 6 November–30 April.
Restrictions Only one splake can be taken.

Splake, a cross between macinaw and fontinalis, have been liberated into this small, reed-infested lake. Very few have been caught and a boat or float-tube is needed to fish the lake.

Broken River

Location Flows northeast from its source in the Craigieburn Range to join the Waimakariri near Staircase.
Access *Upper and middle reaches*
- Crossed by SH 73, with walking access both upstream and downstream along the riverbed. It is 15 km to the Winding Creek confluence down through a limestone gorge.
- Through Flock Hill Station by following the farm track down Winding Creek and walking the last kilometre to the Winding Creek-Broken River confluence. Permission is required from Flock Hill, and an access fee is charged.

Lower reaches From the end of the Craigieburn–Avoca road to the Slovens Creek-Broken River confluence.
Season First Saturday in November–30 April for Broken River and its tributaries. For salmon the season ends on 28 February.
Restrictions Catch and release for Broken River and its tributaries.

Broken River is a spawning tributary for the Waimakariri River although it does hold resident fish throughout the year. The river is lively, clear, small and easily crossed and waded, although the stones are slippery. There are gorgy sections but these can be negotiated by crossing the river at selected fords. Because the river is fast-flowing and turbulent, trout are difficult to spot, so likely looking water should always be fished blind. Early in the season some of the trout will be in poor condition after spawning, but after Christmas fish will be in better shape and will fight well. Stocks are reasonable, with the majority of fish being rainbows, which will respond well to weighted nymphs. Late in the season, salmon enter the river from the Waimakariri.

The Porter River tributary also holds spawning trout early in the season but these drop back downstream when water levels drop around Christmas.

Broken River is now catch and release

Winding Creek

Location Drains Lake Pearson when the lake is high, and the swamp close by on Flock Hill Station. Flows southwest through pasture, tussock and scrub to join Broken River about 6 km above Staircase.
Access With permission from the runholder at Flock Hill Station, and the payment of an access fee. A farm track leads down the creek some 4 km northeast of the homestead.

Season First Saturday in November–30 April.
Restrictions Catch and release.

This is a deep, clear, meandering spring creek with good stable pools and swift runs. The trout are mainly rainbow, which can be sight fished, although casting in the matagouri and manuka scrub poses problems at some locations. Carry a landing net as the fish are lively and can't always be followed downstream. The creek can be crossed at a few selected fords.

Late in the season quinnat salmon from the Waimakariri River enter the creek to spawn. These are often followed by good-sized rainbow trout feeding on the salmon eggs.

Slovens Creek

Location and access Flows south after draining Lake Hawdon and follows the railway line from Craigieburn to Avoca where it enters Broken River.
Access From the Craigieburn road, which follows the creek.
Season First Saturday in November–30 April.
Restrictions Catch and release.

There are falls at Avoca, which prevent salmon spawning higher up. The creek holds brown trout if you can find them among the willows and swamp. It is very difficult to fish and you are wise to carry a landing net, although this is sure to tangle in the scrub. Bow and arrow casting is most useful!

The South Branch

Location This small stream is located just north of Christchurch, near Belfast.
Access Dickeys Road north of the Belfast Hotel leads to Coutts Island and crosses the stream. The Waimakariri Walkway follows upstream.
The stream flows through the Groynes picnic area off Johns Road. Swimmers and canoeists can disturb the fishing at this location.

Season Open all year below Dickeys Road bridge. Above this bridge, 1 October–30 April.

This small tributary of the Waimakariri River is a clear spring creek that follows an old Waimakariri River channel. The lower section of the creek has been polluted in the past and is not worth fishing. Upstream from the raupo below Dickeys Road bridge there is good water, and small brown trout can be spotted and cast to on a weed, gravel and mud bed. Some sections are willow-choked but the fish are a challenge as small flies, long tippets, careful stalking and accurate casting are mandatory.

The final group of Waimakariri River tributaries flow through urban and semi-urban areas near Kaiapoi, Rangiora and Belfast. These are the Cam, Kaiapoi, Styx and Silverstream rivers, the Cust Main Drain and Greigs Drain, all of which hold small and medium-sized brown trout. However, stock pollution, channelling, catchment activities and water extraction have severely affected their value as fisheries. They are fished to some degree by local and junior anglers but are not greatly recommended. The lower reaches of the Cam, Kaiapoi and Styx rivers are open all year.

Within Christchurch city are the Avon and Heathcote rivers and their tributaries, the Wairarapa and Waimairi streams. These small spring creeks offer sport to junior anglers throughout the year, although trout numbers have gone down over recent years due to urban pollution, loss of spawning habitat and a reduction in flow rates.

North Canterbury high country lakes

Season First Saturday in November–30 April. For rivers flowing into these lakes, 1 December–31 March. There is a winter season in lakes Selfe, Lyndon, Pearson, Taylor, Sumner and Loch Katrine from 1 June to 30 September (except within 200 m of any inflowing stream). In Lake Coleridge the winter season opens on 1 June and closes on 31 August.

Restrictions In Lake Sumner the bag limit is six sportsfish, of which only two may be salmon.

In Lake Coleridge the bag limit is also six sportsfish, but all six of these may be salmon. The bag limit for trout is four. In all other high country lakes the bag limit for trout is two fish, except Lake Marymere which is catch and release.

Fly fishing only in lakes Ida, Little Ida, Monck (Catherine), Sarah, Marymere and Sheppard.

Fishing from a mechanically powered boat is only permitted in lakes Coleridge and Sumner. Fishing from a non-mechanically powered boat (or float-tube) is permissible in lakes Coleridge, Sumner, Taylor, Pearson, Lyndon, Georgina, Selfe and Evelyn, and Loch Katrine.

Lake Pearson

Location and access SH 73 parallels the shoreline between Flock Hill and Grasmere stations. There is easy access off this road and from tracks at the north end of the lake.

This attractive, medium-sized lake is shaped like an hourglass and holds mainly brown trout along with the odd rainbow and macinaw (North American char). The macinaw have never done well and rarely reach 1 kg in weight. In their native environment in North America and Canada they often reach 12 kg, but this lake becomes too warm in summer and is too short of food in deep water for them to thrive. However, the brown trout average 1.3 kg, although fish up to 4 kg have been caught. The shoreline is tussock, pasture, willows and scrub, and casting is a problem along the steep eastern shore and some sections of the western shore. Both ends of the lake are relatively free of casting obstructions. Cruising trout can be spotted in bright conditions and ambushed with nymphs, dry flies or terrestrial imitations.

In windy conditions, which are not uncommon, trout can be seen and caught in the waves along the Flock Hill shore. Although there is a winter season, the lake can partially freeze over in cold periods and trout seek shelter and warmth in deeper water. Useful flies include Black Gnat, Coch-y-bondhu, Love's Lure and Green Beetle dry flies, Hamill's Killer and Woolly Bugger lures, and small, dark-bodied nymphs.

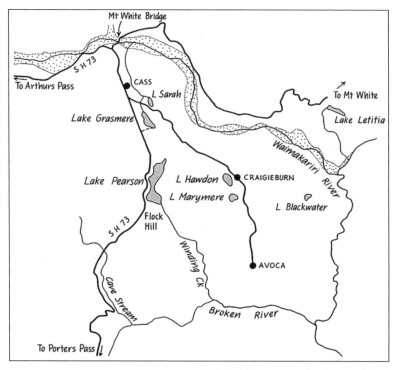

Lake Pearson and adjacent lakes

Lake Grasmere

Location and access A few kilometres beyond Lake Pearson, a vehicle track leads off SH 73 on the right to a basic campsite on the lakeshore, beneath a clump of poplars.

This small, scenic high country lake has for the most part a swampy shoreline. The northeastern shore is rocky, steep and bush-clad. At present the lake holds mainly brown trout averaging 1–2 kg, although in the past it has been stocked with rainbow trout. On a bright, sunny day, fish can be ambushed while cruising the drop-off. However, the water quality has deteriorated over the years because of cattle, run-off from a swamp and a high bird population in this wildlife refuge. The outlet stream at the northern end is overgrown and impossible to fish.

Lake Sarah

Location and access Between Lake Grasmere and Cass the metalled Craigieburn road leaves SH 73 and crosses the railway line. Lake Sarah is the first lake on your left.

Sarah is a small lake stocked with browns and rainbows averaging around 1.3 kg, although there are larger fish present. In ideal conditions cruising trout can be spotted, but often there is glare on the water and spotting is difficult. In some areas, swamp and raupo impede shoreline access. Damsel and dragon fly nymphs fished on a slow-sinking or sink-tip line are very effective in this weedy lake.

Lake Hawdon

Location and access 10 km beyond Lake Sarah on the Craigieburn road (beware of the rail crossings) there is a sign indicating a track up over the hill to Lake Hawdon. It is only a few minutes' walk on this four-wheel-drive track to the lake.

Hawdon is larger than Sarah and oval in shape. It is a shallow lake that holds both brown and rainbow trout, with some very large fish present. Recent stocking should help this lake as fish numbers have been low in recent years. Trout cruise the shallows and are easy to spot on sunny days but not easy to catch. As the season progresses they become even more of a challenge. The western shore beneath Purple Hill is steep, rocky and scrub-covered but shoreline access elsewhere is good. However, tread warily around the swampy northern shore as it is easy to sink in up to your thighs between the clumps of raupo. As with all these lakes, trout will accept dry flies and nymphs but a small wet fly or damsel imitation can be more effective on wary fish.

Lake Marymere

Location and access Lies over the hill at the south end of Lake Hawdon. There is a steep four-wheel-drive access track to the lake further south along the Craigieburn road. Deep ruts on this track create havoc for a conventional vehicle but it is only a short walk from the road. If the ground is wet, anglers should walk to the lake.

This small, clear, high country lake holds Loch Leven brown trout only and is catch and release. Apart from a patch of bush along the western shore, access is easy along the tussock banks. When trout are feeding, they cruise the shallows and can be ambushed. They are easily spooked so it is often an advantage to fish with a friend and take turns spotting. It is best in moderate northwesterly conditions, when fish cruise in close looking for food stirred up by the waves. A large attractor-type buoyant dry fly works well in these conditions, provided you can cast in strong winds! Stocks are not high as trout spawn naturally along the lake shore and are not artificially replenished. However, an occasional fish reaches trophy proportions. Good fish inhabit the rocky western shore and a small weighted nymph is ideal for these cruisers.

Lake Blackwater

Location and access There are two small, shallow tarns lying on Flock Hill Station halfway between the Craigieburn Railway Station and the Waimakariri River. There is a four-wheel-drive track to the lakes but permission must be obtained from either Flock Hill or Craigieburn Station.

These tarns are windswept, shallow and exposed, but they hold a few rainbows which apparently spawn along the gravel shore. Trout are very difficult to spot because of glare on the water. Not worth a special visit.

Lake Rubicon

Location and access Lies beneath Mt Torlesse on Brooksdale Station, 6 km beyond Springfield on SH 73. Permission required from the homestead.

This small lake, partly surrounded by rushes, holds small rainbow trout.

Location Lies between the Torlesse and Mt Hutt ranges near the Rakaia headwaters.

Access From Rakaia Gorge or Hororata take the Lake Coleridge Road, which follows up the true left bank of the Rakaia River. There are a number of access points, including the intake, the Ryton River mouth and the Harper River diversion at the top of the lake but a boat is a great advantage. There are boat launching facilities at either end of the lake.

This is a large, cold, deep, snow- and glacier-fed lake that has been modified for hydro-electric power generation. It is very prone to the nor'wester that sweeps down the lake with great intensity, much to the delight of some hardy windsurfers. The lake is 18 km long, and

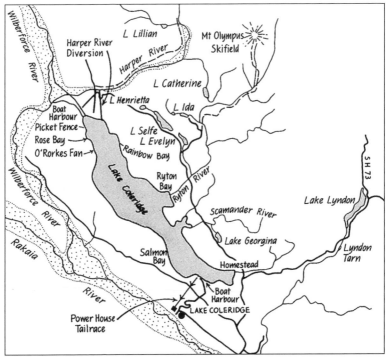

Lake Coleridge and surrounding lakes

because of fluctuating lake levels the shoreline is rather devoid of weed beds and insect life. There are rainbows, browns and land-locked quinnat salmon, with the latter providing most of the sport on opening day for threadline anglers and trollers come rain, hail, snow or shine. However, fishing for salmon has deteriorated in recent years. Hot spots for spin anglers include the Harper River diversion, the Picket Fence, Rose Bay and the Ryton River mouth.

Most trout are caught in Coleridge trolling a spinner. Because of the clean stones and gravel in the shallows, there is limited shoreline fishing for cruising trout except in the vicinity of stream mouths. In April, night stream-mouth fishing for hardy anglers using a black lure can be most effective on trout congregating prior to their spawning runs. Fish up to 4 kg have been caught in recent seasons. However, there are many other fishing locations close by that offer more for the shoreline fly angler.

Lake Georgina

Location and access This is the first lake reached on Harper Road, which skirts the western shore. There is a campsite behind pine trees at the northern end of the lake.

Georgina is a small, exposed lake surrounded by tussock and matagouri scrub. Fish are difficult to spot in this lake, which holds rainbow trout, some of which are the late-maturing 'r' type strain. There is easy shoreline access, safe wading and no swamp. Blind fly fishing over the drop-off or fishing to rising fish is the usual method employed by anglers.

Lake Evelyn

Location and access Harper Road skirts the western shore, while the private toll road to Mt Olympus Skifield passes close to the southeastern shore.

Holds mainly brown trout, but because of raupo and swamp shore-line access is restricted. However, there are stretches of firm tussock along the southeastern and northern shores. Fish are difficult to spot and a float-tube would provide much easier access. Birdlife is prolific on this lake.

Lake Selfe

Location and access Lies a few kilometres beyond Lake Evelyn. Harper Road skirts the southwestern shore. There are basic camping facilities at the southern end of the lake, where small boats can be launched off the beach.

This is the most attractive lake in the area, with bush clothing the steep hillside along the northeastern shore. Elsewhere the shoreline includes tussock, briar rose and matagouri, but there are plenty of spots to fly fish. Trout are difficult to see except on bright, still days, but they tend to cruise the shoreline in summer. Browns and 'r' type rainbow can be caught in this lake on dry flies, nymphs and damsel imitations.

Lake Henrietta

Location and access Lies just north of Lake Selfe, off Harper Road.

This is a very small lake that reputedly holds some large rainbow and brown trout, but because the shoreline is swampy and infested with flax, scrub and raupo, fishing is not easy. If you can find solid ground to stand on, try a sunk Black and Peacock or a slowly retrieved damsel imitation.

Lake Ida

Location and access First left off the Mt Olympus toll road.

Ida is a small lake that lies in a cold, steep-sided basin with tussock and beech trees lining the shore. It holds rainbow trout averaging 1 kg but these feed on snails and damsels deep in the lake until the water warms in summer. Green beetles and other terrestrials blown from the banks then attract fish closer to the shore. The skating pond always holds a few fish.

Little Lake Ida

Location and access A short walk from the top end of Lake Ida takes you to Little Ida.

Also holds a reasonable stock of small rainbows, which are generally fished to blind. Both Ida and Little Ida are fly fishing only.

Lake Catherine (Monck)

Location and access Lies a few kilometres further up the Mt Olympus Road on the left. There is a four-wheel-drive track across the outlet creek into an old station hut.

This small fly-fishing-only lake is the most popular lake in the area for fly anglers. Surrounded by tussock, matagouri scrub, beech bush, willows and raupo, the lake holds both brown and rainbow trout. Fish numbers have dropped in recent years but cruising trout can usually be spotted along the eastern shore. The lake is reasonably sheltered from the nor'west wind.

Lake Mystery is a small tarn overlooking Lake Catherine from the northeast. It has held trout in the past but up-to-date information suggests they are no longer present.

Lake Lillian

Location and access Permission must be obtained from Glenthorne Station, which charges a fee to use its farm track up the true right bank of the Harper River. Opposite the Harper-Avoca river confluence and near the station huts, either follow up the outlet stream or climb the hill behind the huts. It is a 40-minute walk to the lake.

This small high country lake holds rainbow and brown trout averaging 1–2 kg. The top end of the lake is raupo-infested and swampy, but elsewhere there is good access. Cruising trout can be seen and ambushed, especially from the steep northern hillside.

Creeping down without spooking the fish is another matter, and it pays to have an angling friend. In a strong nor'wester, fish can be seen cruising in the waves at the eastern end of the lake.

The Red Lakes and Lake Spectacles are small tarns in the headwaters of the Dry Acheron Stream. They reputedly hold a few browns. The Harper and Ryton rivers, both of which enter Lake Coleridge, are subject to the same regulations that apply to all rivers entering western zone lakes. Anglers have been observed fishing both rivers before the season opens on December 1.

Lake Lyndon

Location and access Reached from SH 73 at a rest area just beyond Porters Pass. It is only just over an hour's drive from Christchurch. The Lake Lyndon to Coleridge road follows the eastern shore.

Lyndon is a small, cold, windswept, high country lake lying in a barren tussock basin. In previous years the lake has held an abundance of small rainbow trout but over the past few seasons, while fish numbers have dropped, their size has increased. They are difficult to spot and most fishing is done by spinning or blind fly fishing. The lake is safe and easy to wade, and fish will rise within casting distance of the shore. In winter, providing the lake is not frozen over, some good fish can be caught on a sinking line and a Woolly Bugger, but survival gear may be necessary!

Lyndon Tarn

Location The Lyndon–Coleridge road passes just west of the tarn.

This small tarn, with a swampy, willow-lined shore, holds small rainbows.

Harper River

Location Drains the Craigieburn Range, flows south and then west to enter the Wilberforce River north of Lake Coleridge. Part of the lower river has been diverted into Lake Coleridge, forming the Harper Diversion.

Access The Harper Road to the top of Lake Coleridge crosses the diversion, while the road to Glenthorne Station crosses the lower river. Foot access is readily available. The Glenthorne Station farm road follows up the true right bank. Permission is required from the station to use this road, and it charges an access fee.

Season 1 December–31 March.

Restrictions Bag limit is two trout.

The Harper River, a spawning stream for Lake Coleridge, is flood-prone, shingly and unstable. It is often silt-laden, but when low and clear it does hold rainbow trout in the more stable runs and pools. Likely looking water should be fished, especially early and late in the season, as fish are difficult to spot especially in the lower reaches. The upper reaches above Hamilton Hut are more stable, but are only of interest to tramper-anglers walking the Lagoon Saddle track. Trout tend to drop back downstream in low water summer conditions.

The Avoca tributary also carries few fish early in the season but it is even more unstable than the Harper River.

Ryton River

Location and access Drains the Craigieburn Range and Lake Catherine. Flows southwest to enter Lake Coleridge at Ryton Bay. Harper Road crosses the lower reaches, there is a vehicle track to the mouth, while the Mt Olympus toll road follows the river upstream.

Season 1 December–31 March.

Restrictions Bag limit is two trout.

This is another Lake Coleridge spawning stream, which is also best fished early in the season before trout drop back downstream to the lake. The best water lies off the Mt Olympus road where the stream is narrow, windy and scrub-covered in some stretches. Fish can be spotted in clear pools but become easily spooked after being fished over a few times. They will accept small weighted nymphs and dry flies that are accurately presented and drag-free.

Action on a headwater stream in Canterbury

Okana (Little River) and its tributary the Okuti

Location and access From SH 75 at Little River. The Okana drains Little River Valley; the Okuti drains the Okuti Valley. The Little River–Te Oka Bay Road crosses both streams. Walk downstream from either bridge.

Season Open all year below the bridges. Elsewhere, 1 October–30 April.

These two small streams join to form the Takiritawai River before discharging into Lake Forsythe. In years gone by anglers experienced great lure fishing for large sea-run browns, but due to increasing eutrophication from farm run-off, the trout habitat has become undesirable. Rather surprisingly, the sluggish lower reaches still hold the odd good fish, especially early in the season. Upstream, the small, overgrown Okuti is worth a look early in the season before fish drop back downstream after spawning.

Lake Forsythe

Location SH 75 follows the shoreline just south of Little River township.

Season Open all year.

Restrictions Bag limit is four trout.

This rather unattractive lake is heavily polluted and eutrophic in summer. Before the water warms, some large sea-run brown trout are caught on spinners and smelt or bully type lures. The hot spot is adjacent to the New Brighton Power Boat Club's pavilion, which is easily seen from SH 75. Wade out carefully onto a shingle bar but beware of sinking mud. Trout tend to school while chasing silveries into the shallows. Birds working, splashy rises and bow waves usually indicate a school of fish approaching. Eels are plentiful in the lake.

The Kaituna River, which is also crossed by SH 75, has deteriorated as a fishery but the mouth sometimes attracts feeding browns, usually after rain. To reach the mouth, walk down the disused railway line from a carpark.

Location and access Rises from springs near Halswell village, flows south across farmland, through Taitapu, and enters Lake Ellesmere near Greenpark Huts. The lower reaches and mouth can be accessed from Hudsons Road via Greenpark Huts. Seabridge Road south of Motukarara also leads to the mouth. Many roads, including SH 75, cross the middle reaches, although permission is often required to cross private property.
Season Open all year below Seabridge Road bridge. Elsewhere, 1 October–30 April.

The mouth offers night lure fishing, while the middle reaches hold a few small brown trout. Unfortunately this spring creek has also suffered from farm run-off, with nitrates and phosphates promoting weed growth and choking the stream. Regular weed cutting is not conducive to good fishing.

L I I River

Location and access Flows south from Lincoln to enter Lake Ellesmere near Selwyn Huts. Access from Wolfes Road or the Selwyn Huts road. Before you reach Selwyn Huts there is a vehicle track on your left that runs to the river between some houses and adjacent to a macrocarpa hedge.

Only the lower reaches and mouth are worth a look as sea-run browns from Lake Ellesmere chase silveries, especially at night. Willows and weed make fishing difficult but at times some good fish are taken. Use a floating or sink-tip line and a large black night lure.

Selwyn River

Location Rises from Big Ben Range, flows east to Glentunnel, Coalgate and Greendale, then across the Canterbury Plains to Lake Ellesmere. The stretch of river crossed by SH 1 usually flows under the shingle riverbed.
Access *Upper reaches* Take the Glentunnel–Whitecliffs road to the Selwyn Gorge.

Middle reaches There are roads on both sides of the river, with popular picnic spots at Chamberlains and Coes fords. These can be reached from the Lincoln–Leeston Road or from Lake Road south of Lincoln.

Lower reaches and mouth From the road to Selwyn Huts south of Springston.

Season Open all year below the Upper Selwyn Huts. Elsewhere, 1 October–30 April.

Upper reaches At times there is a reasonable stock of small brown trout near Glentunnel (75 small fish/km of river). In the head-waters a lot of walking is required to explore the Selwyn Gorge and it holds very few fish.

Middle reaches Upstream from the Upper Selwyn Huts the river is willow-lined and shingly, and above Coes Ford it is rather braided. Dairy farming and water abstraction over recent years have severely affected this once popular river and the trout population has suffered as a result. Drought in 1998 and 2001 also adversely affected the fishery, and few trout now inhabit the river above Chamberlains Ford. Many of the holes beneath willows held large numbers of fish but most of these have now filled in with shingle. The river is a spawning stream for Lake Ellesmere but because of low water flows fishing is best early in the season. In the 1950s the spawning run was estimated to be around 40,000 fish, but it is now only 300!

Trout can be spotted and will accept dry flies and nymphs. However, because of the river's close proximity to Christchurch, angling pressure, and people swimming and picnicking, make the fish here extremely wary.

Lower reaches Forty years ago the lower Selwyn River was famous as a fishery. Most trout were caught at night on lures, many of which originated from and were specifically designed for this river. However, for the reasons given above, the fishery is now a shadow of its former self. There are still some large trout caught in these brackish, muddy, slow-flowing lower reaches, as fish from Lake Ellesmere chase silveries into the river at night. To be successful one must wade carefully, use a slow-sinking or sink-tip line and a large black night lure. It pays to explore the river well during daylight before fishing at night. Eels will occasionally take your lure!

Hawkins River

Location Drains the Russell Range southwest of Springfield, flows east near Sheffield then south to Greendale, where it enters the Selwyn River.

Access From many roads including Dalethorpe, Auchenflower and Mill Road at Annat, and roads west from Sheffield, Racecourse Hill and Aylesbury. Permission must be obtained to cross private farmland.

During the 1998 drought this small, rain-fed, willow-infested tributary of the Selwyn ran dry. Fortunately, it is naturally restocked from the Selwyn River. Although fish stocks are unreliable, prior to the drought the stream held some surprisingly good brown trout. These tended to be sophisticated fish lying in deep holes under overhanging bank vegetation. Careful spotting and accurate, innovative casting is required. The river has not fully recovered from low water flows.

Irwell River

Location and access Flows east across farmland, through Doyleston just north of Leeston, and into Lake Ellesmere. Road access is restricted in the middle reaches and permission from local farmers is required. Lake Road crosses the lower reaches, and the mouth is reached from Aitkens Road via Hanmer Road.

This small spring creek also ran dry during the 1998 drought, with disastrous effects on the trout population. Except in the lower reaches, there were virtually no fish in the stream during the 1999–2000 season. As well as the lack of rain, removal of ground water for irrigation was partly responsible for the creek drying. Hopefully, trout will be attracted back into the stream from Lake

Ellesmere, providing water flows remain consistent. The creek is small, weedy and willow-choked in parts, but a good test of spring creek fly fishing skills. At times there is reasonable night lure fishing at the mouth. The Hanmer Drain close by also holds fish at times.

Harts Creek

Location and access This small, deep spring creek rises north of Leeston and flows south to enter Lake Ellesmere north of Lakeside. From Lake Road, turn onto Timber Yard Road and follow south until the creek can be seen on your left. There is no legal access but local landowners readily give anglers permission to fish. The mouth can be reached from either bank by walking downstream from the farm bridge.

From 1997 until 1999, this creek deteriorated from a clear spring creek to a silt-laden, sterile drain. However, due to the initiative and effort of local landowners, the North Canterbury Fish and Game Council and a group of enthusiastic volunteers, the creek has improved a little. It is an important Canterbury fishery historically, and now there is a chance the creek will be fully restored.

Brown trout from Lake Ellesmere spawn in the creek, feed on silveries, especially at night, and congregate in the cold oxygenated waters near the mouth when Lake Ellesmere warms in summer.

During the day trout can be spotted and stalked in the middle reaches and the Birdlings Brook tributary, but night lure fishing near the mouth is the traditional method of catching browns up to trophy proportions. Not all anglers enjoy this style of fishing, especially when a large eel takes your night lure! Use a strong tippet, a medium-sinking line, and cast across and downstream on this sluggish waterway. It pays to prospect the fishery before dark to familiarise yourself with the area. A landing net, a pair of artery forceps to remove lures from eels and a strong torch should also be carried.

Rakaia River

Location Rises in the Southern Alps west of Lake Coleridge, flows east, at first through mountainous terrain and through a gorge, then spills out over the Canterbury Plains. Enters the Pacific Ocean south of Lake Ellesmere.

Access The river is well served with roads, although many of these run on high river terraces some distance from the river. Many anglers, especially salmon anglers, find jetboats a more practical form of access.

Upper reaches From SH 72 near Rakaia Gorge, roads follow upstream on both banks. The Lake Coleridge Road follows up the north bank while the Blackwood–Double Hill Road follows up the south bank.

Middle reaches SH 72 crosses the river at Rakaia Gorge. SH 1 crosses the river near Rakaia township. The Rakaia–Highbank Road follows up the true right bank.

Lower reaches Follow tracks and roads downstream from the SH 1 bridge.

Mouth The Rakaia Huts and the mouth can be reached via Southbridge.

Season Rakaia River and tributaries for trout and salmon fishing; in the western zone, 1 October–28 February; in the eastern zone, open all year.

Restrictions Bag limit is two trout.

The Rakaia River is a very large, snow- and glacier-fed river with an unstable shingle bed. Like its counterpart the Waimakariri River, the Rakaia is prone to flooding as well as changes of course. Nevertheless the Rakaia has a high reputation as a salmon-fishing river.

The river water is often loaded with silt and glacial flour, and nor'west rains rapidly create flood conditions. The most productive time for salmon anglers to fish the river, especially in February and

March, is when the flow rate drops to less than 180 cumecs immediately following a fresh.

Except for a few high country tributaries and at the mouth, the main river is not generally recommended for trout fishing. However, at the mouth some excellent sea-run browns are caught, mainly by salmon anglers.

Some anglers fish specifically for sea-run trout by using well-weighted lures cast sling-style from a very heavy rod. The sea-run fish often lie deep in fast water along the edges of channels looking for whitebait, elvers or silveries.

In low water summer conditions, a few trout are caught on spinners near The Great Island and at the back of the Rakaia Golf Course.

In the headwaters, especially near the mouth of the Glenariffe Stream, some good rainbows and browns can be fished for with heavily weighted nymphs.

Glenariffe Stream

Location Drains the Palmer Range and lowland swampy country, flows north then east to join Double Hill Stream just above the road bridge. Enters the Rakaia River just downstream from the salmon hatchery.
Access From SH 72 take the Blackwood–Double Hill Road up the south bank of the Rakaia River. At the salmon hatchery there is a bridge over the Glenariffe Stream in a grove of pines. Walk upstream and take the left fork (true right) of the river.

This is a small, clear, winding spring creek and a spawning stream for the Rakaia River. The banks are tussock and scrub, which overhang the stream in some sections. If trout are feeding they are easy to spot but many lie hidden beneath the banks. They become progressively more wary as the season advances and it pays to fish likely looking stretches blind, as fish will suddenly emerge from beneath the bank to take a fly. Holds small numbers of good-sized rainbow and brown trout. There are 2–3 km of fishing water requiring careful stalking and accurate, delicate casting. Carry a landing net.

Location Also drains the Palmer Range, flows generally east through tussock and scrub, and joins the Glenariffe just upstream from the road bridge.

Access

- Walk upstream through the pines from the road bridge and take the right fork (true left).
- Drive beyond the hatchery and turn left at the first side road to Glenariffe Station. This road crosses the stream.
- Drive to where the Blackwood–Double Hill Road crosses the stream and walk upstream.

Although this stream flows parallel to and close by the Glenariffe, its character is entirely different. The stream is a rusher, and early in the season the water can be discoloured by snow-melt. At times it holds a good stock of brown trout but, as in the Glenariffe, these

Double Hill Stream

often seek shelter beneath the tussock banks. If the water is slightly discoloured try a well-weighted nymph with an indicator. When the stream is low and clear trout can be spotted, but look long and hard in likely places as many are hard to see. By Christmas, many fish will have dropped back downstream to the Rakaia. The stream can be forded at the tail of most pools but these are not well-defined. Above the second bridge, a farm pond in the pines occasionally holds a large fish.

Hydra Waters

Location The Hydra Waters lie on Mt Algidus Station, opposite Double Hill Stream on the true left bank of the Rakaia River.
Access Permission should first be obtained from Mt Algidus, and this is not readily given. Some anglers arrive by jetboat, while others fly in to an airstrip close by. Still others wade the Wilberforce River or cross it by four-wheel-drive. This is often a tricky operation unless the river is low and clear. Still others ford the Rakaia — an even more daunting task!

The Hydra Waters comprise a succession of spring-fed streams winding through the red tussock flats of the Rakaia riverbed. The streams are usually clear, and brown trout can be spotted and fished. On a still, bright, sunny day the scenery is quite spectacular, and at times the fishing can match the scenery. In a strong nor'wester, pack up and go home. A landing net must be carried as fish race off downstream when hooked and it is very difficult to run through waist-high red tussock and obscured sinkholes! Trout will take dries and nymphs carefully presented and are not very fussy as to the pattern. Presentation is all-important.

The Hydra Waters are the most important salmon spawning streams for the Rakaia River. Hence the premature closure of the season on 28 February.

Goat Hill Stream

Location This small stream flows into the Wilberforce River almost beneath the Mt Algidus homestead.

Access The Wilberforce River must be crossed to reach the stream and great care must be taken unless this river is very low and clear.

A small, clear spring creek that holds some resident fish and spawners early in the season. Both browns and rainbows can be sight fished but careful stalking and delicate, accurate casting is required. Catch and release is suggested on this fragile stream as fish stocks are not high.

The Wilberforce River holds some good-sized rainbow trout in a few of the more stable holes but these are few and far between. Fish habitat is extremely limited in this unstable, flood-prone, shingly river. The Wilberforce Canal, which enters the top end of Lake Coleridge, also holds a few trout but is uninspiring to fish except with a spinner.

Central South Island Fish and Game Council region

This multifarious region offers all types of water, including high country rivers, lakes and tarns, hydro-electric canals and dams, rain-fed streams, spring creeks and large snow- and glacier-fed rivers. Many of the smaller low country streams have deteriorated over the years as a result of water abstraction and farm run-off. However, there is still some interesting fishing in these waters.

Ashburton River

Location The south branch rises in the Arrowsmith Range of the Southern Alps, flows east through a gorge, and then across the Canterbury Plains to join the north branch just west of Ashburton. The north branch drains the Black Hill and Old Man ranges and flows southeast. The main river flows through Ashburton and enters the Pacific Ocean southeast of the town.

Access

Main river

Mouth From SH 1 in Ashburton take Moore and Beach roads to the Hakatere Huts on the north bank.

Lower reaches Below SH 1, Moore and Beach roads and side roads off these offer easy access to the main river.

Middle reaches Access from side roads on the north bank of the river from the Ashburton–Staveley Road is relatively easy between the SH 1 bridge and the SH 72 bridge at Mt Somers.

South Branch

Upper reaches From Mt Somers take the Ashburton Gorge Road to Lake Heron. This road follows the river.

North Branch

SH 77 parallels the north bank for 15 km. Thompsons Track

crosses the middle reaches, while SH 72 crosses near Alford Forest.
Season South Branch, upstream from and including Taylors and
Bowyers streams, 1 October–31 March. Between SH 1 and Taylors
Stream, and the North Branch, 1 October–30 April. Below SH 1,
1 October–30 April and 1 June–31 August.

Restrictions Bag limit on the South Branch and tributaries above
Taylors Stream, and the North Branch, is four sportsfish, of which
no more than two may be salmon and two may be trout. Bag limit
elsewhere is six sportsfish, of which no more than two may be
salmon and four may be trout. In the winter season, only two trout
may be taken.

The North Branch of the river is smaller than the South Branch
and prone to drying in summer. It is shingly and willow-lined, and

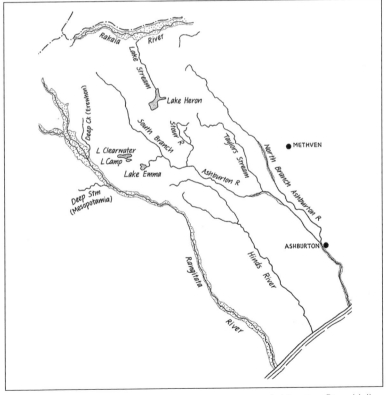

Ashburton River Valley

only worth fishing early in the season upstream from SH 72. Trout averaging 1 kg can be spotted in bright, clear conditions.

The moderate-sized South Branch sometimes carries snow and glacial melt up until Christmas, making sight fishing impossible. In these conditions try blind nymph fishing with an indicator, provided the river is not carrying too much water. The South Branch is rather swift and unstable, and fish stocks are not high. Brown trout are the predominant species, although there are a few rainbows in the vicinity of the forks. Both Taylors and Bowyers Streams are worth a look early in the season.

The main river from the forks to the mouth is shingly, willow-lined and rather unstable. The riverbed stones have been washed clean of algae. Stocks are not high, although there are some good-sized browns in the permanent holes beneath the willows, especially downstream from the SH 1 bridge. Fishing is generally best after Christmas when the river is low and clear, although early in the season some excellent sea-run browns are taken at the mouth, usually on spinners. Best fished when the flow rate is less than 50 cumecs.

Trout become selective and easily spooked in clear, low water summer conditions, and the evening rise is often the best time to deceive them. Try a soft hackle wet fly or a caddis imitation. In late summer, willow grub is useful.

Provided the flow rate is adequate, a small run of quinnat salmon enters this river from December to March.

Hinds River

Location Rises in the Moorhouse Range and flows parallel to but some 20 km south of the Ashburton River. Enters the sea at Longbeach.

Access Although there are a few trout upstream from SH 1, the best section of river lies downstream from this highway. Turn off SH 1 onto Longbeach Road 8 km south of Ashburton. The end of this road takes you to the mouth and lower reaches. Side roads including Newpark, Lynnford and the Hinds River Road offer easy access to other sections of the river

Restrictions Fly fishing only for adults. Bag limit is four trout.

This small, shingly, willow-lined, rain-fed stream holds a good stock of brown trout averaging 1–1.4 kg, which can be sight fished with small nymphs and dry flies. The stones are algae-covered and slippery but attract mayfly and caddis nymphs. Some fish lie in short, deep pools beneath the willows and these are difficult to fish to without drag. A thick screen of willows along both banks provides good shelter from the wind and the stream only discolours after heavy rain. The small lagoon at the mouth also holds trout.

The Ashburton lakes

These exposed high country lakes lie in beautiful, barren, mountainous surroundings but are subject to the vagaries of nor'west storms. They are located in tussock country near the Ashburton River headwaters. Snow can fall at any time of the year, although it is unusual in February. There is a small permanent fishing village on the shores of Lake Clearwater, and basic camping grounds at lakes Heron, Camp and Clearwater.

As I am personally keen on sight fishing, I find these lakes quite difficult to fish. The lakebeds are weedy and greenish-brown in colour. There are few trees or steep hills close by to cast a shadow and reduce light reflection on the water. Unless trout are rising, I struggle to spot cruising fish except in lakes Heron and Donn. If trout are not rising, blind fly fishing requires infinite patience and much barren water is needlessly covered. Calm days are rare and fishing in a nor'wester can be most unsatisfying, especially when you can't see any trout. On one occasion, while I was eating lunch beneath willows on the shores of Lake Clearwater trout began to rise frenetically — much to my chagrin, I had just concluded that fish stocks were low in this lake, and here were these fish going crazy! Ten to fifteen trout were rising, but only near the willows. All my efforts to catch the fish, including using a willow grub imitation, were a waste of time. Despite my seining the water in an effort to determine the identity of the food source, and trying all manner of flies and bully patterns, the fish totally ignored my attempts at deception. In 30 minutes the rise had ceased and not a fish could be seen.

Access From Mt Somers on SH 72, take the Ashburton Gorge Road for 23 km to Hakatere Junction. The branch road to the right passes the Maori Lakes and Lake Emily, and leads to Lake Heron and Lake Stream. The branch to the left leads to Spider Lakes and lakes Donn, Emma, Roundabout, Denny, Camp and Clearwater.

Season First Saturday in November–30 April. Lake Camp has an extended season from the first Saturday in November–31 May. For salmon in Lake Heron the season opens on the first Saturday in November and closes on 28 February.

Restrictions The daily bag limit is four sportsfish, of which no more than two may be trout and no more than two may be salmon. Fly fishing only in Maori, Spider, Denny, Donn, Emily and Roundabout lakes. Fishing from boats is prohibited in lakes Spider, Denny, Donn, Emily, Roundabout and Camp. Fishing from an unmoored boat is prohibited in Lake Emma and Maori Lakes. Minimum length for salmon taken in Lake Heron is 25 cm.

Lake Heron

This is the largest of the Ashburton lakes, and lies 15 km from Hakatere Junction. It is a long day's fishing to walk round this lake, which holds rainbow and brown trout averaging 1.5–2.3 kg and a few landlocked quinnat salmon. In addition, large sea-run salmon enter the lake from the Rakaia River and spawn in Mellish Stream on the eastern shore during March and April. Tussock, scrub and a few patches of willow line the shore, and trout can be spotted cruising the shoreline and drop-off in clear water. Fishing is permitted from rowing boats and canoes but boaties must be very wary of the nor'wester as the lake can rapidly become rough. Trout will accept dry flies, terrestrials, nymphs and bully imitations. Many fish are caught on spinners.

Lake Stream

Location and access Drains the northern end of Lake Heron and joins the Cameron River before entering the Rakaia. Permission should be obtained from Lake Station.

Season 1 October–29 February.

From the outlet, the upper reaches of this stream flow over a gravel bed, but the stream is narrow and choked by willows. The middle reaches are swampy and difficult, while the lower reaches become quite boisterous. Trout can be sight fished but stocks are not high.

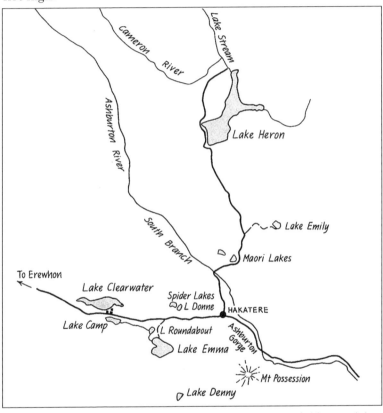

Ashburton lakes

Lake Emily

Access A marked access track on your right near willows leaves the Lake Heron road 3 km beyond the Maori Lakes. The gate is locked but Lake Emily can be reached after a 20-minute walk.
Restrictions Fly fishing only.

This small, shallow, exposed lake lies in a barren tussock basin. The

185

shoreline is swampy in parts with lumpy tussock, but access is possible to most of the shore. Contains fontinalis, or American brook trout, but spotting is not easy and blind fishing with a damsel or dragon fly nymph is the most effective method. The 'brookies' tend to swim in schools and these are often hard to locate. If you hook a fish, stay in the same place and try again.

Maori Lakes

Location and access These two small lakes lie to the left of the Lake Heron road. A track to the lakes leaves the Lake Heron road 0.5 km beyond the Ashburton South Branch bridge.
Restrictions Fly fishing only. A boat or float-tube may be used provided it is anchored.

There is limited shoreline access as the lake margins are swampy and rush-covered. Both lakes hold some good-sized browns but these are wary and not easily fooled. When hooked, they dive for the weed beds. Spotting is very difficult, and blind fishing with damsel and dragon fly nymphs, Woolly Bugger or Hamill's Killer is the best method. At times, a Midge Pupa will bring results. Carry a landing net.

On a bright day, the outlet creek draining into the Ashburton River is worth a look.

Lake Emma

Access A track to the lake leaves the left side of the road to Lake Clearwater, 4.5 km beyond Hakatere Junction. Take a car in fine weather only; best with a four-wheel-drive vehicle.
Restrictions Fishing from an anchored boat, artificial bait and fly are all permitted.

Unless the day is calm and sunny, trout are hard to see in this shallow, medium-sized lake, so blind fishing with dry flies, nymphs or lures is the most popular method. There are browns and rainbows present. Try bully and damsel imitations, midge pupae and small nymphs. It is easier to fish when trout are rising.

Lake Roundabout

Location Seen on the right from the track to Lake Emma.
Restrictions Fly fishing only.

This small lake holds brown trout but they are hard to spot from the swampy shore.

Lake Camp

Location Lies opposite Lake Clearwater.
Restrictions Note the extended season to 31 May. This is the only lake in the area where power boating is permitted.

This lake is often disturbed by water-skiers and swimmers, but it does hold both rainbow and brown trout. Best fished early and late in the day. The shore is easy to walk in most places but fish are hard to spot unless rising.

Lake Clearwater

Location and access This is the largest lake on the Erewhon Road. It lies opposite Lake Camp, 10 km from Hakatere Junction, and has a permanent fishing village on its shore.
Restrictions Artificial bait and fly only. Boats are permitted.

The lake is surrounded by tussock and pasture with a few patches of willow. There are good stocks of brown trout averaging 1.5 kg, but these are hard to see unless the lake is calm and the conditions bright. Another access track branches off the Erewhon Road 2 km past the village. A wide variety of flies and lures will take fish but bully, damsel and dragon fly imitations are popular.

Spider Lakes and Lake Donn

Location and access The access track is signposted almost opposite the track to Lake Emma. It is a 15-minute walk to the lakes.
Restrictions Fly fishing only.

These small lakes hold a few brown trout but they are hardly worth visiting as fish numbers in recent years have been low.

Lake Denny

Location and access A four-wheel-drive track runs south for 3 km from Hakatere Junction across pastoral land to this small lake. **Restrictions** Fly fishing only.

Lying in a tussock basin, this small lake has one patch of willows along the northern shore and some straggly looking beech trees along the southern shore. It holds a reasonable stock of brown trout and in calm, sunny conditions cruising fish can be spotted through the beech trees from an elevated bank.

 Rangitata River and tributaries

Rangitata River

Location Rises in the Southern Alps and, after emerging from a gorge, flows east in braided fashion across the Canterbury Plains to enter the sea south of Hinds.
Access
Mouth
North bank Turn off SH 1 onto the Hinds–Rangitata mouth road 2 km south of Hinds township. The Ealing–Coldstream road just north of Rangitata Bridge also leads to the mouth, and provides access to the river at the irrigation outfall and Old Main South Road.
South bank Turn off SH 1 onto Edgar Road at the Rangitata Store. There are fishing huts on both sides of the mouth.
Middle reaches
North bank From the Arundel Bridge continue on SH 72 for 6 km and turn off at Five Crossroads corner onto the Ealing–Montalto road. There is only one access from Klondyke Terrace Road via the Ealing–Montalto road. There is foot access to the gorge but please respect private property.
South bank There are many access points along the south bank.

From the mouth to SH 1 these include Wades Crossing (Badham Road) 12 km from the mouth, Dip Road (15 km) and Brodie Road (18 km). From the Arundel–Rangitata road there is access from Lewis Road until Arundel Bridge (SH 72) is reached.

From the Arundel Bridge there is access on Ferry Road to Peel Forest and at the Peel Forest camping ground. From the Rangitata Gorge Road there is access at Lynn Stream, Mt Peel Station, Raules Gully, Rata Peaks (Fishermans Lane) and Forest Creek.

Season Above Turn Again Point, 1 October–28 February. Between SH 1 and Turn Again Point, 1 October–30 April. Below SH 1, 1 October–30 April and 1 June–31 August. The Rangitata Diversion Race is open all year from Rakaia River Road to the intake.

Restrictions Daily bag limit is six sportsfish, of which only two may be salmon and four may be trout. In the winter season, the bag limit is two sportsfish.

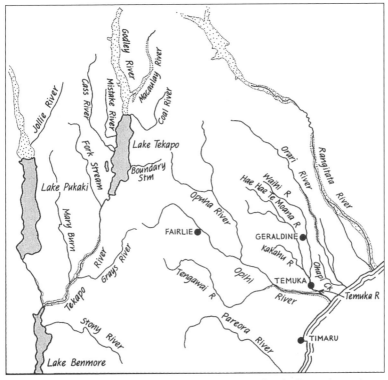

South Canterbury rivers

The river is best fished when the flow rate is less than 90 cumecs. Like its northern neighbour the Rakaia, the Rangitata River is a highly regarded salmon fishery. Very few anglers fish exclusively for trout, except upstream above Peel Forest. Some good sea-run browns are taken at the mouth, usually by salmon anglers on spinning gear. The river is very large, flood-prone and braided once it leaves the gorge, and trout habitat is limited in this unstable environment. Snow-melt and glacial flour often colour the river until after Christmas. However, when the river is low and clear there are some very good brown trout caught in the upper reaches. Fish over 4 kg are not unusual, and the occasional rainbow adds to the excitement. Most trout are taken on spinners as the opportunities for fly fishing are limited in this large river.

Only two tributaries are described here, and they lie almost opposite each other in the upper reaches. Both become unfishable in strong nor'west conditions as they are very exposed.

Deep Creek (Mt Potts)

Location and access Take the Erewhon Road beyond Lake Clearwater. At Mt Potts Station, the stream can be seen winding its way across the Rangitata River flats. It joins the Rangitata River upstream from the Potts River. There is access through private land across the Mt Potts airstrip, but permission should be obtained from Mt Potts Station.
Season 1 October–28 February.
Restrictions The daily bag limit is four trout, but catch and release should be practised.

This deep, clear spring creek is a favoured salmon spawning tributary of the Rangitata River on the north bank. However, it holds both brown and rainbow trout. These can be spotted and stalked with dry flies and nymphs, but as the season progresses they become extremely wary. Stocks are not great and on a fine, calm day it is unusual to have the stream to yourself. Trout enter the mouth of this creek when the Rangitata River is silt-laden.

A Canterbury high country spring creek

Deep Stream (Mesopotamia–Garondale)

Location and access Take the Rangitata Gorge Road beyond Peel Forest to Garondale Station. This creek rises on Mesopotamia Station and flows across the Rangitata River flats on Garondale Station before entering the north bank of the Rangitata River. The creek flows past the Garondale woolshed.

Season 1 October–28 February.

Restrictions Although the bag limit for trout is four, catch and release should be practised.

This is another deep, clear spring creek favoured by spawning salmon on the south bank of the Rangitata River. It holds both brown and rainbow trout, which can be sight fished with weighted nymphs and dry flies on a bright, calm, sunny day. There are patches of willows along the banks, which are swampy in parts. Only a few fish inhabit the creek upstream from the woolshed.

With increasing angler pressure, trout become more easily spooked as the season progresses.

Orari River

Location Rises in the Ben McLeod Range, flows southeast parallel to but south of the Rangitata River, and enters the sea north of Temuka.
Access *Lower reaches* From roads south and east of Clandeboye and northeast of Temuka. Take Farm Road off SH 1, 49 km south of Ashburton, to the dairy factory at Clandeboye. A number of roads run south to the river.
Middle reaches There is access from both sides of the river between Orari township on SH 1 and Orari Bridge on SH 72.
Upper reaches The gorge can be reached from roads running northwest from Arundel or from Orari and Blue Mountain stations on the true right bank. Clayton Road from Fairlie leads to the top of the gorge.
Season 1 October–30 April.
Restrictions Bag limit above Slip Panel Stream is four sportsfish (two salmon and two trout). Below this stream, two salmon and four trout.

The river is best fished when the water flows are less than 30 cumecs.

The lower reaches below Rolleston Road offer good brown trout fishing. The river is willow-lined and the shingle riverbed reasonably stable. Trout can be sight fished in some sections on a bright day but many will hide in deep holes beneath the willows and only emerge at night to feed. There is good water below where Ohapi Creek enters, although early in the season whitebaiters can be a problem. The river is safe to cross and wade, although the stones are very slippery. It holds fish in the 0.5–1.5 kg range. Caddis and mayfly imitations work well, as does willow grub later in the season. Trout can be selective, however. Best fished early and late in the season.

The middle reaches suffer from water abstraction and low water flows in summer, and are braided and unstable. The water often flows beneath the shingle.

There are a few fish in the gorge, but access is difficult and a lot of walking is required between fish. Deep pools and bluffs can cause problems and there are very few access tracks either into or out of the gorge once it has been entered.

When river flows are adequate and the mouth is open, an occasional salmon enters the river to spawn.

Ohapi Creek

Location and access Flows parallel to but south of the Orari and joins this river 1 km upstream from its mouth. Access is difficult across private farmland just north of Milford School and northeast of Temuka. Permission is readily given by local farmers.
Season 1 October–30 April.
Restrictions Fly fishing only.

This small spring creek has previously been valued by fly anglers, but unfortunately over recent seasons farming operations have almost destroyed it. The water is now often silt-laden and the weed beds have been covered with mud. In the past the creek offered excellent sight fishing for brown trout, and being narrow and clear was a real test of angling skill. The banks are grass, with a few willows on some stretches. This stream might be restored in the future, provided local farmers keep their stock out of the water.

 Opihi River and tributaries

Opihi River

Location Drains the Ben McLeod and Richmond ranges west of Fairlie, and follows an easterly course through rolling hill country to enter the sea east of Temuka.
Access Mouth and lower reaches accessed from Wareing Road and Milford Huts. Many roads offer access to the middle reaches, including SH 1 at Temuka and roads round Pleasant Point, Opihi, Hanging Rock, Raincliff and Rockwood. There are marked anglers' access points off River and Main Waitohi roads.

Season 1 October–30 April. Below SH 1 there is a winter season from 1 June to 31 August.
Restrictions Bag limit is six sportsfish (two salmon and four trout) below the Opuha junction. Above this junction and during the winter season the bag limit is two trout.

The river is best fished when the flow rate is less than 10 cumecs. This river has recovered remarkably well following the bursting of the Opuha Dam in 1996. Now the water flows from the Opuha Dam are reliable, fishing has greatly improved. The two most popular stretches for fly anglers lie below SH 1 and downstream from the Opuha confluence. There is productive water either side of Hanging Rock Bridge, and well-conditioned brown trout averaging 1.2 kg can be sight fished. However, all likely looking water should be fished or many trout will be missed, especially in the faster runs. The gorge above Rockwood Bridge is worth exploring early in the season. The river has a shingle bed, long rippling runs and well-formed pools, and is lined by willows. Wading and crossing are safe, although the algae-covered stones can be very slippery.

Opuha River

Location and access The north and south branches drain the Ben McLeod and Two Thumb ranges and enter the top end of Lake Opuha. From this dam the river flows southeast through a gorge, beneath SH 79, and joins the Opihi River at Raincliff. There is access from the dam by walking downstream or walking upstream from the SH 79 bridge. There is also access from Gudex Road.
Season 1 October–30 April.
Restrictions Bag limit is four trout.

This small to medium-sized river has also made a remarkable recovery since the Opuha Dam was breached in 1996. Being a tailwater, conditions should now be ideal for trout. The best water lies upstream from SH 79. There are some large, deep, slow-flowing, dark-looking holes, and feeding trout treat these like a lake and cruise the edges. Provided trout are feeding in shallow water they can be spotted and stalked, but it pays to fish other likely looking water as well. Browns up to 2.3 kg are present and fish stocks seem to be improving. Unfortunately, broom, gorse and scrub cleared out by the flood have begun to grow back, and this makes bank access more difficult. The river is not easy to cross as the water is brownish looking and the rocks are slippery. It pays to carry a wading stick. It is more than one full day's fishing from SH 79 to the dam. The river becomes unfishable when the flow rate exceeds 20 cumecs.

Lake Opuha

Location and access Lies northeast of Fairlie. Turn off SH 8 onto Clayton Road just before Fairlie. It is 12 km to the lake.
Season First Saturday in November to–30 April.
Restrictions Power boats are permitted and there are launching facilities. Bag limit is six sportsfish, of which only four may be trout.

This artificial lake was formed in 1997 by damming the Opuha River. Unfortunately the original earth dam collapsed before it was completed, leading to a catastrophic flood that affected the Opuha and Opihi rivers. Both branches of the Opuha River enter the top of the dam. It has been stocked with brown and rainbow trout and sockeye salmon. Most fish are caught trolling from a boat or spinning from the shore, and the sockeye salmon have been a great attraction. Water quality is poor in summer due to rotting vegetation and water warming, but hopefully this will improve with time. The lake is used for water-skiing, boating and swimming in summer, but it almost dried during the drought in 2001.

Hae Hae Te Moana River

Location and access Rises northwest of Geraldine and joins the Opihi near Temuka. Crossed by SH 79 southwest of Geraldine. Side roads off Earls Road offer access.
Season 1 October–30 April.
Restrictions Bag limit is four trout.

This small, shingly, willow-lined stream holds small brown trout. It is best fished early in the season in the lower reaches, before water abstraction and warming cause trout to drop back downstream. There is reasonable water at Geraldine Flat.

Kakahu River

Location and access Drains Waitohi and Kakahu Hills west of Geraldine, flowing east on a convoluted course to join the Hae Hae Te Moana River west of Winchester. Access from roads running between Kakahu and Hilton.
Season 1 October–30 April.
Restrictions Bag limit is four trout.

This small stream is very overgrown with willows, gorse and scrub. There are some very deep, dark, slow-flowing pools, which are difficult to fish. It is best to explore the stream during the day and return for the evening rise. Holds some good-sized browns that do not remain on station but rather cruise the holes. If you are brave enough to fish this stream, take a landing net. It tends to become warm in long, hot summers.

Waihi River

Location and access Rises from the Four Peak Range, flows through the Waihi Gorge to Geraldine, then turns south to join the Hae Hae Te Moana River. SH 72 follows the river from Geraldine to Winchester. There are a number of access roads off SH 72 to the stream.
Season 1 October–30 April.
Restrictions Bag limit is four trout.

This small stream holds a reasonable stock of brown trout in the 0.5–1.3 kg range, especially upstream from Winchester. Fish can be spotted but often lie beneath the banks during the day and only emerge at dusk to feed. Trout respond to small mayfly and caddis imitations accurately presented.

Location and access Formed by the confluence of the Hae Hae Te Moana and Waihi rivers just northwest of Temuka. Flows south just west of Temuka, then east, before joining the lower reaches of the Opihi River. Access from the SH 1 bridge south of Temuka and Manse Bridge on the Temuka–Waitohi road.
Season 1 October–30 April.
Restrictions Bag limit is four trout.

This small, shingly, willow-lined stream is only 12 km long. It is best fished when the flow rate is less than 20 cumecs. It holds a good stock of browns averaging 1 kg, which can be spotted and stalked. Best early in the season before swimmers and picnickers make the trout wary. There are stable pools and riffles, the stream is easily waded and crossed, and it is a delight to fish. Small caddis and mayfly imitations work well but a long fine tippet and gentle casting are required.

Tengawai River

Location and access Drains the Richmond Range and follows SH 8 from Albury to Pleasant Point, where it joins the Opihi.
Season 1 October–30 April.
Restrictions Fly fishing only. Bag limit is four trout.

The final Opihi River tributary is another small, shingly, willow-lined stream that holds brown trout. Like most of these South Canterbury streams, it is best early in the season before water draw-off, low flows and water warming causes weed growth and eutrophication. The most productive water lies in the region of Cave. It becomes unfishable when the flow rate exceeds 20 cumecs. Mudstone along the banks makes walking hazardous on some stretches.

Most of these streams were once highly regarded fisheries, and although there is still some interesting angling, many have unfortunately deteriorated because of changing farming practices.

Pareora River

Location Drains the Hunter Hills southwest of Timaru, flows southeast and enters the sea near Pareora township.
Access The best access is from Pareora River Road, which follows up the true right or south side of the river.
Season Above SH 1, open 1 October–30 April. Below SH 1 there is a winter season from 1 June to 31 August.

This river also suffers severely from water abstraction and is best fished early in the season when river flows are adequate. It still yields brown trout below the dam at Evans Crossing, and sea-run browns enter the river early in the season.

Becomes unfishable when the flow rate exceeds 15 cumecs.

Waihao River

Location and access SH 1 crosses the lower reaches; road access to the 'Box' at the mouth. Above Bradshaws Bridge access obtained from Gum Tree Flat Road and at McCulloughs Bridge.
Season 1 October–30 April.

This small stream offers good blind fishing for sea-run brown trout from the 'Box' to Bradshaws Bridge. Many anglers use bait in this section of the river. Upstream, the river gorges. There are stable deep pools holding a small stock of brown trout. Can dry in summer.

Kakanui River

Location Both branches rise in the Kakanui Mountains west of Oamaru. After they join, the main stream follows a southeasterly course to enter the sea south of Oamaru at Kakanui.
Access SH 1 crosses the river just north of Maheno, and a number of roads both upstream and downstream of this bridge offer access to the river. Above SH 1, these include Gemmells Crossing, Robbs Crossing, Five Forks Bridge and Dunrobin Road Bridge. Below SH 1, access is mostly across private farmland although the Kakanui township bridge crosses near the mouth.

Season Above the SH 1 bridge, 1 October–30 April. Below this bridge there is a winter season from 1 June to 31 August.

Restrictions Above Five Forks Bridge, two trout. Below this bridge, four trout.

The best water lies below Clifton Falls where there are good stable pools and shallow, shingly runs. The banks are willow-lined and fish are easily spotted in clear water. The river is not heavily fished, and a good stock of brown trout (80 fish/km at Pringles below SH 1) averaging 1 kg can be anticipated. There are only a few fish above Clifton Falls. Caddis, mayfly and willow grub imitations can all be effective. The river fishes best early in the season before water is extracted for irrigation. The lower estuarine reaches and mouth offer good fishing for sea-run browns, especially early in the season and after a fresh. Most of these fish are taken on spinners, although night lure fishing with a large black lure is worth trying. The water is slow-flowing and deep in this section.

The Waianakarua River, crossed by SH 1 south of Herbert, also holds a few browns below the SH 1 bridge, but the river warms and becomes low and weedy in summer.

Waitaki River and tributaries

Lower Waitaki River

Location The Waitaki River rises in the Southern Alps, drains three large high country lakes and three large hydro lakes, flows generally east and enters the Pacific Ocean at Glenavy, north of Oamaru. The lower Waitaki River runs from Lake Waitaki to the sea. The upper Waitaki River has been severely modified for power generation and only exists for short stretches between dams.

Access

Waitaki mouth

North bank From Glenavy on SH 1 take Fisheries Road to Waitaki Huts. The mouth involves a long walk round the lagoon or a short trip across by dinghy.

South bank Take Kaik Road, 1.5 km south of the Waitaki Bridge on SH 1, which leads to the Kaik Camp Ground and river mouth.

From SH 1 to Waitaki Dam

North bank From the Glenavy–Tawai road there is access from Henstridges Road and Ferry Road. Then from the Tawai–Ikawai road there is access from Ross Road (Bells Pond). From SH 82 there is access from the eastern end of the Stonewall at the irrigation intake. Just before Hakataramea township, there is access through an unmarked gate and along a stopbank. Twin Bridges over the river to Kurow offers further passage to the river, as does Old Slip Road upstream through Hakataramea township.

South bank Travelling upstream on SH 83, many roads lead close to the river. These include Ferry, Jardine, Wilson and Goulding. Further upstream there is access at Black Point, Duntroon (west side of the Maerewhenua River), Priests Road, Otekaike River (east side) and Otiake River. There is also access at the Awakino River, 4 km from Kurow.

Season Above SH 1, open 1 October–30 April. Below SH 1 there is a winter season from 1 June to 31 August. The salmon season closes on 30 March between the Waitaki Dam and the mouth of the Maerewhenua River.

Restrictions Bag limit is six sportsfish, of which only two may be salmon and four may be trout. Jetboats are permitted on the river and can be launched at the Kaik Motor Camp, the south side of the SH 1 bridge, Ferry Road, Duntroon and Twin Bridges.

This very large river, which has been severely modified for power generation, is famous as a salmon fishery. Quinnat (chinook) salmon were first liberated from the Hakataramea Hatchery in 1901. Despite the severe modifications to the upper river, a good run of salmon appear each year from January to March and most spawn in the Hakataramea River.

Despite the river carrying glacial flour from Lake Pukaki for much of the year, it also holds some excellent brown and rainbow trout. The river is subject to flow fluctuations, and only becomes fishable when the flow rate is less than 500 cumecs. In summer when the river is low and clear there is excellent sedge fishing in

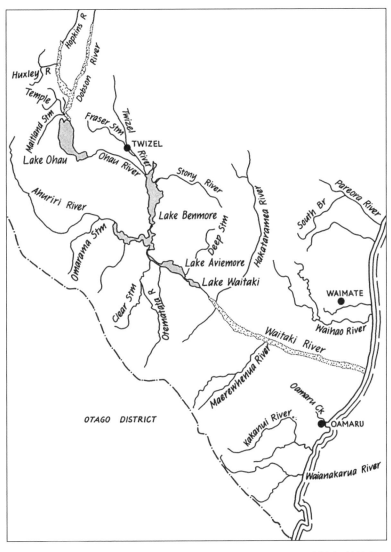

Waitaki Valley

the area adjacent to the Twin Bridges at Kurow. This hatch is best in a light northerly. As with all the Waitaki Valley, the easterly kills the fishing. Below this area, the river becomes braided and willowed and access to good water is not easy unless you have a jetboat. The rainbow trout can be very lively, and fish around 3 kg make use of the current when escaping downstream. At night, it pays to use 4 kg tippet and have plenty of backing available.

In the lagoon and mouth there are good sea-run browns, which respond to spinners or weighted smelt flies sunk very deep. Birds working on silveries and splashy rises usually indicate the presence of sea-run trout. A boat is very useful.

Maerewhenua River

Location Rises near Danseys Pass, flows north and enters the Waitaki River at Duntroon.
Access Danseys Pass Road from Duntroon follows up the river.
Season 1 October–30 April.
Restrictions Bag limit is two trout.

Before water was extracted for irrigation, the Maerewhenua was a highly regarded fishery. Now, because of low water flows, the river is best fished early in the season. The lower reaches are willowed and shingly and only hold small fish. There is reasonable fishing at Kellys Gully but the fish are small.

The upper reaches and branches provide more stable water, with deep pools in gorgy tussock terrain, although falls above Mt Alexander Station obstruct fish in the north branch. Both branches require a lot of walking, and some scrambling in certain sections. Fish can be stalked but a careful approach and one accurate cast is required.

Hakataramea River

Location Rises near the Hakataramea Pass, flows south and enters the Waitaki River at Hakataramea township opposite Kurow.
Access *Lower reaches* McHenry's Road, on the true left or east side of the river, follows upstream for 12 km to Wrights Crossing.
Middle and upper reaches Above Wrights Crossing access can be obtained from the Hakataramea Valley Road.
Season 1 October–30 April.
Restrictions Fly fishing only. Bag limit is two trout.

This popular, medium-sized river offers 30 km of fishable water, although in long dry summers trout drop back downstream after Christmas. Fish can usually be spotted but some difficult sections should be fished blind as stocks are good. In the lower reaches trout tend to be smaller (140 small to medium-sized fish/km). Higher upstream in the gorge there are well-established pools holding larger rainbow and brown trout. The river can be waded and crossed but the bed of rock and stone can be slippery. In some sections, the stream is willow-fringed. The river becomes unfishable when the flow rate is more than 15 cumecs. Salmon spawn in the river late in the season.

A Hakataramea rainbow about to be beached

Lake Waitaki

Location This is the first hydro lake in the Waitaki Valley, sited just upstream from Kurow.
Access SH 83 follows the southern shore. There is a boat ramp below the Aviemore Dam on the northern side. Basic camping facilities are available at Fishermans Bend.
Season 1 October–30 April.

Restrictions Bag limit is six sportsfish, of which only four may be trout.

Holds brown and rainbow trout averaging 1 kg, which are generally caught deep trolling or bait fishing. The lake water is often milky from glacial sediment but there are some shallow inlets close to SH 83 where fish can be spotted cruising the edges.

Lake Aviemore

Location This is the central lake of three on the Waitaki River.
Access Encircled by roads, including SH 83 and Te Akatarawa Road.
Season Open all year.
Restrictions Bag limit is four trout.
Boat launching facilities At Otematata on the southern shore and Waitangi Station on the northern shore. There are basic camping facilities at Waitangi.

This 16-km-long hydro lake holds good stocks of browns and rainbows averaging 1–2 kg. Although most fish are taken by trolling from a boat or spinning from the shore, there are some opportunities for shoreline fly fishing as trout can be sighted cruising the shallow bays alongside SH 83. The Otematata River delta and Deep Stream delta on the northern shore are also recommended. Some hardy anglers fish the deep water above the Aviemore Dam and the Deep Stream delta at night with a sunk black lure. Wind is the main problem in the Waitaki Valley; the nor'wester blows down the valley and the sou'wester blows up. Fishing is usually poor in an easterly.

Deep Stream

Location Drains the Kirkliston Range, flows south and enters Lake Aviemore just above the dam.
Access From Te Akatarawa Road on the north side there is a marked anglers' access track. An easy 20-minute walk to the mouth.
Season First Saturday in November–30 April.
Restrictions Fly fishing only. Bag limit is two trout.

Only the mouth and lower reaches of this freestone stream are worth fishing. The middle reaches are willow-lined, shingly and unstable, and by the time the season opens spawning fish will have dropped back downstream. The stream dries in long, hot summers. Cruising fish can be stalked around the mouth and delta.

Otematata River

Location Rises in the Hawkdun and Ida ranges of Central Otago and flows north to enter Lake Aviemore at Otematata.
Access The lower reaches can be accessed by walking downstream and upstream from SH 83 at Otematata. Permission to fish the middle and upper reaches must be obtained from Otematata Station. A four-wheel-drive vehicle is required.
Season 1 October–30 April.
Restrictions Bag limit is two trout above the Clear Stream confluence.

The upper reaches of this small to medium-sized freestone river are unstable, with the riverbed stones washed clean of algae. It is a spawning river for Lake Aviemore but when the stream warms, fish drop back downstream. Early in the season they tend to be in poor condition. The Otematata river flows through barren, rocky country, with briar rose and matagouri the only impediments to casting.

In the middle reaches, below Clear Stream, the river is more stable and the algae-covered stones harbour plenty of mayfly and caddis nymphs. A few willows line the banks and fish stocks are greater, with trout averaging 1–1.5 kg. Early in the season both rainbows and browns can be sight fished but many of the rainbows drop back to Lake Aviemore by Christmas. Although there are some good-looking pools in the gorge, fish stocks are not high there.

The mouth is worth prospecting for cruising fish, and at times reasonable night lure fishing can be experienced.

The Clear Stream tributary offers 10 km of small stream sight fishing but the middle and upper reaches are gorgy and hard going.

Briar rose and matagouri grow thickly along the banks in some sections. Like the Otematata, this stream can be waded and crossed without difficulty. Trout are not selective, but careful stalking and casting is required.

Lake Benmore

Location Lies in the Mackenzie country between Twizel, Omarama and Otematata.

Access There many access points, including the following:

- SH 83 runs close by the Ahuriri Arm. There is walking access to the Ahuriri Delta and lakeshore 5.5 km from Omarama through Glenburn Station.
- Turn off SH 8 at Dog Kennel Corner near Burke Pass and take the Haldon Road to the camping ground, boat harbour and east side of Haldon Arm.
- From SH 83 opposite Godley Peaks Road, take the Tekapo Canal road and the Tekapo–Pukaki River road down the true right bank of the Tekapo River from the Tekapo Power House to the Iron Bridge and Haldon Arm. This road is rough and shingly, and a four-wheel-drive vehicle is recommended.
- From Ruataniwha Dam on SH 83, take Falstone Road to the west side of Haldon Arm.
- From Ohau B Power Station, the canal road leads to Haldon Arm and the Ohau River mouth. This mouth can usually be crossed by four-wheel-drive and the Haldon Camp reached after fording the Tekapo River. Extreme care should be taken!

Season Open all year.

Restrictions Bag limit is four trout.

Boat ramps At Sailors Cutting on Ahuriri Arm and at the Haldon Camping Ground and boat harbour on Grays Road. There are camping facilities at Haldon Camping Ground, Falstone and Sailors Cutting on SH 83.

Formed in 1964, this large, rather inaccessible hydro lake has 116 km of shoreline. There are two arms: Haldon Arm, which has rather milky glacial water from the Tasman Glacier, Lake Pukaki and spillway discharges; and Ahuriri Arm, which has clear snow-fed water. The lake holds a vast stock of brown and rainbow trout averaging 1–2 kg. Sockeye salmon have been liberated in the past. Much of the shoreline can only be reached by boat.

Most fish are taken trolling from boats or live-bait fishing with worms, with some hardy anglers using these methods in winter when snow covers the surrounding mountains. Both the Ahuriri and Tekapo river deltas offer good fly fishing where cruising trout can be ambushed. The tussock-covered shore either side of the Ahuriri Delta is also a top spot for sight fishing provided the wind is not gale force. Fish will take dry flies but a small nymph, midge pupa or wet fly cast well ahead of a cruiser is usually more effective. From the Haldon Boat Harbour, on summer evenings there is good fly fishing from a boat. Trout cruise beneath the willows and will take dry flies such as Coch-y-bondhu, Humpy and Black Gnat.

Although access to many locations is difficult without a boat, much of the shoreline is rather barren of vegetation and fish. Anglers should concentrate on the locations described, where trout numbers are high.

Stony River

Location and access Flows down through Haldon Station and into the Haldon Arm of Lake Benmore. Permission from Haldon Station is required to fish the middle and upper reaches.

This small rock and stone type stream tends to dry in long hot summers. Water extraction for irrigation by Haldon station has adversely affected this stream. However, it still holds a few resident fish in more stable pools well upstream in the gorge. Best fished early in the season.

Omarama River

Location Drains the St Bathans Range south of Omarama and flows north to join the Ahuriri River just above Lake Benmore.
Access Lower reaches from the Omarama Camping Ground; middle and upper reaches from Omarama Station — permission must be obtained.

Season 1 October–30 April.
Restrictions Above SH 8, fly fishing only and a bag limit of two trout.

This small, lightly peat-stained stream winds its way across pastoral land. The stream can be discoloured by irrigation water and fish are difficult to spot. After rain, the water may take three days to clear. The banks are grass, briar rose and willow, with the latter being very thick in the upper reaches. The stream holds mainly brown trout averaging 1–2 kg but stocks are not high. The larger trout lie in short, deep pools and are best fished to blind with weighted nymphs and short casts. There can be a rise during the day but these are often the smaller fish. There's a day's fishing beyond a row of pines to the Tara Hills Research Station where the water becomes rather thin.

Ahuriri River

Location Rises in the Southern Alps below Mt Huxley and between lakes Ohau and Hawea. Flows on a curving easterly course down the picturesque Ahuriri Valley to enter Lake Benmore near Omarama.
Access *Delta* There is an anglers' walking access from SH 83 through Glenburn Station 5.5 km from Omarama. It is a 20-minute walk to the delta.
Lower reaches Walk downstream from the SH 8 bridge. There is vehicle access through Ben Omar Station but a fee is charged.
Middle reaches SH 8 parallels the true right bank of the river from Omarama to Dunstan Downs Station. There is walking access across private farmland to the river. Access to the true left bank is from Quail Burn Road and the branch road to the Clay Cliffs.
Upper reaches Beyond Dunstan Downs Station 17 km south of Omarama take the metalled Birchwood Road to Ben Avon and Birchwood stations. This follows upstream for 25 km, although the river is often some distance away from the road. Permission should be obtained before walking across private farmland on Ben Avon or Birchwood stations. The river can also be reached by walking down Avon Burn.

Season Above Longslip Creek, the Ahuriri and tributaries open on the first Saturday in December and close on 30 April. Below Longslip Creek, 1 October–30 April.

Restrictions Bag limit above Longslip Creek is two trout. Below this creek, four trout.

This medium to large river has a reputation for trophy fish in the upper reaches and is protected by a Water Conservation Order. Over recent years the angling pressure, especially from overseas visitors, has made it more difficult to secure a stretch of unfished water. The river winds in ox-bow fashion across pastoral land in a very exposed valley and the prevailing nor'wester can make upstream angling impossible by 10 a.m. There are long, slow, deep glides where some fish can be spotted on a bright, still day. However, others remain hidden under banks and only emerge to feed at dusk. In the Native Cutting section on Ben Avon Station, the river comes to life. There are well-developed stable, deep pools

A typical nor'west storm in the Ahuriri basin

and runs over a rock and stone riverbed. Some trout along the edges can be stalked but many remain hidden in the rocky crevices and deep holes. Fish stocks are not great in the upper reaches but most are well worth catching. Both rainbow and brown trout average over 2 kg in the upper reaches, with some browns over 4 kg. Weighted nymphs account for many of the fish caught, but in high summer cicada and grasshopper imitations can provide exciting fishing. The river can be crossed at a few selected fords in low water conditions only. Above Birchwood Station fish are few and far between as the riverbed of fine silt and sand is usually on the move. The middle reaches below Longslip Creek are more swift, unstable and braided but still hold good stocks of browns and rainbows that can be sight fished in ideal conditions. Many of the rainbows are small in this section but the browns average 1–2 kg. This section is not subject to the same angling pressure as the upper reaches and often provides a good alternative. Trout can be taken on a down-stream lure but most of these will be small rainbows.

Below the SH 8 bridge the river braids through willows but stocks of fish averaging 1 kg are high (90 trout/km).

This snow- and glacier-fed river can flood in an alarming fashion during nor'west storms, and remain unfishable for three or four days at a time. It is best fished when the river flow is well below 29 cumecs and on hot summer days.

The East Branch is shingly and unstable but holds a few fish recovering from spawning early in the season.

Ahuriri Valley lagoons

Location and access These lagoons are accessible from the right side of the Birchwood road, some 2 km north of Ben Avon Station. Although the present Ben Avon runholder is happy for responsible anglers to fish, it is polite to gain prior approval. The lagoon on the left side of the road is private.
Season First Saturday in December–30 April.
Restrictions Fly fishing only. Bag limit is two trout.

These lagoons — Ben Avon, Horseshoe, Watson and Yellow — are old ox-bows of the Ahuriri River that have been cut off after floods. Most have some connection with the main river, as they can become silt-laden when the Ahuriri River is in high flood. Their shores are swampy tussock dotted with a few willows, and the soft silt lake beds are dangerous to wade. Large browns cruise the weed beds and these can keep you interested all day in relatively calm and bright conditions. They are very difficult to stalk and deceive. A long fine tippet is required, with the fly cast well ahead of cruising fish. Just when you think the fish is on track towards your fly, it turns and goes the other way. Try small unweighted nymphs and emergers or even a small damsel fly. In February, a cicada imitation either scares the fish or induces a smash and grab take.

Green Tarn

Location and access This tarn lies on Ribbonwood Station, north of the Ahuriri River. The Ahuriri River must be forded below Birchwood Station, and the true left bank of the Snowy Creek gorge followed for one hour. The lake lies in a basin on your right.
Season First Saturday in November–30 April.
Restrictions Bag limit is two trout.

This small, exposed, high country lake holds rainbow trout but fish stocks are unreliable. Some large fish have been caught in the past, but the shallow lake warmed during the summer of 1998 and this affected the trout. Fish can be sight fished on a calm bright day, and seem most receptive to a damsel imitation. There are plenty of water fowl. A small creek at the northern end is probably used for spawning.

Lake Ohau

Location and access This large high country lake lies southwest of Twizel between the Ben Ohau and Barrier ranges. Turn off SH 8 at Clearburn onto the Lake Ohau Lodge road. This skirts the southern shore and provides access to the head of the lake. The road from Twizel to Glen Lyon Station provides access to the northern shore and the Dobson River at the head of the lake.

Season Open all year.
Restrictions Bag limit is four trout.
Boat ramps At the control gates and 3 km beyond the lodge turn-off. There are pleasant camping grounds at Lake Middleton and at Temple Forest at the head of the lake.

This lake is very exposed to the nor'wester and can become hazardous for boating. The lake itself can become milky from silt brought down by the Dobson River when in flood. Ohau is 16 km long and in fine weather is very picturesque. It holds good stocks of brown and rainbow trout averaging 1–2 kg, and tends to be under-fished. Sockeye salmon are also present but these are generally in poor condition. Most trout are caught trolling from a boat or spinning from the shore but some areas are conducive to fly fishing. The shoreline between Lake Ohau Lodge and the head of the lake is good for cruising fish, and night lure fishing at stream mouths can be productive. If the lake is high, manuka and matagouri scrub can interfere with the back cast. Round the top of the lake, beware of sinking sand and gravel near the Dobson delta.

During the day attractor type dry flies and small wet flies are good for cruising fish, while at night a Mrs Simpson lure or Woolly Bugger seems effective.

Lake Middleton

Location and access Lies adjacent to the southern shore of Ohau, where there is an attractive, sheltered campsite.
Season Open all year.
Restrictions Fishing from a boat is only legal if the boat is anchored.

This small lake holds small brown and rainbow trout, but in summer water-skiers and swimmers disturb the fishing.

Maitland Stream

Location Drains the Barrier Range, flows northeast to join the Dobson River near the head of Lake Ohau.

Access The Ohau Road crosses this stream near the head of the lake.

Season First Saturday in November–30 April.

Restrictions Bag limit is two trout.

This clear mountain stream rushes out of a gorge and across the flats at the head of Lake Ohau. The stream is best early in the season when it holds fish recovering from spawning, but fish numbers are generally low. Walk upstream from the road and look for trout in the gorge pools. Only the fit, active angler should attempt to fish the middle reaches above the gorge.

Temple Stream

Location The north and south branches drain the Barrier Range northwest of Lake Ohau and join near the road end at the Temple Forest picnic and camping ground. The river then leaves the bush and flows south in braided fashion across pastoral land to join the Dobson River just upstream from its mouth.

Access The Ohau Road crosses Temple Stream 5 km beyond the Maitland crossing. A branch road leads to Temple Forest and the forks.

Season First Saturday in November–30 April.

Restrictions Bag limit is two trout.

This fast-flowing mountain torrent holds few fish above the forks but across the farmland the river changes character, slows and becomes braided. The best water lies in the lower 2 km, although there are a few fish in the gorge downstream from the Temple Forest camping ground. Best fished early in the season, and despite the willows the lower stretch can be sight fished on a bright day.

Larch Stream, a small spawning spring creek for sockeye salmon, enters the Dobson River just upstream from the mouth. It holds a few trout early in the season.

The Hopkins and Dobson rivers hold a few fish in the deeper, more stable water of the lower reaches, but generally these rivers are too unstable, flood-prone and full of glacial flour, shifting silt, shingle and snow-melt. Nor'west dust storms in the riverbed can make life very unpleasant in this area.

The Huxley River holds a few fish for tramper-anglers.

Swan, Raupo and Red lagoons

Location and access These small lagoons lie on either side of the road into Lake Ohau, some 8–10 km from the lake. Swan lies on the right, while Raupo and Red are on the left. A short walk across tussock country is required to reach the lagoons.
Season First Saturday in November–30 April.
Restrictions Fly fishing only. Bag limit is two trout.

These small, shallow lagoons hold rainbow and brown trout, and Raupo also has fontinalis. Fish are not easy to spot unless rising. Try damsel and dragon fly nymphs or a Woolly Bugger fished on a floating or slow-sinking line.

Ohau River

Location This river has been severely modified for hydro-electric power generation. However, the stretch of river between Lake Ohau and Lake Ruataniwha has been made fishable by increasing the flow. The lower reaches below Ohau B Power Station are just a series of interconnected pools that drain into Haldon Arm on Lake Benmore.
Access Roads follow up both banks of the upper river from Twizel and from SH 8. The lower river can be accessed from the canal road below Ohau B Power Station.
Season First Saturday in November–30 April.

Below Lake Ohau there is a good-looking stretch of water with stable pools and runs. The river is moderate in size but seldom sufficiently clear for sight fishing. Best fished with weighted nymphs or spinners. Fish stocks do not seem to be very high. Access is easy but the river is rather formidable to cross. The pools in the lower reaches below Ohau B Power Station hold some very large fish that are most difficult to deceive.

Lake Ruataniwha

Location Lies just south of Twizel and opposite Ohau B Power Station.
Access There is access from SH 8 to the international rowing venue. This road continues to the top of the lake, Ohau A Power Station and the Ohau River Delta.
Season Open all year.
Restrictions Bag limit is four sportsfish.
Boat launching Facilities are available. There is also a camping ground close by the rowing headquarters.

This lake is frequently disturbed by rowers and other water sports. It carries glacial flour from Lake Pukaki via the Pukaki–Ohau Canal and Ohau A spillway. Most fish are caught trolling from a boat but there is some shoreline fishing in the clear water of the Ohau River delta. Some large browns can be spotted cruising the shallow bays in bright, still conditions or even at dusk, and ambushed with small weighted nymphs.

The Wairepo Arm on the east side of SH 8 is similarly coloured by glacial flour but trout are caught from the tussocky shore on flies and spinners. The swampy Wairepo Creek, which enters this arm, is worth exploring, especially early in the season after the first Saturday in November.

Kellands Pond

Location and access Just west of SH 8 and opposite Wairepo Arm. Easy access from SH 8.
Season Open all year.

This small pond has reasonably clear water and trout can be sight fished while cruising the shoreline. The pond is very exposed to the wind, but in ideal conditions attempts can be made to fool these sophisticated browns. I tried once and used small nymphs, midge pupae, soft hackle wets and damsel flies, all to no avail. Fortunately this was only a lunch break, so the frustration was tempered by good food.

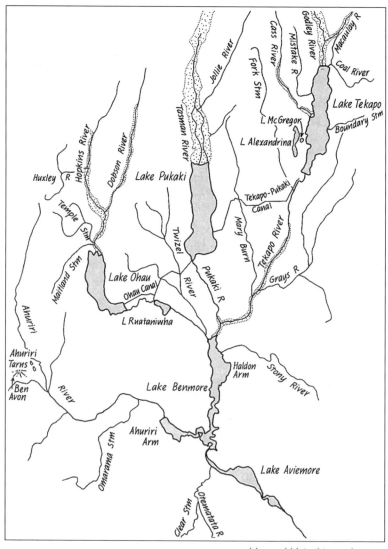

Upper Waitaki catchment

Location Drains swampy country near Burke Pass, flows south across the McKenzie Plains, round the western foot of Grays Hills and into the Tekapo River.

Access *Lower reaches* From Haldon Arm, follow up the true left bank of the Tekapo River and past Iron Bridge. After a long, bumpy ride this gravel road eventually fords the Grays River on a series of concrete posts. A four-wheel-drive vehicle is recommended.

Middle and upper reaches There are two marked anglers' access points off Haldon Road, one opposite the McKenzie Pass Road, and a number of private vehicle tracks to the river. Permission is required from local landowners to use these tracks.

Season First Saturday in November–30 April.

Restrictions Bag limit is two trout.

Upper Grays River

This small to medium-sized spring creek holds a good stock of trout, with a few rainbows in the lower reaches and browns elsewhere. Most fish weigh from 1 to 2 kg, but there are larger fish present. The lower reaches are choked with willows, but upstream beyond these there can be excellent sight fishing. At times, however, especially early in the season when the river is full, trout can be difficult to spot as the water can be slightly cloudy. For this reason it is also well worth fishing likely looking water. On some stretches where there are no willows, glare on the water can also make spotting hard and several fish will inevitably be spooked. There are some deep corner holes and hides beneath banks and the river is very stable. This creek is best in calm, sunny conditions when the trout are rising. The river has a sand, weed and mud bottom and the banks are grass in between willows. The more sheltered stretches can be fished in a nor'wester, and there are 20 km of fishable water. If a vehicle is already parked at your chosen site, find another section of river. It is heavily fished.

Tekapo River

Location Drains Lake Tekapo and flows south to enter Haldon Arm on Lake Benmore. The upper river has been severely modified for hydro-electric power generation and there is very little worthwhile fishing above where Forks Stream enters.

Access Most roads along the Tekapo River are very rough and a four-wheel-drive vehicle is recommended.

Lower reaches

- From Ohau B Power Station on SH 8, take canal road to Ohau River crossing just above the mouth. If this stretch of water is low, it can be forded and Tekapo River reached by vehicle.
- Haldon Road leaves SH 8 at Dog Kennel Corner and leads to Haldon Camping Ground; drive through the camp to the river.

Middle reaches Rough gravel roads run along both banks, with side tracks through the willows to the river.

- Iron Bridge crosses the river, provided the approaches haven't been washed out.
- Turn off SH 8 onto the Tekapo Canal Road 1.5 km south of Tekapo township, opposite Godley Peaks Road. Cross the canal

A trophy brown from the Tekapo basin

and continue on a rough metal road down the true right bank of the Tekapo River. This runs for 35 km and joins up with roads following upstream. There are many access tracks off this road.
Season Below the lower power pylons 1 km upstream from the mouth, the river is open all year. Above these pylons, first Saturday in November–30 April.
Restrictions Bag limit is two trout.

Although this medium-sized river is subject to fluctuating flow rates as a result of power generation, the river holds very high numbers of trout (250 trout/km). The river has a mean residual flow of 12 cumecs but becomes unfishable when the Tekapo Dam is fully open.

The riverbed is wide open, shingly, somewhat unstable and exposed to the nor'wester. On a sunny day in spring when the orange Californian poppies (eschscholtzia) are in flower there is no better sight than looking upstream towards snow-covered Aoraki/Mt Cook. The river is heavily willowed in some sections and braided in others. Wading is not difficult and the tails of most pools can be crossed. Trout can be spotted along the edges in optimum conditions, but generally the water should be fished blind or many fish will be missed. There are long, deep glides and ripply shallow runs. After heavy rain the river dirties from silt brought down by Forks Stream, and it may take three days to clear.

The larger fish will often lie deep beneath the drop-off at the head of the deeper pools, and only heavily weighted nymphs or a mouse imitation at night will interest them. The majority of fish are browns but some well-conditioned rainbows in the lower reaches can be exciting. Trout will respond to a wide selection of flies and lures, although during a rise they can be selective. This is an ideal river for beginners, with plenty of fish, plenty of safe water and few casting obstructions. However, beware of the nor'wester.

There are a number of side channels and ponds in the Tekapo Valley and most contain trout. Pattersons Ponds, below the Tekapo spillway, hold some good-sized browns.

Lake Pukaki

Location and access SH 8 skirts the southern shore while the Mount Cook road follows up the western shore.
Season Open all year.

This lake is very unattractive for angling as it contains water that is heavily laden with glacial silt from the Tasman Glacier. Despite fluctuating lake levels and the discoloured water, there are trout in the lake, but most are found near the mouths of incoming clear-water streams.

Glentanner Spring Creek and Tarn

Location and access On Glentanner Station. The small tarn lies on the right side of Mount Cook road 4 km beyond the Glentanner Visitor Centre. The spring creek can be seen from the visitor centre winding its way across the Tasman River flats. Permission must be obtained from the Glentanner Visitor Centre.
Season First Saturday in November–30 April.
Restrictions Bag limit is two trout.

In the spring creek, trout can be spotted in optimum conditions but numbers are not high. Best early in the season as angling pressure has increased over recent seasons. This is a freestone stream that is very exposed to the nor'wester.

The tarn is very weedy but holds a few good fish. These can be spotted from the hill on the west side.

Hydro canals

Location and access These include the Tekapo–Pukaki, Pukaki–Ohau, Ruataniwha–Ohau B and Ohau B–Ohau C. The locations are self-explanatory, and access is generally good with roads following down both banks of the canals.
Season Open all year.
Restrictions Bag limit is six sportsfish, of which two may be salmon and four may be trout.

All contain rainbow and brown trout, and the Tekapo–Pukaki canal also holds salmon, these having escaped from the salmon farm. The aesthetics of all the canals leave a little to be desired but some amazing trout have been caught, especially those feeding downstream from salmon farms. Recently, a 9-kg rainbow in prime condition was landed.

Trout will rise at times and some can be spotted along the edges waiting for wind-blown terrestrials. Generally, however, glacial flour, especially from Lake Pukaki, makes sight fishing impossible. Some trout cruise the canals on a regular beat, and can be ambushed by watching their rise forms.

Lake Poaka

Location and access Lies just north of the Pukaki–Ohau canal. Access along the canal road off SH 8 just south of Rhoboro Road
Season First Saturday in November–30 April.
Restrictions Fly fishing only. Bag limit is two trout, but catch and release is encouraged.

There is good shoreline sight fishing for cruising brown trout in this small lake. Stocks are not great and success comes to anglers with patience and skilful stalking techniques.

Lake Merino

Location and access Lies northwest of Twizel and opposite Loch Cameron on the north bank of the Pukaki canal.
Season First Saturday in November–30 April.
Restrictions Fly fishing only; the bag limit is two trout.

This small, shallow lake holds a small stock of good-sized browns that can be spotted and stalked on a bright sunny day.

Loch Cameron

Location and access Lies on the south side of the Pukaki hydro canal opposite Lake Merino.
Season First Saturday in November–30 April.
Restrictions Fly fishing only; the bag limit is two trout.

Slightly larger than Merino, this lake also holds brown trout which can be stalked and ambushed along the shore in bright conditions. There are a number of other small lakes and ponds in the Mackenzie country, and nearly all hold brown trout.

Twizel River

Location Drains the Ben Ohau Range, flows generally south through the outskirts of Twizel and across the McKenzie Plain to enter the Haldon Arm of Lake Benmore.
Access *Upper reaches* From SH 8 take Rhoboro Station Road, which crosses the river.
Middle reaches SH 8 crosses near Twizel. A private farm road follows down the true right bank; permission is required. There is also access across farmland from the continuation of the road to the black stilt research centre.
Lower reaches Walking access upstream from the Ohau River crossing near the mouth.

Season First Saturday in November–30 April.
Restrictions Bag limit is two trout.

The upper reaches of this small, freestone stream are flood-prone and unstable but are worth a look early in the season, as is the Fraser tributary reached from the Glen Lyon Road.

The middle and lower reaches offer 20 km of sight fishing for browns averaging 1–2 kg. Avoid nor'west conditions as the wind blows downstream and there is no shelter here apart from an occasional willow.

Mary Burn

Location The upper reaches flow south, parallel to the eastern shoreline of Lake Pukaki. The middle reaches are crossed by SH 8 then wind across flat Mackenzie country pastoral land before entering the Tekapo River in the Grays Hills area.
Access *Upper reaches* Permission required from Irishmans Creek Station.
Middle reaches From SH 8, although permission must be obtained from local runholders on Mary Burn and Simons Hills stations.
Lower reaches The Tekapo–Pukaki canal road crosses the lower reaches where there is a sheltered campsite.
Season First Saturday in November–30 April.
Restrictions Bag limit is two trout.

This small, exposed, stable, shingly stream has been heavily fished over recent seasons. It holds mainly brown trout, but early in the season rainbows add some spice. There are good stocks of fish averaging 2 kg which can be stalked on a bright, sunny day. It is impossible to fish in strong nor'west conditions, and on cloudy days sight fishing is very difficult due to glare on the water. The stream is easily crossed and the banks of grass, briar rose and matagouri scrub do not impede casting to any great extent. The lower reaches near the campsite are willow-choked. Trout rise avidly to dry flies presented without drag and will just as avidly accept small weighted nymphs. There are two days of fishing from the campsite to SH 8.

Fork Stream

Location Flows parallel to but east of the Mary Burn and joins the upper reaches of the Tekapo River.
Access *Upper and middle reaches* SH 8 crosses the river near the Tekapo Military Camp. Braemar Road off SH 8 leads upstream before crossing and leaving the river.
Lower reaches From the Tekapo–Pukaki canal road.
Season First Saturday in November–30 April.
Restrictions Bag limit is two trout.

Fork Stream holds a few browns and rainbows, especially early in the season. However, this small, freestone stream is unstable and flood-prone. Most of the fish have dropped back downstream by Christmas as the clean river stones offer little in the way of nymph life. A few resident fish remain in the more stable pools well upstream.

Jollie River

Location Drains the Southern Alps and follows a southerly course before entering the Tasman River at the head of Lake Pukaki.
Access Take Braemar Road from SH 8 and follow up the eastern side of Lake Pukaki to Mt Cook Station. This road crosses the river.
Season First Saturday in November–30 April.
Restrictions Bag limit is two trout.

This mountain torrent usually contains glacial flour, is flood-prone and unstable. It holds a few fish in the more stable pools of the middle reaches but the gorge is difficult to negotiate before this water is reached. On a clear and sunny day the scenic vistas of Aoraki/Mt Cook are quite magnificent.

Lake Alexandrina

Location Lies west of Lake Tekapo.
Access From SH 8 take Godley Peaks Road, 2 km south of Tekapo township. For the southern end of the lake and fishing huts turn onto a track to the left about 3.5 km from SH 8. For the middle

arm, turn off at Lake McGregor and continue to the outlet and fishing huts. For the top end of the lake and huts, drive to Glenmore Station. A track through deer paddocks leads to the huts.

Season First Saturday in November–30 April; there is also a winter season from 1 June to 31 July.

Restrictions Fishing from non-mechanically powered boats is permitted but boats must be anchored if fishing within 200 m of the shore. Bag limit is four sportsfish.

This moderate-sized, cold high country lake is very popular with anglers, especially those who enjoy harling. The lake lies between tussock-covered hills, and with its backdrop of snow-covered mountains it is most picturesque. It is exposed to the nor'wester, which blows down the lake and can make boating hazardous. Apart from a few willows lining the shore, the lake edge is fringed with tussock.

Both brown and rainbow trout averaging 1–2 kg can be caught, by far the most popular method being rowing and harling a lure on a sinking line. Early in the morning and at dusk are the favoured times. In summer the area round the island is popular, where rainbows tend to congregate in the deeper holes.

There is some shoreline angling but cruising trout are hard to spot unless conditions are ideal. Blind lure fishing accounts for some trout. In winter the browns continue to cruise the shore, whereas the rainbows stay in deeper water until September. Popular lures include Mrs Simpson, Woolly Bugger, Yellow Dorothy, Hamill's Killer, Parsons' Glory, Woolly Worm and Rabbit patterns.

Lake McGregor

Location and access Lies on the left side of Godley Peaks Road about 8.5 km from SH 8. A vehicle track to Lake Alexandrina follows the lake shore.

Season First Saturday in November–30 April.

Restrictions Bag limit is two trout. Fishing from a boat is only permitted if the boat is anchored.

Snow can fall any time of the year (even in November) in the South Island high country

The outlet from Lake Alexandrina drains into this small, willow-fringed lake. It holds good stocks of fish, which are not easy to spot. Most are caught fly fishing with a lure, bully or damsel imitation, as listed for Lake Alexandrina. Best in the early morning or at dusk. Fly casting from a dinghy near the outlet creek delta usually brings results.

The outlet creek from Lake McGregor flows under the Godley Peaks Road and is worth fishing if the level of Lake Tekapo is reasonably high. Browns can be spotted cruising under the willows.

Lake Tekapo

Location and access Tekapo is the northernmost lake in the Upper Waitaki basin and has also been modified for hydro-electric power. SH 8 passes the southern shore at Tekapo township. The Lilybank

Road follows up the eastern shore to the head of the lake, while Godley Peaks Road provides some access near Lake McGregor on the western shore.

Season Open all year.

Restrictions Bag limit is four trout.

Although this lake is coloured by glacial flour brought down by the Godley River, brown and rainbow trout survive. Generally, the best spots for shoreline fishing are the mouths of the various clear-water creeks flowing into the lake. These include the Mistake, Cass, and the outlet of Lake McGregor and Glenmore Station Tarn on the western shore, and the Coal, Boundary and Macauley on the eastern shore. However, most fish are caught by trolling a spinner from a boat.

Glenmore Station Tarn

Location and access Take the farm track that leaves Godley Peaks Road opposite Lake Murray.

Season First Saturday in November–30 April.

Restrictions Bag limit is two trout.

This small tarn on the shores of Lake Tekapo has been fenced off for black stilt nest protection. Permission to fish should be obtained from either Glenmore Station or the Department of Conservation.

The weedy tarn holds a few good-sized rainbow and brown trout, which can be stalked along the shore. Use small unweighted nymphs or midge pupa imitations to avoid the weed beds.

Cass River

Location Drains the Hall and Gammack ranges, flows south between these mountains and enters Lake Tekapo just north of Lake McGregor.

Access The Godley Peaks Road crosses the lower reaches. Walk upstream from the bridge.

Season First Saturday in November–30 April.

Restrictions Bag limit is two trout.

At the road bridge the river is unstable, shingly and flood-prone. It can take a week to clear after heavy rain. About 2 km upstream there is more stable water in a gorge. There are 3 km of fishing up as far as Joseph Stream, where the river again becomes very unstable. In clear, low water conditions, both browns and rainbows can be stalked.

Mistake River

Location and access Flows parallel to but east of the Cass River on Godley Peaks Station. Permission is required from the station.

This stream is a rusher but early in the season it does hold a few rainbows in the gorge and upper reaches. A lot of walking and scrambling is required for few fish. The mouth is worth a look but access is much easier by boat.

Boundary Stream

Location and access Drains the Two Thumb Range and enters the eastern shore of Lake Tekapo. The Lilybank Road crosses the stream.

This small, shingly stream almost dries in long, hot summers. Only the mouth is worth fishing.

Coal River

Location Drains the Two Thumb Range near the old Round Hill Skifield and flows west into the head of Lake Tekapo.
Access Crossed by the Lilybank Road.

This small clear-water stream holds a few fish in the lower reaches early in the season, but the mouth can be fished all year round. The middle and upper reaches are turbulent and swift.

Location and access Drains the Main Divide, flows south and joins the Godley River near Lilybank Station. Access to the lower reaches from Lilybank Road. Permission should be obtained from Mt Creighton Station to fish the middle reaches.

This is a spawning river for Lake Tekapo and fish numbers vary from a few to very few. There are some stable pools in the Northeast Gorge, but on a recent visit we found no trout. The stones had been washed clean by floods.

There are a few spring creeks on both sides of the Godley Valley that hold a few trout. These should be sight fished on a fine, clear day but the nor'wester can be devastating in this area. Permission is required from local runholders.

Otago Fish and Game Council region

Climatic conditions vary enormously within the Otago district. In West Otago, the country is mountainous, remote and bush-clad, with a rainfall in the region of 3000 mm per year. In Central Otago the climate is more continental, with hot dry summers and cold frosty winters. Rainfall can be as little as 250 mm per year. Coastal Otago's rainfall is greater, at 600–1200 mm per year, and the climate cooler. Hydro-electric power generation and irrigation schemes have modified a number of rivers and produced lakes and ponds, nearly all of which have been stocked with trout. Some of the rivers affected include the Clutha, Fraser, Manuherikia, Teviot, Taieri and Waipori.

Brown trout were first introduced in 1869 and are now well-established in most rivers. Rainbow trout were liberated in 1883 and have thrived in the mountainous waters of West Otago. Sea-run browns provide sport at the mouths of the Shag, Waikouaiti, Taieri, Clutha and Catlins rivers, while quinnat salmon run in the Clutha and Taieri rivers from January to April.

Just as creeper fishing has played a significant part in the trout fishing scene in Taranaki, so live-bait fishing has played a similar role in parts of Otago and Southland, and indeed is very popular in some of the lower reaches of rivers and their estuaries.

North Otago

Shag River

Location Rises in the Kakanui Mountains, flows southeast and enters the Pacific Ocean at Shag Point just east of Palmerston.

Access *Lower reaches* From SH 1, which crosses the river.

Middle and upper reaches From SH 85 and the many side roads that cross the river between Palmerston and Dunback. These include Horse Range, Switchback, Munro, Craig, McLew, Jones, Limekiln and Dunback. Above Dunback, Waynestown and Loop roads offer access. There is no Queen's chain on this river so permission should be obtained from landowners.

Season Below the SH 1 bridge, open all year. Above this bridge, 1 October–30 April.

Restrictions Bag limit is six trout.

The estuary and lower reaches of this small to medium-sized river offer sea-run browns early in the season when whitebait are running, and again in February when they run upstream to spawn. Most fish are taken on small gold and silver spinners, but smelt and bully imitation lures also work well on a fly rod, especially at night. The water is dark and slow-flowing.

The middle reaches from Palmerston to above Dunback are heavily overgrown with willows, gorse, blackberry and broom. However, there are small clearings where improvised casting is usually possible. Clear water and easily spooked fish add to the angling difficulties; perhaps that's the reason for the bag limit being left at a high six fish! There are good stocks of brown trout averaging 1–2 kg (44 takeable fish/km near Dunback) and these can be spotted easily in most sections above SH 1. Wading will disturb fish but the river can normally be crossed easily. By the middle of December, low flows and farm run-off contribute to weed growth and this makes fishing even more difficult. Trout tend to cruise in the slow-moving pools rather than remain on station, and expert stalking techniques, a long fine tippet and delicate casting are necessary.

Trout numbers decrease in the upper reaches above Dunback although a few larger fish inhabit the deeper holes.

Try small, lightly weighted nymphs, emergers, beetles, Midge Pupa, Willow Grub and Corixa. Small mayfly dry flies can be useful, especially early and late in the day. I suggest carrying a landing net.

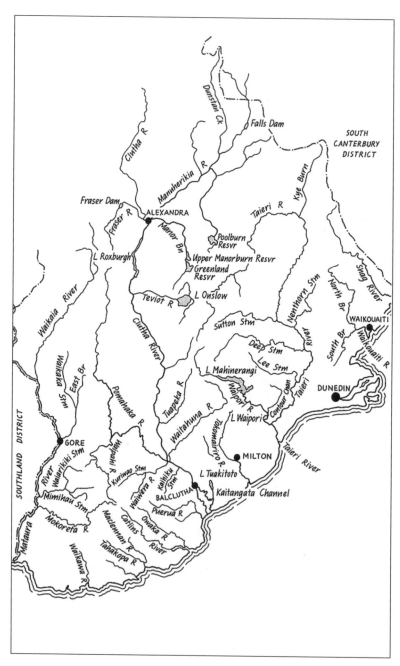

Otago District

Location Rises from the steep, tussock-covered hills west of Waikouaiti. The north and south branches meet near Orbells Crossing and enter the sea at Karitane.
Access From SH 1 on Ramrock Road just south of Waikouaiti, McGrath Road, Mill Road at Orbells Crossing, and Kiatoa Road at Bucklands Crossing.
Season Below SH 1, open all year. Above SH 1, open 1 October–30 April.

The South Branch holds few fish, whereas the North Branch above Bucklands Crossing is well worth exploring early in the season before weed growth becomes a problem. There are long, deep, slow-flowing pools that hold some reasonable brown trout, but a lot of walking, wading and crossing is required.

Below Orbells Crossing the river becomes slow-flowing, sluggish and choked with willows. These lower reaches are better fished with spinners or live bait. The estuary welcomes a run of sea-run browns in February and these can be caught on smelt flies or bully imitations as well as spinners.

South Otago

 Taieri River and tributaries

Taieri River

Location Rises in the high tussock country of the Lammerlaw and Lammermoor ranges of Central Otago, flows north to Waipiata then bends south round the Rock and Pillar Range to eventually enter the sea 30 km south of Dunedin.
Season Below the SH 1 bridge at Allanton the river is open all year. Above this bridge, 1 October–30 April.
Restrictions Bag limit is six trout. Trolling from boats is only permitted below Henley Ferry Bridge.

The river has been modified for hydro-electric generation and irrigation. It is over 250 km long and hence described in three sections.

Upper reaches from the headwaters to Waipiata
Access Many roads lead to and cross the river. These include the Loganburn, Upper Taieri, Styx–Patearoa, Puketoi–Patearoa, Patearoa–Maniototo, and Ranfurly–Patearoa roads.

Because the river drains a vast swamp the water is heavily peat-stained, making sight fishing difficult unless the trout are rising. There are very few fish above Canadian Flat. At Serpentine Flat there are deep pools and runs, and although the river is rather narrow, some excellent nymph and dry fly fishing can be experienced on calm days with accurate casting. Below Serpentine Flat the river deepens and becomes more sluggish and convoluted. Weed growth can be a problem so carry a landing net. The banks are open tussock but swampy and this section of river is very exposed to cold winds. A variety of flies including the usual Pheasant Tail and Hare's Ear nymphs, Corixa, Midge Pupa, damsel and mayfly imitations, Coch-y-bondhu, Black Gnat and, in high summer, cicada and cricket patterns will take fish. There are some large browns in this section but they are not easy to fool.

The upper Taieri Gorge above Hores Bridge is very difficult to fish except with a spinner. A lot of rock scrambling is required.

Below this gorge there is excellent still water fishing across the Upper Taieri Plains. The river is deep, weedy and sluggish, with ox-bows, while the banks are swampy tussock and willows. There is a good stock of browns, and some double-figure fish have been landed from this section of river. Use the same flies as listed above, although emerger and CDC patterns can also be useful. Anglers using small spinners and live bait also take fish here.

Middle reaches from Waipiata to Outram
Access SH 87 follows the true right bank downstream to Middlemarch. There are numerous roads off this highway which offer river access.

Between Waipiata and Kokonga there is excellent accessible water for the angler. The nature of the river changes, with well-defined pools and runs and a shingly bed. Willows dot the banks in some stretches but fish stocks are reasonable and the river is more easily managed in this section. Between Kokonga and Hyde (Horseburn Road at Tiroiti), the river again enters a rough gorge, which can be negotiated by active anglers, especially when the river is low. From Hyde to Sutton the riverbed opens out again, with shingly runs and pools flowing through pastoral land. Below Sutton a third rocky gorge is entered and this is even more difficult to negotiate. The Mosgiel–Mt Allan and Outram–Hindon roads give limited access to this gorge and 'mountain goat' type fishing.

Lower reaches from Outram to Taieri Mouth
Access There are many access roads across the Taieri Plain between Henley Ferry and Outram, including School, Bruce, Otokia, Henley, Riverbank and Ferry roads. The mouth can be accessed through Brighton on the coast road south of Dunedin, or from SH 1 at Waihola.

The river is tidal below Allanton, and difficult to fish without a boat in the dark, deep, gorgy, slow-flowing section below Henley Ferry. In summer the water can be disturbed by water-skiers. Between Outram and Allanton the river is willow-lined, has deep holes and a shingle bed. Spinning and live-bait fishing accounts for the majority of trout taken, although lure fishing at night or a smelt fly during the day can pick up the odd sea-run brown. Having been modified for flood protection, this is not an attractive stretch of river to fish, but because it is close to Dunedin usage is high.

The mouth offers sea-run browns, kahawai, flounder and mullet fishing.

Kye Burn

Location Drains the Ida Range, flows south through Kye Burn Diggings and joins the Taieri near Kokonga.
Access SH 85 crosses at Kye Burn. The Danseys Pass Road to Kye Burn Diggings follows upstream.

Season 1 October–30 April.
Restrictions Bag limit is six trout.

This rather unstable, shingly stream has been turned over in the past by goldminers. However, it is a spawning stream for the Taieri River and holds trout in the more stable pools early and late in the season in the lower reaches, especially below SH 85. In summer the river is dewatered for irrigation and trout drop back downstream.

Nenthorn Stream

Location Rises near Macraes Flat and enters the Taieri in the vicinity of Middlemarch.
Access From the Middlemarch–Macraes Flat road and side roads off this road, including Mt Stoker, Hummock Runs and Nenthorn roads.
Season 1 October–30 April.
Restrictions Bag limit is six trout.

This small, tea-coloured tributary holds a few reasonable brown trout. The lower reaches are best fished with a spinner but there is fly fishing in the upper section above Hummock Runs Road.

Deep Stream

Location Drains the Lammermoor Range and flows east to join the Taieri near Hindon.
Access SH 87 crosses the stream, while the Old Dunstan Trail branches off SH 87 at Clarks Junction and reaches the stream at Rocklands Station.
Season 1 October–30 April.
Restrictions Bag limit is six trout.

A small, peat-stained, rock and stone type stream holding brown trout in the 0.75–1 kg range. The stream winds through tussock-covered hills and is gorgy in parts but quite negotiable. Mayfly, caddis and beetle imitations are worth trying.

Lee Stream

Location Drains the Lammerlaw Range, flows east parallel to but south of Deep Stream, and joins the Taieri downstream below Traquair.

Access SH 87 crosses at Traquair. A small road branches off the Traquair–Mahinerangi Road just over the Lee Stream bridge on SH 87. This follows upstream to Lee Flat. Black Rock Road leaves SH 87 beyond the Lee Stream school and leads to the upper reaches.

Season 1 October–30 April.

Restrictions Bag limit is six trout.

This is another typical small, peat-stained Taieri tributary draining swampy land. It holds a reasonable population of brown trout. The best water lies upstream from SH 87, as a little way downstream the river enters an impassable gorge. As the trout cannot be sight fished, morning and evening are the best times for dry fly fishing.

Waipori River

Because this river has been severely modified for hydro-electric power generation it is divided into two sections: the Upper Waipori above Lake Mahinerangi, and the Lower Waipori River.

Upper Waipori River

Location Drains the Lammerlaw Range and flows southeast through exposed tussock and matagouri country into Lake Mahinerangi.

Access From the Waipori–Lawrence road take Gardiners Track and then walk to the river. A four-wheel-drive vehicle is recommended.

Season 1 November–30 April.

Restrictions Bag limit is six trout.

A short distance above Lake Mahinerangi the river enters a steep-sided gorge, which can be waded through with some difficulty in low water, summer conditions. The river holds only a few trout but these are well worth catching. Fish stocks are very unreliable. Best in high summer when the cicadas are whistling.

Lower Waipori River

Location Drains Lake Mahinerangi, flows down through a rough gorge, gathers together other drainage canals and tributaries and enters lakes Waipori and Waihola. Below these lakes, the now large, slow-flowing river enters the Taieri above Henley Ferry Bridge.

Access *Above Lake Waipori* From SH 1 on the Henley–Berwick– Waipori Falls Road up the gorge to the village of Waipori Falls.
Below Lake Waipori From SH 1 or from the old Main South Road southwest of Henley.

Season 1 October–30 April.

Restrictions Bag limit is six trout.

Four kilometres above Lake Waipori, the gorge section offers a real challenge. It holds a few nice browns in rough pocket water but should only be attempted by fit, active anglers. The rocky shelves and rocks are slippery to wade and the possibility of water level fluctuations makes crossing hazardous.

Below Lake Waipori, the river is large, dark, slow-flowing and uninteresting but still holds fish. Most are taken on spinners and live bait.

Lake Mahinerangi

Location This lake was created by damming the Waipori River for hydro-electric power.

Access From SH 87 near Traquair on Mahinerangi Road, the Waipori Falls Road through Waipori village or from SH 8 at Lawrence on the Lawrence–Waipori road.

Season 1 October–31 May.

Restrictions Bag limit is six trout. Boats are permitted.

This relatively large lake suffers from fluctuating levels depending on power usage. However, it has been stocked with brown and rainbow trout and perch. The shoreline is very accessible, but the lake lies at an elevation of 400 m and is often cold and windswept. The western shoreline is forested. Trout can be taken on all legal methods but fly fishing is best in summer in warmer conditions. Trolling and harling from a small boat account for many fish, as do spinning and live bait fishing from the shore. For the fly angler, damsel, midge and mayfly patterns are effective, as are bully type lures. By December the manuka beetle should be tried, and in February a cicada or cricket imitation will provide exciting fishing.

Contour channel

Location Drains swampy farmland near Woodside, flows south and empties into the Waipori River below Berwick.
Access Landowner permission is required. A number of roads lead to the channel, including Mangatua, Miller, Otokia, Berwick and Henley.

This is another slow-flowing, unattractive waterway that holds brown trout and perch. It is fished by local anglers, mainly with spinners and live bait.

Lake Waipori and Lake Waihola are tidal, freshwater lakes on the Taieri Plain, which hold trout and perch. Both are uninspiring to fish. Local anglers use a boat and live bait methods. Both lakes can become muddy and discoloured in strong winds.

Other tributaries of the Taieri River that hold a few brown trout are Sutton Stream, Meggat Burn, Three O'Clock Stream and Silverstream, but they are not highly recommended.

Two ponds on the Taieri River that are part of the Maniototo power and irrigation scheme are stocked with trout. These are Hore's Control Pond and McAtamney's Head Pond, which are both reached from the Styx–Patearoa road. Both are on private property and it is necessary to obtain permission before fishing. The season is 1 October–30 April; the bag limit is six fish.

Two of Dunedin's water supply dams are stocked with trout, mainly for junior anglers. These are Sullivans Dam at the top of the northern motorway, and Southern Reservoir off Kaikorai Valley Road. Tomahawk Lagoon behind Tomahawk Beach is similarly stocked.

Tokomairiro River

Location and access The east and west branches of this small stream flow southeast down through the town of Milton and join just south of the town. SH 1 crosses both branches south of Milton. The west branch is reached from SH 8 at Glenore and Mt Stuart, while access to the east branch is from North Branch Road off SH 1 and Springfield Road.
Season Open all year below Coal Gully road bridge. Above this bridge, 1 October–30 April.

This small stream, which winds its way through hilly farmland, becomes sluggish and weedy once the two branches join. Both branches offer small stream fly fishing early in the season, while the main river is usually fished with live bait and spinners. The river holds a reasonable stock of browns averaging around 1 kg.

 Lower Clutha River and tributaries

Lower Clutha River (Clyde Dam to the mouth)

The Upper Clutha is described under the Lakes Wanaka, Hawea and surrounding district section.

Access SH 8 parallels the river between Clyde and Balclutha. Some sections can only be reached by boat, while others require permission from local landowners. Below Balclutha the river divides into the Koau and Matau branches. There is good access from roads in the region of Inch Clutha.
Season Open all year.

This is a huge river, and unless you have a boat, angling opportunities are limited. Between Clyde and Alexandra the river is deep, swift and swirly, and occupies one channel. It holds small numbers of brown and rainbow trout, which can be fished to with spinning gear. Lake Roxburgh is deep and rather sterile, hence holds few fish. Access is by boat.

In February and March, quinnat salmon congregate immediately below the Roxburgh Dam and are heavily fished with spinning gear.

Between the Roxburgh Dam and Balclutha, the sheer size of the river makes angling almost impossible. It is large, deep and swirly, with little definition. Willows line the banks but unless a boat is used much of the best water cannot be reached. It holds brown and rainbow trout, with the hot spots being stream mouths such as the Pomohaka and Waitahuna.

Below Balclutha the river divides into two branches, the Matau to the north and the Koau to the south. Both branches flow deep between stopbanks. The Matau branch is heavily fished by anglers using live bait whereas the Koau branch is more difficult to access and is polluted. Both sea-run browns and salmon are caught by anglers using threadline methods.

Waiwera River

Location Drains the Kaihiku Range and flows north to enter the Clutha on its true right bank downstream from Clydevale.
Access SH 1 crosses the river 15 km west of Balclutha. Kuriwao Siding Road, Hillfoot Road and Waiwera Gorge Road offer access to the river, although some stretches are difficult to reach because of private farmland.
Season 1 October–30 April.

Below SH 1 this small, rain-fed river is overgrown with willows. At SH 1, the stream appears sluggish and uninviting but upstream there is good water, especially in the gorge. Browns average 1 kg and are best fished early in the season before weed growth and easily spooked fish make it difficult. Caddis, mayfly and beetle imitations work well.

Location This long river, which is protected by a Conservation Notice, rises in the Umbrella Mountains south of Roxburgh and winds its way for 125 km through West Otago farmland to enter the Clutha River below Clydevale, not far from the mouth of the Waiwera River. Because the river is so long, it is described in three sections.

Season 1 October–30 April.

Upper reaches above Switzers Bridge

Access From the following roads running northeast of Heriot, Kelso and Tapanui: Aitcheson's Runs Road to Hamiltons Flat and the headwaters, Switzers Road to Park Hill Domain, Hukarere Station Road and Spylaw Burn Road.

The headwaters run deep in a rocky gorge lined with beech bush. Access is tricky and river crossings can be hazardous. The country above the gorge is barren and windswept, and can become very cold even in February. Only fit anglers should attempt this section as you really need to be a mountain goat. The attraction in this river is the large sea-run browns, up to 4–5 kg, which run upstream from the Clutha to spawn from January to March. By mid-April most fish have paired up for spawning and they become unresponsive to anglers. There are stable, deep holes and fish can be spotted but they are wary unless approached with finesse.

From Hamiltons Flat to Switzers Bridge the river runs through tussock and grazing country. The river is very manageable in this section and can be safely waded and crossed. The water is clear and fish can be spotted on the rock, stone and gravel bed. They respond to carefully presented weighted nymphs, especially stonefly and caddis varieties, and to cicada imitations, Black Gnat, Coch-y-bondhu and small mayflies.

Middle reaches between Switzers Bridge and Conical Hill

Access From Dusky Forest, Kelso township, Paradise Flat Road, Tapanui–Waikaka bridge, Gore–Tapanui bridge, Waipehi–Conical road and Waikoikoi Road.

Trout are smaller in this section and average around 1.2 kg, but stocks are good. The water becomes brownish in colour and sight fishing is hardly an option. There is a variety of water, some of which is overgrown with willows. The best stretch is in Dusky Forest where the river rushes through on a slippery rock and stone bed. Wading and crossing can be treacherous but blind nymph and dry fly fishing can be exciting. Carry a landing net for this section of river. Below Dusky Forest the river slows and is heavily willowed, but between Kelso and Tapanui another gorge offers more challenging fishing.

Lower reaches from Conical Hill to the mouth
Access Many roads provide access but some sections of the river are very overgrown with willows and impossible to fish. Burkes Ford, Ross and Taumata roads, along with the Clinton–Clydevale and Waiwera–Clydevale roads, lead to or cross the river.

Below Conical Hill the water becomes even more peat-stained and the river more willow-choked. There are swift, rocky runs and deep guts, with spinning the best option in this section. Below Burkes Ford the river slows, deepens and becomes more muddy and weedy, and most fish in this section are caught on live bait. The mouth can be accessed on foot from Swans Bridge across private land.

The size and number of resident trout in this popular river has diminished over recent years. Even the numbers of sea-run fish are considerably lower than a few years ago. Water abstraction and farm pollution are thought to be the cause.

Waipahi River

Location Rises from swampy country west of Clinton and winds its way north across open, swampy farmland to join the Pomahaka River south of Conical Hill.
Access *Lower reaches* SH 1 crosses the river near Arthurton, 20 km east of Gore.
Middle reaches Jeffs Road off the Clinton–Mataura road crosses the river.
Upper reaches The Clinton–Mataura back road crosses the river,

while the road to Wyndham follows upstream. The best stretches of river are reached through private farmland.

There are over 35 km of fishable water on this small stream, which hosts the Waipahi Gold Medal competition in late October each year. The stream is tannin-stained from its swampy origins so sight fishing is generally impossible unless fish are rising. Although reasonably small, this river has some deep holes and rocky runs, and brown trout stocks are excellent. Fish average around 1 kg. There are prolific hatches on the river, especially early in the season, and trout can be very selective. Best fished either early or late in the season, as low water in summer heralds the onset of weed growth.

Small mayfly nymphs, emergers, No Hackle Duns and mayfly dry flies account for most fish taken. Caddis patterns can be useful at dusk.

Catlins district

Most rivers in the Catlins district rise from swampy tussock country or from dense rainforest, and as a result are heavily peat-stained. This makes spotting trout virtually impossible unless the fish are rising. Nearly all sizeable streams and rivers hold brown trout, with sea-run or estuarine-living fish providing much of the sport. The middle and upper reaches of many of these rivers are overgrown and difficult to fish. This district has a relatively high rainfall and strong, cold winds often blow.

Owaka River

Location Rises from the Wisp Range, flows southeast across farmland and empties into the Catlins River estuary at Pounawea just below Catlins Lake.
Access SH 92 crosses east of Owaka and the Owaka–Clinton road follows upstream. Side roads off this main road offer access, although the best water is often reached through private farmland.
Season Open all year below the Pounawea–Newhaven bridge. Above this bridge, 1 October–30 April.

This small, peat-stained stream has deteriorated over recent years due to farming practices. It now colours readily after rain and can remain silt-laden for some time thereafter.

It holds small numbers of brown trout but most fish are caught by local anglers on live bait in the lower reaches. The estuary provides good spin fishing for sea-run fish off Newhaven Road, but beware of sea-lions!

In the middle reaches the river is well-contained by stable, grassy banks. There are long, sluggish, deep pools and short riffles. Browns up to 2 kg respond well to caddis and mayfly dry flies but stocks are not great. There is often a good evening rise but carry a landing net for the steep banks and beware of large eels. Best between Mason and Forsythe roads.

Catlins River

Location Drains the Beresford and Wisp ranges and tussock swamp in the Wisp area, flows southeast through the Catlins State Forest Park to empty into the tidal Catlins Lake south of Owaka.

Access *Upper reaches and headwaters* Take the Chloris Pass Road off the Clinton–Owaka road or Cairn Road off the Clinton–Wyndham road. The eastern end of Cairn Road crosses the river.

Middle reaches From forestry tracks in the Catlins State Forest Park. From the Owaka–Clinton road take Morris Saddle Road to Tawanui. This leads to an excellent DoC camping area at the Tawanui Recreation Reserve. From this reserve, a well-maintained walking track follows up the true left bank to Franks Creek (2½ hours). The track then crosses the main river on a swingbridge and follows up the true right bank, eventually reaching the Wisp Recreation Reserve (2½ hours). It is also possible to drive to Franks Creek on a forestry road where a side track leads down through the bush to the swingbridge.

Lower reaches SH 92 crosses the river just above Catlins Lake. Hinahina Road from SH 92 offers good access to the main channel — the best area for sea-run fish.

Season Open all year below SH 92. Above this bridge, 1 October–30 April.

Although this river holds a good population of brown trout, it is severely peat-stained and unless trout are rising they cannot be spotted.

The upper reaches flow through barren tussock and grazing land but have become overgrown with giant gorse. Where the banks are clear, fly fishing can be productive. It is best to wade upstream from the bridge on Cairn Road but the rock shelves and river stones are very slippery. There is plenty of river to fish but the bank vegetation makes it very frustrating to fly fish.

The best stretch of river to fish lies in the Catlins State Forest. There are deep, stable pools and frothy runs, and when trout are rising to mayflies some reasonable angling can be enjoyed. It is worth visiting the area round Franks Creek, where trout averaging 1–2 kg rise enthusiastically to dry flies. The river can be crossed and waded but beware of healthy eels!

Below Tawanui, the river slows. Larger fish are caught in the section of river immediately upstream from tidal influence but the river is less attractive and access more difficult. Catlins Lake is just a large estuary, and in high summer some large sea-run browns are caught in the channels on spinners, live bait and smelt imitation lures. A boat is useful for the estuary.

The Catlins River

Location Rises from Table Ridge in the Catlins State Forest Park, flows southeast and empties into Tahakopa Bay.
Access From Maclennan, follow upstream on the Tahakopa Valley Road. The upper reaches can also be accessed from Mokoreta.
Season Open all year below the Maclennan confluence. Above this confluence, 1 October–30 April.

This medium-sized river is similar to the Catlins in being heavily peat-stained. Many stretches of river are rather inaccessible due to overhanging scrub and gorse. The middle reaches hold good numbers of browns averaging 1 kg, while the deep, slow-moving lower reaches near Papatowai hold larger sea-run fish. Most anglers fish this river with spinners and live bait, but early in the season some reasonable fly fishing is available for anglers adept at 'bow and arrow' casting and crawling through scrub. Access is easier where exotic forest has been planted and the banks cleared, but after Christmas long grass can snag your flies! There is plenty of river to fish but bank vegetation tends to detract from the angling experience.

The Tahakopa River

Maclennan River

Location This tributary of the Tahakopa River also flows through the Catlins Forest and joins the Tahakopa 2 km from the mouth.
Access From the Tahakopa Valley Road turn right over Mouat's Saddle to Kahuika. Alternatively, branch off SH 92 near Caberfeidh. Puketiro Road crosses the river. Elsewhere, access is across private farmland, but permission can be readily obtained.
Season 1 October–30 April.

This heavily peat-stained stream is even more overgrown than the Tahakopa. It runs down through dense native bush in the upper reaches, and manuka scrub, gorse and cleared pastoral land in the middle reaches. Trout cannot be spotted unless they are rising. In the forested section there are stable pools and runs, and although fish stocks are low, most browns in this overgrown section are worth catching.

The lower tidal reaches upstream from the Tahakopa confluence hold sea-run browns, which are fished for by anglers using live bait and spinners.

Waikawa River

Location Rises in the Forest Range of the Catlins State Forest Park, flows southeast and empties into the sea at the small village of Waikawa.
Access From the Waikawa–Wyndham road and side roads off this.
Season 1 October–30 April.

This small, peat-stained stream holds well-conditioned browns averaging 1 kg, both in the main stream and up both branches. There are long, stable pools and shallow ripply runs but, as with the other Catlins rivers, trout cannot be sighted unless they are rising. The banks are partially bush- and scrub-lined but there are open sections of farmland where fly casting is possible. The stream is tidal below the falls on Progress Valley Road.

Other smaller streams in the Catlin district that hold brown trout include the Tautuku, Waipati and Waipapa but they are not recommended as dense bank vegetation generally prevents fly fishing.

Central Otago

With hot, dry summers and limited rainfall, water is a precious commodity in Central Otago. Many dams have been built for irrigation and most rivers have water abstracted for this purpose. Most dams have been stocked with trout, and although many of these are on private property permission to fish is generally readily given provided anglers enquire before fishing.

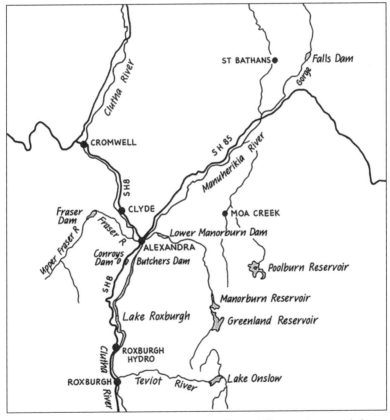

Central Otago rivers and dams

Location Rises in the tussock-covered Ewe, Wether and St Bathans ranges close to Lindis Pass, flows south down the Manuherikia Valley to enter the Clutha at Alexandra.

Access *Upper reaches above Falls Dam* From Hawkdun Hills Run Road off the Ranfurly–St Bathans road, or Home Hills Run Road off the Ranfurly–Alexandra road. These gravel roads join up at the top bridge over the upper Manuherikia River above Falls Dam. Fiddlers Flat Road provides access to the gorge and the lower end of Falls Dam.

Middle and lower reaches From SH 85 and side roads off this. Between Alexandra and Ophir, SH 85 lies some distance away from the river.

Season 1 October–30 April.

Restrictions Bag limit is six trout.

The water in the lower and middle reaches of this long, medium-sized river can be low and warm in the Central Otago summer, as water is abstracted for irrigation. The river is heavily willowed as it winds across pastoral land, but this does not affect fishing to any great extent. Crossings and wading are safe although the shingly riverbed can be slippery. Stocks are reasonable, with browns out-numbering rainbows and averaging 0.75 kg (75 fish/km at Ophir). Trout are difficult to spot in the brownish water. The river improves upstream from Becks but the best section lies above the St Bathans Bridge. The river rises after rain but usually remains fishable. During the day fish will accept small mayfly imitations but sedge fishing in late evening often brings the best results.

There are some large trout in the gorge but you need to be a rock-climbing angler to fish some sections. In low water progress can be made, with frequent deep fords, but anglers need to be agile and sure-footed. Some pools are so deep that double weighted nymphs are required to cover fish.

Above Falls Dam a lot of walking is required between fish. The country is typical of Central Otago, being barren, windswept and tussock-covered, but it has a beauty all its own. The river is small and shingly with few pools likely to hold fish. These can easily be

Attractive water in the Manuherikia Gorge

spotted on a bright day and are best fished to early in the season before they drop back down to Falls Dam.

Dunstan Creek

Location Drains the Dunstan Range, flows southeast and joins the Manuherikia River at Becks.
Access From the St Bathans–Becks road, which crosses the stream, and from a farm track up the true right bank, but permission from the local farmer is required to open the locked gate.
Season 1 October–30 April.

This small, clear freestone stream draining tussock-covered hills holds only a few trout. It is best early in the season before low water flows in summer. The lower reaches hold more fish but these are heavily willowed and overgrown with broom, making casting frustrating. In places, one needs to wade quietly up the stream itself. In the middle and upper reaches a lot of walking is necessary between fish. The gorge has a few stable pools.

Falls Dam

Location This dam lies east of St Bathans, and was formed by damming the Manuherikia River for irrigation.
Access From the Ranfurly–St Bathans road take Fiddlers Flat Road to the lower end and the dam. From the Ranfurly–Alexandra road take Home Hills Run Road to the top end.
Season 1 October–30 April.
Restrictions Bag limit is six trout. Boats are permitted.

This large dam lies in exposed, bleak, windswept country surrounded by typical Central Otago tussock-covered hills. On a warm summer's day with the cicadas chirping it is a beautiful place to be. On a cold windy day, it is another matter! The lake is shallow at the Manuherikia delta but deep at the dam. It holds plenty of small brown trout (averaging 0.5–1 kg), which can be caught by all legal methods of angling. Cicada fishing in February can be fun but the dam is generally not an appealing angling venue.

Butchers Dam

Location and access SH 8, 6 km south of Alexandra, skirts the western shore.
Season Open all year.
Restrictions Bag limit is six trout.

This shallow, medium-sized lake has a number of inlets and islands, and holds brown trout averaging 1 kg, as well as perch. Most fish are caught on live bait and spinners but some stalking is possible around the edges of the shallow inlets. Midge pupa, damsel and bully imitations, small nymphs and Black and Peacock for the snails are worth trying.

Conroys Dam

Location and access Lies on the opposite side of SH 8 from Butchers Dam and, like Butchers, is used for irrigation. Take Conroys Road off Earnscleugh Road and then a former Ministry of Works road to the dam. It's worth stopping at Black Ridge Winery on the way!
Season Open all year.
Restrictions Bag limit is six trout.

This is another shallow dam that holds small brown trout.

Fraser Dam

Location and access Lies 15 km west of Alexandra. From Earnscleugh Road turn onto Blackman Road and travel to the end.
Season 1 October–30 April.
Restrictions Bag limit is six trout.

This small, steep-sided dam holds a moderate population of small brown trout, which are best fished to with spinners.

The Upper Fraser River flows into the top of the dam and is worth exploring if you are fit and sufficiently dexterous to tackle a rough, bouldery gorge. There aren't many fish but they can be spotted and stalked. The bag limit for this small river is one trout.

Upper Manorburn Reservoir (includes Greenland Reservoir)

Location Lies in high tussock country southeast of Alexandra.

Access Moa Creek Road, a gravel access road to the dam, leaves Ida Valley Road at the Poolburn Hotel. Continue to the road end at the dam. The road to the right takes you over Manorburn Creek to a few baches and is then private. The road to the left leads to the boat-launching area and more fishing huts further up the lake. A four-wheel-drive vehicle is an advantage as the last section of road is narrow, unmetalled and rough.

Season 1 November–31 May.

Restrictions Bag limit is six trout.

Boat launching Small boats can be launched near the dam and from a gravel beach further up the lake.

This large, exposed, irrigation reservoir is 700 ha in area and was built in 1914. Since 1948 the dam has been stocked with rainbow trout only, and these average around 1.4 kg. Although the dam is deep in parts, the water is not sufficiently clear for sight fishing. The lake fishes best early and late in the season, as in January and February the trout go deep into cooler water. Anglers use live bait, spinners, flies and boats for trolling and harling. Fly anglers should try damsel and corixa imitations over the weed beds, attractor type dry flies, lures such as Woolly Bugger, Mrs Simpson and Kilwell No. 1, and in February a cicada pattern. The lake is safe to wade, trout stocks are good and angling pressure is minimal. Greenland Reservoir is very shallow.

There is little shelter at this lake and rapid weather changes are common. Take sunburn lotion, polypropylene thermal underwear and a parka!

The Lower Manorburn Dam between Alexandra and Galloway holds small brown trout. It is used for ice skating in winter.

Poolburn Dam

Location and access Lies north of Manorburn Dam and can also be reached from the Poolburn Hotel on Ida Valley Road. Take Moa

Creek Road and just past the school turn left onto Webster Lane. Beyond the former Moa Creek Hotel, turn right. The dam is signposted from here. There are several access points around the lake and three spots to launch small boats.

Season Open for fishing all year.

Restrictions Bag limit is six trout.

This exposed dam, which covers 300 ha, was completed in 1931. It holds brown trout averaging around 1.5 kg. The landscape is unique, and characterised by interesting rock formations on land and in the lake. The latter pose a hazard for outboard motors and trollers. There are numerous fishing huts dotted around the tussock shores, some of which are very basic. Sight fishing is again difficult and most trout are caught spinning or live bait fishing. In the warmer months trout cruise the shoreline, and these can be tempted with bully and damsel type lures fished on a floating line, corixa and midge patterns. Dry flies such as Black Gnat and Coch-y-bondhu take fish, while cicada imitations can be very useful in February.

Good still water angling in the Poolburn Dam

Location Lies 22 km east of Roxburgh at the northwestern end of the Lammerlaw Range.

Access *From Miller's Flat* Turn off SH 8 at Miller's Flat Hotel and cross the Clutha River, then turn left onto Timaburn Road. The lake is signposted from there.

From Roxburgh Cross the Clutha to Roxburgh East and turn right. After 1 km turn successively left onto Wright, Sanders and Lake Onslow roads.

From the Upper Taieri River and Styx Basin This is a rough, unmetalled, dry weather, four-wheel-drive road.

Season Open all year.

Restrictions There is no bag limit.

Boat launching There is a boat ramp at the fishing huts at the southwestern end of the lake.

This large irrigation dam, lying high on a tussock grassland plateau, covers 830 ha. Formed by damming the Teviot River in 1888, the lake has been enlarged on four occasions, the last in 1982. Like Manorburn and Poolburn, the lake is very exposed, windswept and cold in winter, but on a calm, sunny summer's day with the cicadas chirping, the golden tussock and blue lake present a special kind of Central Otago beauty.

The lake was originally stocked with brown trout and these are now self-sustaining. Trout average 1.4 kg, but fish over 3 kg are not unusual. There are good numbers of fish and during the warmer months these cruise the shoreline. In ideal conditions some can be spotted, but generally fly anglers fish to rising fish. Access is good around the shore except for a few swampy patches, and the lake can be safely waded.

Most fish are taken by trolling and harling from a boat and spinning from the shore, but from December to the end of February there is good shoreline fly fishing. Early in the season use bully and damsel imitations such as Woolly Bugger, Mrs Simpson, Hamill's Killer, Kilwell No. 1 or Monsum's Bully fished on a floating or slow-sinking line.

When the weather warms in December, a green beetle or Coch-y-bondhu is useful, but the most exciting fishing is in February when the cicadas arrive. It is important to leave your cicada imitation on the water even if a fish smashes it. Sometimes they do this to stun it and return soon after to take it. Wait until your fly line starts to move before tightening. In the evenings clouds of midges hatch, so Midge Pupa and Griffiths Gnat are also worth carrying.

Teviot River

Location Drains into and out of Lake Onslow, flows west and joins the Clutha River at Roxburgh.
Access From Lake Onslow, Bridge Huts and The Dip.
Season 1 October–30 April.

The best water to fish on this small, peat-stained stream lies between Bridge Huts and Lake Onslow. Trout cannot be spotted but blind fly fishing usually yields results as brown trout numbers are very high. The stream flows down a rock and stone bed and the tussock banks are easy to negotiate. The fish are small but respond to a wide variety of dries, nymphs and small spinners. When the wind isn't blowing this is a great learner fly stream.

Maniototo dams

Coalpit Dam

Location This old mining dam lies in the Naseby Forest 1 km northwest of Naseby.
Access From the Naseby–Ranfurly road turn off at Coalpit Bridle track to the carpark and picnic area.
Season Open all year.
Restrictions Bag limit is three trout.

Brown and rainbow trout averaging 1–2 kg cruise the margins of

The Coalpit Dam, Naseby

this small dam in summer, but they are not easy to catch. The lake is open to spinning, bait fishing and fly fishing. Midge pupa, corixa and damsel imitations are useful, as are green and brown beetle patterns from November to January. Although surrounded by pine forest, casting is generally unhindered.

Hoffmans Dam

Location and access Lies close by Coalpit Dam in the Naseby Forest, but turn off the Naseby–Ranfurly road at Wet Gully Road.
Season Open all year but the ice may need to be broken in winter!
Restrictions Bag limit is three trout.

Like its neighbour, this old mining dam holds both rainbow and brown trout and is regularly stocked. The dam is shaped like an hourglass, with the deepest section close to the carpark. The top section is shallow and there is a good access track to most of the

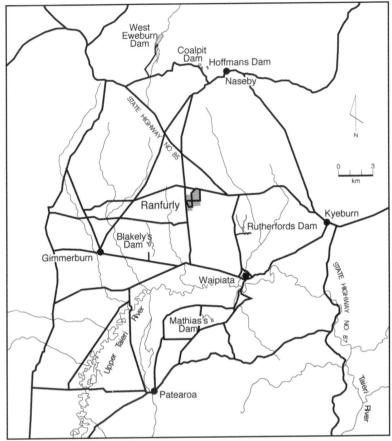

Maniototo dams

dam. Trout are much harder to spot in this dam but use the same methods as for Coalpit. Most fish are taken on spinning gear. Coalpit tends to be more productive.

West Eweburn Dam

Location and access Lies behind the Naseby Forest. Turn off SH 85 onto the Wedderburn–Naseby Plantation road then left onto Reservoir Road.
Season 1 October–30 April.
Restrictions Bag limit is six fish.

Holds a good stock of small brown trout, which can be fished with all legal methods.

Rutherfords Dam

Location and access Turn left off the Naseby–Waipiata road 1.5 km past Barney Lane. Permission must be obtained from the farmhouse.
Season 1 October–30 April.
Restrictions Bag limit is three trout.

This small dam has a reputation for large trout. It is regularly stocked with rainbows and browns by the Otago Fish and Game Council. The dam is weedy and obviously provides plenty of food for trout. Fish are hard to spot unless rising, and usually feed below the surface on damsels, corixa and midges. However, they will rise in midsummer, especially to something worthwhile like a deer hair attractor pattern or a cicada imitation.

Blakely's Dam

Location and access Travelling from Waipiata to Gimmerburn, turn right just part Creamery Road onto the access road to the dam. Permission to fish is granted unless there is a sign on the gate.
Season 1 October–30 April.
Restrictions Bag limit is three trout.

This dam is similar in size to Rutherfords Dam and is regularly stocked with brown and rainbow trout. The food supply is also plentiful and trout grow to a good size. Use fishing methods similar to those on Rutherfords Dam.

Mathias's Dam

Location and access From the Waipiata–Patearoa road. The access road lies beyond the Hamilton turn-off on your left beside a large willow. Unless there is a note on the gate, anglers have permission to fish.

Season 1 October–30 April.
Restrictions Bag limit is three fish.

This small dam is connected to the Taieri River so small brown trout enter from time to time. The Otago Fish and Game Council also stocks the dam with rainbows. Use similar methods to those described for Rutherfords Dam.

Loganburn Dam

Location This irrigation reservoir lies high on the southern end of the Rock and Pillar Range west of Sutton.
Access Turn west off SH 87 at Clarks Junction onto the Old Dunstan Road. The road climbs high over the Rock and Pillars, crosses Deep Stream and eventually reaches the dam. From the Maniototo Plain near Styx, the other end of the Old Dunstan Road takes you to the dam.
Season 1 October–30 April.
Restrictions Bag limit is six trout.

This 1200-ha irrigation reservoir was built in 1985 from creeks supplying the Great Moss Swamp. Lying at 800 m, it is cold and windswept in winter. It holds a reasonable stock of brown trout averaging 1.3 kg but these are not easy to catch on a fly until the cicadas arrive in late January. The water is brownish in colour and fish cannot be spotted unless they are rising. The best fishing is from the southern and western shores, with most fish caught on live bait, spinners and trolling from a dinghy.

Malones Dam and Phoenix Dam

Location and access Both lie northeast of Lawrence at Weatherston, along the road to the golf course.
Season Open all year.

Both these small dams hold a small population of brown trout, which are impossible to spot in the peat-stained water. Not highly recommended.

Three other small dams lie close by in Gabriels Gully. These are the Victoria, Otago and Gray's dams. All three contain small numbers of brown trout and are fished by the locals with live bait and spinners.

Lakes Wanaka, Hawea and surrounding district

Lake Wanaka

Access Road access to many areas of this large lake is somewhat limited and some of the best fishing spots can only be reached by boat. The Glendhu Bay Road generally follows within walking distance of the shore, while the road to West Wanaka offers access to Paddock Bay. SH 6 follows the eastern shore from the head of the lake to The Neck. Aubrey, Beacon Point, Maungawera and Dublin Bay roads give limited access in the vicinity of Wanaka township.
Season The lake is open to fishing all year.
Restrictions Bag limit is six sportsfish. Fishing is prohibited within 150 m of the launch wharf and within 100 m of the marina wharf. Bait fishing is prohibited.
Boat launching From Wanaka marina, Glendhu Bay, and Camp, Waterfall and Wharf streams up the eastern side of the lake.

Lake Wanaka is a very large, scenic lake occupying an old glaciated valley. The lake holds an enormous resource of fish, including brown and rainbow trout and landlocked quinnat (chinook) salmon. Trolling is a popular method of fishing throughout the year, although in winter it can be very cold. Popular spots are the river deltas including the Matukituki and the Makarora, the bluffs at Hells Gate, and Stevenson Arm. Spinning from the shore is productive except on a bright, calm summer's day. Lead lines and outriggers are both legal.

There is plenty of scope for shoreline fly fishing in summer as the water is clear and trout can be ambushed cruising the drop-off and shallows. Small, lightly weighted nymphs, soft hackle wet flies, Black and Peacock snail pattern and damsel imitations are effective on cruisers that are feeding below the surface. Suggested dry flies include Humpy, Coch-y-bondhu, Black Gnat, Green Beetle and Royal Wulff.

In the colder months browns cruise the shallows after spawning and will take bully type lures such as Woolly Bugger, Mrs Simpson, Hamill's Killer and Rabbit patterns. Dublin Bay and Stevensons Arm are popular for this type of fishing.

The weed and sand flats at Paddock Bay, West Wanaka, are a favourite spot to intercept cruising trout. Small, lightly weighted nymphs, Black and Peacock or soft hackles are cast well in front of cruising fish and twitched when a fish approaches. Careful, slow wading, plenty of patience and good spotting conditions are needed to be successful here.

Good fish can be caught at the Makarora and Matukituki deltas late in the season using a smelt fly and a high-density sinking line.

 Lake Wanaka tributaries

Matukituki River

Location Drains Mt Aspiring and the snowfields of the surrounding mountains. After the East and West branches meet, the river flows southeast and enters Lake Wanaka at West Wanaka.

Access *Lower reaches and mouth* From Glendhu Bay take the road to Cattle Flat Station and just past Hells Gate turn right to Paddock Bay and the river beyond. You can walk downstream from the bridge to the mouth.

Middle and upper reaches Continue on up the Matukituki Valley beyond Cattle Flat Station. There is an emergency four-wheel-drive track up the West Branch to the Aspiring Hut. For the East Branch, wade the West Branch and walk across the grassy flats.

Season 1 November–31 May.

Restrictions Bag limit is one trout per day.

This large snow- and glacier-fed river can offer reasonable fishing at times but often carries glacial flour and is very unstable in the lower reaches. The nor'wester can blow down the valley, raising clouds of silt dust. At the mouth there is reasonable smelt fly fishing. For 4–5 km downstream from the branch confluence there are more permanent pools holding a few good rainbows. Most fish are taken from this section on spinners.

In the upper reaches both branches hold a reasonable stock of fish early in the season, but after Christmas many will have dropped back downstream to the lake. Sight fishing is usually possible in the East Branch but more difficult in the West Branch. The West Branch tends to hold a small stock of resident fish almost as far as the Aspiring Hut. The majority of trout are rainbows and they are not particular about whether they take nymphs, dry flies or lures swung across and downstream.

Motutapu River

Location Rises southwest of Glendhu Bay where it saddles with the Arrow River at Roses Saddle. Flows northeast through grazing land before joining the lower Matukituki River.
Access The road from Glendhu Bay to Cattle Flat Station crosses the river beyond Hells Gate.
Season 1 November–31 May.
Restrictions Bag limit is one fish.

This is a small spawning tributary of the Matukituki River, although it does hold a few resident browns and rainbows. The lower reaches are willowed and casting is difficult in some spots, whereas above the road bridge access is reasonably clear. Sight fishing is necessary as fish stocks are not great but the shallow, clear water makes stalking tricky. There are 10 km of fishing before impassable falls are reached. Small dry flies and weighted nymphs carefully presented are usually effective.

Albert Burn

Location Saddles with the East Branch of the Matukituki River, flows east and enters the western shore of Lake Wanaka about 8 km from the head of the lake.
Access Usually by boat, unless one is prepared to ford the Makarora River and walk 8 km along the lake shore.

Season 1 November–31 May.
Restrictions Bag limit is one fish.

Fishing is restricted to the 2 km of river below a rugged gorge. It is a small, clear-water, rock and stone type stream that holds good numbers of trout both early and late in the season.

Makarora River

Location Rises near the Haast Pass, drains the Young Range and the Brewster Glacier before flowing south down a wide valley to enter Lake Wanaka south of Makarora.
Access SH 6 follows upstream from the mouth to a gorge above Davis Flat. The river lies mostly some distance away across farmland to the west of the road.
Season 1 November–31 May.
Restrictions Bag limit is one trout.

This large, freestone river is flood-prone and unstable. More stable pools and runs lie above the Young River confluence. The water is blue and clear, enabling sight fishing, but angling pressure is high as the river flows close to the main highway. Fish stocks are unreliable although better both early and late in the season. It is not worth exploring above the Fish River confluence. The delta fishes well late in the season with a smelt fly on a high-density or shooting head line. The nor'wester whistles down the valley. Wading is safe and fording at the tail of some pools is possible but the river deserves respect below the Wilkin confluence, especially when running above normal.

Wilkin River

Location The headwaters saddle with the East Branch of the Matukituki River and drain the alps of Mt Aspiring National Park. The main river flows generally east to join the Makarora River 9 km above Lake Wanaka.
Access
• The Makarora River needs to be forded, usually upstream of the

confluence, and this is only possible in low water summer conditions. Then the Wilkin River itself must also be crossed about 2 km upstream from the confluence. Both these fords can be dangerous due to soft silt and strong currents. Tramper/anglers should first check river conditions at the Makarora Store or at the DoC office.

- A jetboat service operates from Makarora village and can carry trampers and anglers to within 1–2 km of Kerin Forks Hut. Bookings can be made at a kiosk near the Makarora Store.
- One can also fly into Kerin Forks onto a bush airstrip. The DoC hut at Kerin Forks has ten bunks and is heavily used by trampers.

Season 1 November–31 May.
Restrictions Bag limit is one trout.

This medium-sized river can carry snow-melt and glacial flour until Christmas. As it drains a large alpine catchment, the river rises rapidly in heavy rain and readily discolours. The lower reaches are

Pocket water in the beautiful Wilkin River

unstable and often silt-laden, and generally are not worth fishing. The best water lies at Kerin Forks, 16 km upstream from the Makarora confluence. Here, the pools are more stable and rocky, the water clear and fish stocks are reasonable, especially early and late in the season. The majority of trout are rainbow with a spawning run from Lake Wanaka late in the season, but the occasional brown up to 4 kg has been caught. Sight fishing is possible on some stretches but the deeper pools and runs should not be bypassed without casting a fly. There is a day's fishing above Kerin Forks until the river rises rapidly and pours from a steep gorge. The valley is exceptionally beautiful, with dense beech bush and green grassy clearings overshadowed by sheer snow capped peaks. It is a favourite with trampers. Take insect repellent for the sandflies.

The tributary streams, Siberia and Newlands, offer small stream fishing in their lower reaches only as a series of waterfalls impedes the progress of trout.

Falls prevent trout running up the Blue River.

Young River

Location Flows parallel to but north of the Wilkin River and enters the Makarora River 4 km downstream from the Blue River confluence.
Access From SH 6 look for the access track at Brady's Creek. This leads across farmland to the Young-Makarora confluence. The Makarora River must then be forded, which can be difficult unless all the rivers are running reasonably low. At times the best crossing can be either upstream or downstream from the Makarora confluence. The track follows up the true left bank.
Season 1 November–31 May.
Restrictions Bag limit is one trout.

This small, beautiful mountain river is now heavily fished, especially by commercial operators. The fishing has deteriorated over the past twenty years but the valley is well worth visiting for its scenic qualities alone and there is always the chance of catching a nice rainbow. There are few fish in the lower 2 km but in the gorge, seen well below from the access track, there are usually a few fish. They are very easy to spot but often difficult to get at. The best fishing lies just below the forks but this is a two- to three-hour tramp from the Makarora confluence. Here, there are some pleasant, stable pools that hold rainbows averaging 1–2 kg.

There's also good fishing up the north branch for 1 km before a formidable gorge blocks progress; there are no fish in the south branch. The trout are not fussy and, like most sight fishing in the back country, stalking and presentation with an accurate first cast are all-important. They become spooky as the season progresses, after being fished over many times. Try attractor dry flies, weighted nymphs or even lures swung down and across.

There are good campsites at the forks clearing and the valley is popular for tramping. Take sandfly repellent.

Lake Hawea

Access SH 6 follows the western shore from the outlet near Hawea to The Neck. A branch road continues to the DoC camping ground at Kidd's Bush and beyond to Hunter Valley Station. The road to Timaru Creek follows the eastern shore. Four kilometres beyond Timaru Creek the road to Dingle Burn Station becomes private and permission should be obtained before travelling further up the lake.
Season The lake is open all year.
Restrictions Bag limit is six fish.
Boat launching At Hawea Motor Camp, from SH 6, at The Neck and from Hunter Valley Station.

This lake suffers from fluctuating levels as a result of hydro-electric power generation. However, there is still good shoreline fishing, although it is best when the lake level is low.

There are good stocks of brown and rainbow trout and land-locked quinnat salmon. The latter are caught by trolling spinners from a boat. Hot spots for shoreline anglers are The Neck, the delta of Timaru Creek and the adjacent shore, and the mouths of Dingle Burn and the Hunter River. The latter are best accessed by boat, although it is a long trip to the head of the lake only to find a nor'wester roaring down the Hunter Valley. Trout are easy to spot and ambush on a bright day. Favourite dry flies include Coch-y-bondhu, Black Gnat, Humpy, Royal Wulff and Parachute Adams. Any small weighted nymph is usually acceptable, as are lures such as Mrs Simpson, Monsum's Bully, Hamill's Killer, Yellow Dorothy and other smelt imitations.

Lake Hawea tributaries

Hunter River

Location Rises from the Bealey Range of the Main Divide near the source of the Wills River. From the forks in the headwaters, the main stream flows south for 30 km before entering Lake Hawea.

Access
- By boat to the top of Lake Hawea. (See Lake Hawea for launching sites.)
- Through Hunter Valley Station by four-wheel-drive. Permission required.
- By helicopter or fixed-wing aircraft (valley has two airstrips).
- It is a 16-hour tramp from Hunter Valley Station to Forbes Hut.

Season 1 November–31 May.

Restrictions Bag limit is one trout.

This is a large snow- and glacier-fed river that flows down a wide, picturesque but exposed valley. The nor'wester frequently ends all chance of upstream fly fishing. Trout are difficult to spot as the water usually carries some glacial flour, but stocks are sufficient to warrant fishing the water. It is best fished in low water conditions during February and March, especially when the cicadas are chirping. The river is swift and difficult to cross but there are long, deep runs and stable pools sufficient to entice any angler. It holds mainly rainbow trout averaging 1.5 kg, with a few good browns for variety.

Round the mouth, backwaters and side channels are worth exploring, along with a small spring creek. Lure fishing with a smelt imitation across and downstream can be very productive. Spinning also accounts for many of the trout caught.

From Long Flat Creek (Ferguson Hut) to the forks (Forbes Hut) the river is usually confined to one channel and there is excellent fly water. In summer, when the river is low, use a cicada imitation such as a Stimulator, large Humpy or Irresistible. The river rises rapidly with rain in the headwaters and can take three or more days to clear and return to normal. Despite being rather inaccessible this river is worth a visit, especially on a calm, bright summer's day, although such days are all too infrequent in this valley.

Dingle Burn

Location Drains mountains on the northeast side of Lake Hawea, flows southwest and enters the lake north of Silver Island.
Access
Headwaters and upper reaches
- By fixed-wing aircraft or helicopter.
- By tramping over a saddle from Birchwood Station in the Ahuriri Valley. There is a horse track to follow for some of the way on the three-hour journey.
- By tramping upstream from the mouth and through the gorge (six hours), with many river crossings.
Middle reaches
- The gorge can be reached either from above or by walking upstream from the mouth.
Lower reaches and mouth
- By boat.
- By private road through Dingle Burn Station. Permission is required and the road is very narrow and tortuous.
Season 1 November–31 May.
Restrictions Bag limit is one trout.

The best water lies in the upper reaches where this small stream rushes down a wide tussock valley lined with beech bush. Unfortunately, over recent years the stream has been overfished by guides and their clients. Some of the rainbow trout can be spotted but many will be missed in the fast-flowing, bubbly runs. Fish average 1–2 kg but their condition is often below par, especially after having been caught and released a few times. Most will accept weighted nymphs and attractor pattern dry flies, provided you cast short to avoid drag. A landing net is very useful.

The gorge always holds a few trout in stable, deep pools and most of these can be sight fished. Many of the pools are short and drag is again the most important problem to overcome. It is only fishable in low water, summer conditions.

The lower reaches between the gorge and the mouth are braided and unstable and hold very few fish.

At the mouth, the shoreline close by always presents a few cruising fish that can be stalked.

The Dingle Burn Tarn on Dingle Burn Station holds brook char (fontinalis) and brown trout. Permission is required from the station before fishing. It is best fished from a boat, either with spinners or bully type lures on a medium-sinking line.

Timaru River (Creek)

Location Drains Mt Martha and Mt Melina on the east side of Lake Hawea, flows roughly parallel to but south of the Dingle Burn before entering Lake Hawea.
Access From the Timaru River road along the eastern side of Lake Hawea, which crosses the river at the Peter Muir Bridge. The mouth is 20 km from Hawea township and there is a basic camping area.
Season Above the bridge, 1 November–31 May. Below the bridge, the river is open for fishing all year.
Restrictions Bag limit is one trout.

This small spawning river for Lake Hawea does hold a few resident fish, especially in the upper reaches, but a lot of walking is required. By late December most of the trout have spawned and returned to the lake so it fishes best early in the season, although many of these fish will still be recovering and may not be in the best condition. Most fish are rainbows and once the spawners have dropped downstream only small fish are left.

The lower 3 km above the bridge are gorgy and don't hold many fish. Above the gorge the valley opens out and becomes most attractive, with tussock flats and beech bush. The stream is clear and fish are easy to spot.

Location Drains Lake Hawea and flows on a tortuous southwesterly course for 16 km before joining the Clutha below Albert Town.

Access From SH 6 below the Albert Town Bridge and from Hawea Flat, Newcastle and Camp Hill roads. The river flows beneath high terraces but access is available to both banks. Beware the briar roses!

Season Open all year.

Restrictions Bag limit is six fish.

The Hawea River has been modified for power generation so watch for fluctuating flows. However, it generally remains constant throughout summer.

Rainbow and brown trout are present, and fish up to 4 kg have been caught. The river is difficult to wade because of large slippery boulders, which make night fishing hazardous. It is a large river, and although some trout can be spotted in the shallows most lie in deeper water sheltered by rocks. Fish can be taken on all legal methods, although fly fishing in summer when the flows are low is the most productive.

Clutha River (upper reaches)

Location Drains Lake Wanaka and flows south to Lake Dunstan.

Access There are many access points; these are some of the main ones.

- From Beacon Point Road off Dublin Bay Road.
- From SH 6 and SH 8A at Albert Town and Luggate.
- Deans Bank from Alison Avenue at Albert Town.

In places private farmland needs to be crossed, but please ask permission. The Upper Clutha Angling Club has published an excellent pamphlet detailing all the accesses to the Upper Clutha River and Lake Dunstan. These are available from local sports stores. Before fishing at night it is worth exploring the access and looking at the river. In some places a steep cliff needs to be negotiated before the river can be reached and this might not be easy in the dark.

Season Deans Bank, 1 October–31 May. This section of river is marked by two posts, one near the outlet at Lake Wanaka and the other 600 m above the Albert Town bridge. Elsewhere, the Upper Clutha is open all year.

Restrictions Deans Bank is reserved for fly fishing only. Above the Luggate Bridge, fly and artificial bait only. Bag limit is six fish.

Boat ramps Boats can be launched from the outlet, Albert Town bridge and Luggate.

This very large river has the highest flow rate of any New Zealand river, and consequently is difficult to fish. Draining a lake, the upper reaches are stable and remain clear even after heavy rain, although fishing becomes more difficult when Lake Wanaka is high. Drift dives have established that near the outlet this river holds the highest biomass (kg/km) of fish of any New Zealand river (275 fish/km).

During the day many large trout lie sheltered behind boulders in deep, fast water, and it is nearly impossible to get your fly or spinner down to these fish. At night some of these fish move into the edges of the current and over weed beds and shallows to feed, thereby becoming more accessible to anglers. Wading is safe provided you avoid the strong current. Both rainbows and browns, some over 5 kg, occupy this magnificent waterway, and with the strong current, anglers fishing during the evening and at night would be well advised to use strong tippets and have at least 100 m of backing available on their reel. Trout are virtually impossible to spot but rise freely at dusk in favourable weather conditions, especially to caddis. The best months for this type of fishing are from December to the end of February. Those feeding on caddis usually exhibit a splashy type of rise as caddis emergers leave the water in a great hurry. Frequently this caddis rise may not begin until late at night. If you are fortunate enough to strike a good caddis rise, try a floating line, cast a deer hair or Goddard Caddis or even a soft hackle wet fly across and downstream and swing the fly through the rising fish. The take can be explosive.

During the day, try fishing any shallow run or weed bed with weighted nymphs, or dry flies such as Humpy, Royal Wulff, Coch-y-bondhu, Black Gnat, Irresistible or Parachute Adams. Rainbows especially will also take lures such as Woolly Bugger, Rabbit patterns, Parsons' Glory or Mrs Simpson fished on a sinking or shooting head line. At night, a large black Hairy Dog or similar lure on a sinking line can produce a few surprises. Long casting and a powerful rod are an advantage for this type of water.

Spinning accounts for many fish and again, long casting is required to adequately cover the water.

The stretch of water upstream from Lake Dunstan is braided and more easily reached by boat. However, there is some excellent fishing beneath the willows, and late in the season a good run of fish enter the river from the lake intent on spawning. These can be fished 'Taupo style' with lures such as Red Setter and Orange Rabbit on a heavy-sinking line or weighted nymphs and egg patterns on a floating line.

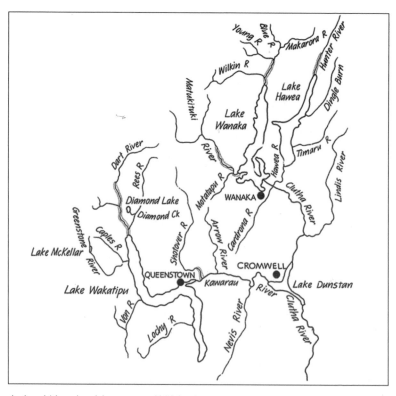

Lakes Wanaka, Hawea and Wakatipu

Location This large hydro lake was formed in 1993 following the construction of the Clyde Dam on the Clutha River.

Access There are three arms to the lake — the Clutha, Kawerau and Dunstan — but the Clutha Arm is by far the most productive fishery.

- SH 6 follows the western shore of the Clutha Arm from Cromwell towards Wanaka. There are marked anglers' access points off this highway.
- SH 8 follows the eastern shore of the Clutha Arm from Cromwell until it bends east towards Tarras.
- Access to the less-favoured Kawerau Arm is from SH 6 to Queenstown and the bridge to Bannockburn, but a boat is a great advantage.
- The Dunstan Arm is also best accessed from a boat but SH 8 follows the northeastern shore from Cromwell to Clyde.

Season Open all year.

Restrictions Bag limit is six fish.

Initially this lake was a very productive fishery but a severe flood in 1994 covered the weed beds with silt and destroyed much of the insect life. The lake has now recovered and good fishing can be expected, especially round the Clutha River delta and the weed beds at the top of the Clutha Arm. Both brown and rainbow trout average 1.4 kg and small landlocked quinnat salmon add some interest, especially for trollers.

Most fish are caught from boats, either trolling or harling a fly, but there is some good sight fishing available from the shore. Spinning from the shore can also be worthwhile, although after Christmas weed beds are a problem. For the fly angler try Midge Pupa, Corixa, Damsel nymphs, Black and Peacock, Green Beetle, Willow Grub and terrestrial cicada and cricket imitations in January and February. Mrs Simpson, Hamill's Killer and other bully-type lures can also attract fish. A float-tube would be most useful and enable anglers to fish the holes between weed beds.

Location Drains the mountains north of the Lindis Pass, flows south and enters the Clutha River above Lake Dunstan.
Access SH 8 follows the river for some distance.
Season 1 October–31 May.
Restrictions Bag limit is six trout.

This very attractive, small, willow-lined stream promises plenty but delivers very little. It does suffer severely from the effects of water abstraction for irrigation, but even before these schemes were developed the Lindis held only a few fish. It is an important spawning stream for the Upper Clutha River and Lake Dunstan but most trout have returned to the lake by the time the season opens. Although there is some wonderful-looking water in the upper reaches away from SH 8 there are very few fish. In the lower reaches around Tarras, there are usually a few browns.

Lake Wakatipu and surrounding district

Lake Wakatipu

Access The eastern shore is well served by roads including SH 6 from Kingston to Queenstown and the Glenorchy Road from Queenstown to Glenorchy. Apart from the Kinloch/Greenstone Station Road down the northwestern shore at the top of the lake, access by boat is necessary to reach the remainder of the western shore.
Season The lake is open all year.
Restrictions Bag limit is six sportsfish. Lead lines and downriggers are permitted.
Boat launching Available at Kingston, Frankton Marina, Kelvin Heights, Queenstown, Sunshine Bay and Glenorchy. Other launching sites are available for four-wheel-drive vehicles.

Lake Wakatipu, which lies in an old glaciated valley, is 80 km long and over 300 m deep. Even in summer this is a very cold lake, and it can become exceptionally rough for small boats in strong westerly winds. This very scenic lake holds browns, rainbows and landlocked quinnat salmon. Although trout average 1–2 kg, 'double figure' fish are caught each year. Some local anglers maintain these originate from the school of tame trout beneath the Queenstown Wharf. It is rare to catch a salmon weighing 1 kg. Most anglers troll or spin fish but fly fishing can be very effective, especially at stream mouths and deltas. Trout will accept nymphs, especially the Green Stonefly, lures representing bullies or smelt, and green beetle and cicada imitations in January and February. From April to July there is good stream-mouth fishing for trout gathering for their spawning run. There is no problem with spotting fish as the water is very clear.

When trolling, many anglers use three to four colours of lead line and 30 m of monofilament. It pays to be flexible and try different depths and speeds. Many lures catch fish, with Cobras and Tobys being popular. Harling with a downrigger using a smelt fly pattern is also effective.

Lochy River

Location Rises in the Eyre Mountains and follows a northeasterly course to enter Lake Wakatipu at Halfway Bay.
Access This is difficult and most overseas anglers use a helicopter.
- By boat to the mouth and walking upstream.
- By tramping over mountainous country from Mt Nicholas Road to the headwaters.
- By four-wheel-drive on private roads from Mt Nicholas and Cecil Peak stations to the middle and upper reaches.
- By helicopter.
Before camping in the area, permission should be obtained from Halfway Bay, Cecil Peak and Mt Nicholas stations. The Long Burn hut has six bunks and is open to the public.
Season 1 November–31 May.
Restrictions Fly fishing only in this river. Catch and release upstream from the Long Burn confluence. Below this confluence, only one fish may be taken.

The Lochy is an excellent medium-sized mountain river that offers over 20 km of sight fishing, mainly for rainbow trout, which average 1.5 kg. Like the Greenstone and the Von rivers close by, the Lochy is an important spawning river for Lake Wakatipu. Although this river holds resident trout, 60 percent of fish will have returned to the lake by Christmas.

The lower reaches flow across developed farmland and become braided at times but there are plenty of fish, especially early in the season. Upriver from the Long Burn the river enters a gorge, with native bush lining the river in some sections. The river is more turbulent here but excellent fishing is available to active anglers who are prepared to rock-scramble and ford the river. This 10-km-long section is best fished in boots and shorts. A tramping track follows up the true right bank.

Above the gorge the river valley opens out again and fishing is much easier. There is excellent water upstream for 3 km beyond Killiecrankie Creek. As fish are easy to spot in stable pools and runs, this section is heavily fished by overseas anglers and their guides.

Trout are rarely selective when recovering from spawning and will accept a wide variety of dry flies and nymphs presented without drag. Try Humpy, Stimulator, Coch-y-bondhu, Green Beetle, Royal Wulff, Dad's Favourite and Irresistible dry flies, and Green Stonefly, Perla and Hare and Copper nymphs.

Von River

Location The North Branch drains the Thomson Mountains, while the South Branch drains the Eyre Mountains. From the branch confluence in the upper reaches, the river flows north to enter the western shore of Lake Wakatipu just north of Whites Bay and Mt Nicholas Station.

Access
- By boat to the mouth and lower reaches.
- From Mt Nicholas Road via Mavora Lakes. This road follows down the true right bank almost to the mouth.

Season 1 November–31 May.

Restrictions Bag limit is one trout. Fly fishing only.

This small to medium-sized mountain stream is a highly regarded rainbow trout fishery. It is a spawning river for Lake Wakatipu, and although it holds fish throughout the year many spawning fish in the upper reaches will have returned to the lake by Christmas. The South Branch enters a steep gorge, which can only be fished through by active anglers in low water conditions. Below the North Branch confluence the river flows through tussock grassland for 15 km before entering the lower gorge. This ends about 2 km upstream from the mouth. The lower gorge is very difficult to access and fishing is only possible when the river is low. Early in the season some mending fish will be in poor condition, but most are hungry and not very selective. Trout are easy to spot in the very clear water and will take many varieties of dry flies and nymphs that are well-presented. Fish average around 1.5 kg. The upper gorge is sheltered and can be fished in westerly winds.

Von lakes

Location and access These two small tarns lie in the headwaters of the South Branch of the Von River, either side of the Path Burn. Access from the Mt Nicholas Road.
Season 1 November–31 May.
Restrictions Bag limit is one trout.

Both tarns hold a stock of rainbow trout that spawn in the gravel edges of the lakes. Cruising fish can be spotted and stalked along the shore, although the open tussock terrain is very exposed to wind. In February try a cicada imitation, especially on a windy day.

Greenstone River and its tributary the Caples River

Location Drain the Livingstone, Ailsa and Humboldt mountains and Lake McKellar. The Caples River flows south and joins the Greenstone 6 km from its mouth. Together they enter the western side of Lake Wakatipu north of Elfin Bay.
Access
- A rough gravel road from Kinloch leads to a carpark 3 km up from the mouth of the Greenstone. From here there is a walking track that leads upstream to both rivers.

- There is a three-hour walk from the Divide carpark on SH 94 (Te Anau–Milford road) to the McKellar Hut on the upper reaches of the Greenstone River. The track is well-defined but steep in parts.
- Overseas anglers often use helicopters.

Season 1 November–31 May.

Restrictions Bag limit is one trout. Fly fishing only.

The Greenstone is a medium-sized spawning river for Lake Wakatipu but the middle and upper reaches are easily waded and crossed. The Caples is smaller, and both have very clear mountain water, making sight fishing possible. Both valleys are very scenic, with bubbling rivers winding across wide tussock flats fringed with beech bush, with a backdrop of snowy mountains. Tramping is very popular, especially in summer, and the DoC huts are often fully occupied. Both rivers are heavily fished, especially by overseas anglers and their guides.

As with the Von River, many of the rainbow trout in the upper reaches of the Greenstone River return to the lake by Christmas. The most productive and easiest water to fish, especially early in the season, lies upstream from the Pass Burn, the route to Mararoa Saddle. The main obstacle to fishing is the westerly wind that blows straight down both valleys. Fish are easy to spot and stalk and are unselective as far as fly patterns are concerned. However, they are readily spooked, especially after they have been fished over a few times. Wear drab colours and adopt the usual stalking techniques. An accurate first cast is very important. Rainbows average 1.4 kg, with the odd brown usually larger. Before Christmas fish stocks are excellent, walking and casting is easy, and the river is safe to cross and wade.

Below the Pass Burn the river becomes more difficult to fish, with rocky gorges and fast runs, but for active, agile anglers it is well worth a look for resident fish. Below the Caples confluence the river is considerably larger. The mouth offers good lure fishing, especially late in the season when trout gather near the delta prior to their spawning run.

The Caples holds slightly larger fish than the Greenstone and not all are easy to spot. When spotting is difficult, it pays to blind fish the likely looking turbulent water. An access track follows up the true left bank until it crosses at a swingbridge. Use similar flies to those suggested for the Lochy River.

Lake Rere, which lies to the south of the Greenstone River and inland from Elfin Bay, holds small brown trout but because the lake margins are overhung with bush is best fished with a spinner.

Lake McKellar in the upper reaches also holds many small trout but few are of takeable size. Fishing is easy from the grassy shore at the north end of the lake but the remaining shores are heavily bush-clad. There is no bag limit for this lake.

Dart River/Te Awa Whakatipu

Location Drains the Forbes and Humboldt mountains, flows south down a wide exposed valley, and in conjunction with the Rees River enters the northern end of Lake Wakatipu.
Access From Kinloch and the Routeburn Road.
Season Below the Dart Bridge, the river is open all year. Upstream from this bridge, 1 November–31 May.
Restrictions Bag limit is one trout or salmon.

This large snow- and glacier-fed river is shingly, flood-prone, unstable and generally provides poor trout habitat. Some of the small side channels and spring creeks along the edges hold a few fish, but generally the river is not highly regarded. In low water summer conditions a few of the more stable pools are worth investigating but a lot of walking is required.

The mouth is popular, however, for both spin and lure fishing, especially during April and May. Access to the Dart mouth is from the Kinloch side.

Routeburn River

Location Drains the Humboldt Mountains and joins the true right bank of the Dart River opposite Paradise.
Access Only the lower reaches are worth fishing as the river goes underground. Take the Routeburn Road from Kinloch and turn off to the carpark for Lake Sylvan. Upstream from the swingbridge

there is access to only a few pools. Below this bridge there is good water right down to the Dart confluence.

Season 1 November–31 May.

Restrictions Catch and release and fly fishing only.

This small, short, clear, rock and stone tributary of the Dart holds a few good-sized brown and rainbow trout and is heavily fished. Fish are usually easy to spot but become extremely wary and more sophisticated as the season progresses.

Lake Sylvan is a small lake that lies 20 minutes' walk from the carpark, as described for the Routeburn River. It is picturesque, being surrounded by native bush, but although the brown trout are prolific they are small and in poor condition. Best fished with a spinner as the water is heavily peat-stained. The sandflies are also prolific. There is no bag limit (for trout!).

Diamond Lake

Location Lies 15 km north of Glenorchy on the road to Paradise.

Access The road follows the eastern shore, enabling easy walking access to the eastern and northern shores. The western shore is heavily bush-clad and steep.

Season Open all year.

Restrictions Bag limit is three trout. Fishing from a mechanically powered boat is permitted.

This small, clear, scenic lake holds a good stock of brown trout averaging 1.2 kg. When the weather is calm and the sun shining these can be stalked and ambushed along the shoreline and in the shallow bays. Unweighted nymphs, Black and Peacock, Midge Pupa and Damsels are all good patterns to try. For rising fish try Parachute Adams, Black Gnat and Coch-y-bondhu dry flies.

Diamond Creek

Location Drains Diamond and Reid lakes, flows south for 4 km before entering the Rees River.

Access There are two marked anglers' access points: one is from Paradise Road and the other is near the Priory Road bridge.
Season 1 October–31 May.
Restrictions Bag limit is one fish. Artificial bait and fly only.

This medium-sized stream resembles a spring creek, with stable undercut tussock banks, native bush and a weedy streambed. Normally the stream is clear but after strong winds when the lakes become rough the discoloured lake water can affect the stream. There are reasonable numbers of good-sized browns and rainbows sufficient to tempt any angler, but these become very shy and well-educated as the season progresses. Careful stalking, small mayfly and caddis imitations and an accurate presentation are required. As is usually the case at the head of Lake Wakatipu, the nor'wester can play havoc with fishing this stream.

Reid Lake

Location and access Lies just south of Diamond Lake. Walking access from Paradise Road.
Season Open all year.
Restrictions Bag limit is three fish. Fishing from a non-mechanically powered boat is permitted.

This small, shallow, weedy lake holds good-sized brown trout, which can be stalked around the swampy lake edges. Try the same fly patterns as suggested for Diamond Lake.

Rees River

Location Drains the Forbes Mountains in Mt Aspiring National Park, flows south and, together with the Dart River, enters the head of Lake Wakatipu.
Access The Glenorchy–Paradise road crosses the lower reaches and a shingle road follows up the true left bank to Muddy Creek.
Season Below Muddy Creek, the river is open all year. Above Muddy Creek, 1 November–31 May.
Restrictions Bag limit is one fish.

Below Muddy Creek this medium-sized river is unstable, often silt-laden, braided and contains glacial flour. Above Muddy Creek there is more stable water, and although stocks are not high, there are 10 km of fishing up as far as Hunter Stream. Fish can be spotted in ideal conditions but early in the season it pays to fish all the likely looking water, including the boisterous runs. A lot of walking is required but the valley is beautiful on a fine day in early summer.

The mouth can be reached from the Glenorchy side and is worth fishing with a lure or spinner.

Glenorchy tarns

Location These lie in a wildlife reserve 1 km north of Glenorchy.
Access Cross the sportsground on your left as you drive north from Glenorchy.
Season 1 November–31 May.

There is good sight fishing for cruising browns in these small, shallow, weedy tarns, provided the sun is shining and the wind is not howling. Use Midge Pupa, unweighted nymphs and emergers, Corixa and Black and Peacock. At times these fish will take small mayfly imitation dry flies.

Lake Luna

Location and access Lies on Mt Creighton Station; permission is required. It is a two- to three-hour walk to the lake on a washed-out four-wheel-drive track.
Season 1 October–31 May.

This small lake holds browns, which surface from deep water to take dry flies. It is overstocked and not worth visiting

Lake Dispute

Location and access Lies off the Glenorchy road. The walking track is signposted 3 km beyond the Moke Lake turn-off. It is 30 minutes' walk to the lake.

Season 1 October–31 May.

Restrictions Bag limit is six trout. Fishing from a non-mechanically powered boat is permitted.

This narrow, swampy, reedy lake lying in a tussock and matagouri basin holds brown and rainbow trout. Fish can be ambushed along the shallow southern end. Splake have been liberated in the past but have now probably died out.

Lake Kirkpatrick and Moke Lake

Location and access The road to these lakes branches off the Glenorchy Road about 8 km from Queenstown. Kirkpatrick is the first small lake.

Season Moke Lake is open all year. Lake Kirkpatrick opens on 1 October and closes on 31 May.

Restrictions Bag limit is three trout for Kirkpatrick but six for Moke Lake. Boats are not permitted on Lake Kirkpatrick. Fishing from a non-mechanically powered boat is permitted on Moke Lake. There is a basic camping area at Moke Lake where the road ends.

Lake Kirkpatrick is a small, shallow lake lying in a tussock basin. In recent years fish stocks have been low, but it holds a few browns, which can be spotted cruising the shoreline. The most favoured shore lies away from the road.

Lake Moke is deeper, larger and more difficult to fish. Spotting is not easy along a narrow shore. The shore surrounding the bush-covered peninsula is worth exploring, especially when the green manuka beetle is in flight. Elsewhere the shoreline is tussock, briar rose and matagouri, with even a few redcurrant bushes.

Lake Johnson

Location and access Lies north of Frankton. Turn off SH 6 opposite the Frankton Golf Course onto Hansen Road.

Season Open all year.
Restrictions Bag limit is three fish. Fishing from a non-mechanically powered boat is permitted.

This small lake holds rainbow trout and perch and is regularly stocked. Best fished with spinners or lures such as Hamill's Killer, Mrs Simpson and Green Woolly Buggers on a slow-sinking line.

Lake Hayes

Location Lies between Queenstown and Arrowtown.
Access SH 6 skirts the southern shore. The lake is most easily accessed from the north shore reserve and from the A & P showgrounds.
Season Open all year.
Restrictions Bag limit is six fish. Fishing from a mechanically powered boat is prohibited.
Boat launching For small boats, from Bendemeer Bay.

The Nevis River runs through barren country in summer

This moderate-sized lake holds a good stock of brown trout averaging 1–2 kg, as well as perch. As willows restrict shoreline fishing a small boat or float-tube is an advantage. Most browns are caught on lures such as bully imitations, damsel and dragon fly nymphs, and small smelt flies fished on a slow-sinking line. Harling from a rowboat is a popular method. Use a high-density line and a Mrs Simpson, Woolly Bugger or Hamill's Killer. Water quality has deteriorated over recent years.

Other spots to explore in the Queenstown area include the Kawerau River from the outlet down to the Shotover confluence. This is best fished from a drifting boat, and most trout are caught on spinners. The Shotover River holds a few trout, especially in the upper reaches, but the water is usually silt-laden. The Arrow River holds small trout only. The season for the Arrow and Shotover rivers is 1 October–31 May. The Roaring Meg dams hold a few trout but the road access is very difficult and you need to be desperate to visit this spot for fishing.

Nevis River

Location Drains the Hector and Garvie mountains, flows northeast behind the Remarkables and joins the Kawerau River 1 km downstream from the Victoria Bridge.

Access
- From Cromwell, take the Cromwell–Nevis road through Bannockburn. This is a gravel road that climbs high over barren mountains before descending into the Nevis Valley. The views from the top are superb but be wary of the prickly spaniard plants when taking photos!
- From Garston on SH 6, take the narrow, fine-weather four-wheel-drive road over the mountains into the upper Nevis Valley. There are more than twenty fords on this road and washouts are common. A shovel may come in handy.

Season 1 October–30 April.

Restrictions Fly fishing only. Bag limit is one trout.

This moderate-sized river flows through dry, barren, inhospitable tussock country with scenery reminiscent of Western movie sets. In winter the valley is very cold, while summers are generally dry and hot. The river holds a moderate stock of good-sized brown trout, which can be spotted and stalked. At times there are trophy fish in the river but fish have been smaller in recent years. Fishes best before Christmas as the river can warm in long hot summers and fish become easily spooked after they have been fished over. The gorge downstream from Nevis Crossing bridge is very rough and hardly worth the effort of exploring. The middle reaches are the most popular, with 15 km of easily accessible water to fish upstream from Nevis Crossing. Gold sluicing is still carried out in the upper valley and the piles of tailings throughout are a reminder of the early prospecting days in this harsh, remote location.

Southland Fish and Game Council region

The Southland region includes the southernmost part of the South Island and Fiordland. In Southland there are four major river systems draining to the south coast. To the west lies the severely modified Waiau River, draining lakes Te Anau and Manapouri. East of the Waiau, the Aparima River flows south from its source in the Takitimu Mountains while the Oreti and Mataura rivers rise from mountainous bush- and tussock-covered country south of Lake Wakatipu. All four rivers flow gently south across the fertile plains of Southland and empty into Foveaux Strait.

Most rivers and streams hold brown trout, which were introduced in 1870. Rainbow trout are only present in the Waiau River system and Lake Thomas. Atlantic salmon were also introduced into the Waiau River but these have not thrived.

The township of Gore in central Southland has laid claims to the title of 'Trout Fishing Capital of New Zealand'. There's little doubt that Southland has some superb trout streams, but the inclement weather very often restricts the fishing opportunities. Summer is the best time to visit, when the weather is temperate and the prevailing westerly winds moderate. There is a long twilight in the south, and from December to the end of January it remains daylight until after 10 p.m.

Fiordland, to the west of the region, is a World Heritage Park, but as it encompasses precipitous bush-clad fiords and rugged mountains, many valleys are largely inaccessible. With a rainfall exceeding 6000 mm in some areas, ferocious swarms of sandflies and few tracks or roads, anglers need to be rugged individuals indeed to tackle some of these steep, gorgy rivers. However, there is a wide variety of fishing water available and even the most

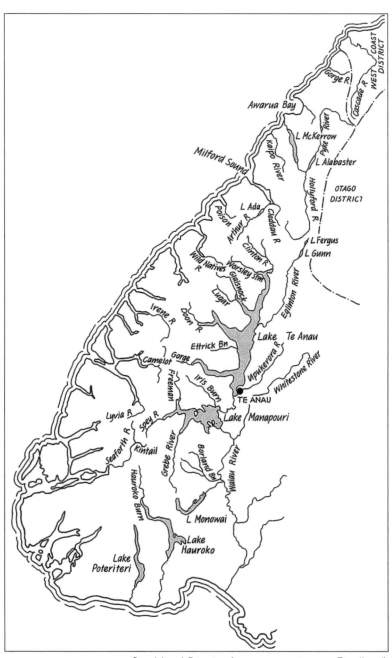

Southland District (western section — Fiordland)

remote river or mountain tarn can be reached by helicopter or floatplane from Te Anau. Some spots are very seldom visited by anyone. Anglers spending time in this area should be experienced in bushcraft, possess adequate maps, and tell others of their plans. Rivers can rise to frightening levels overnight, but they return to normal just as rapidly. Remember the insect repellent and have an insect-proof tent.

Brown trout were first introduced into Lake Manapouri in about 1875, and into the Hollyford River as early as 1884. The browns have migrated down the coast from the Hollyford mouth and spread to most Fiordland rivers. Rainbow trout were first introduced into Lake Te Anau in the mid-1920s; Atlantic salmon were released into Lake Ada in 1891 and into Lake Te Anau about 1910. It is rare to catch a salmon nowadays.

Fiordland rivers and lakes

Awarua River

Location and access This medium-sized river drains swampy country and the Waiuna Lagoon behind Big Bay, flows west through dense native bush and empties into the Tasman Sea at the northern end of Big Bay. Trampers reach the river from either the Hollyford or Pyke valleys, but fixed-wing aircraft can land on the Big Bay Beach at low tide.
Season Open all year.
Restrictions Bag limit is three trout.

This very remote river is only of interest to trampers. It is a prime whitebaiting river and these small delicacies form the diet of the resident and sea-run browns that inhabit the river. Trout are hard to spot but accept smelt lures and spinners fished across and downstream. The estuary is the only clear area to fish but there is a dinghy in the bush at the Waiuna Lagoon, which also holds a few browns.

Location Begins near the Gertrude Saddle on the Milford Road and drains the Darren and Humboldt mountains. Flows generally north down a very beautiful valley to enter the top end of Lake McKerrow, then drains this lake by flowing into the sea at Martins Bay. The river is 80 km long.

Access Branch off the Milford Road onto the upper Hollyford road to Gunn's Camp. The road follows down the valley for a short distance beyond the camp. From here you can either tramp or hire a jetboat. A tramping track follows down the true right bank to Lake McKerrow. Fixed-wing flights can be arranged to Martins Bay or a floatplane from Te Anau or Queenstown to Lake McKerrow.

Season Open all year.

Restrictions Bag limit is four trout.

This large, wonderful, wild and scenic river holds brown trout averaging 2 kg, with an occasional fish up to 4.5 kg. The upper reaches above Hidden Falls hold only a few fish, but below the Hidden Falls confluence the valley flattens out and the river flows more sedately through deep pools and runs. The river seldom discolours after rain but can rise in an alarming fashion and crossings can become extremely hazardous. Tree falls, logs and snags provide ample evidence of the high rainfall in this bush-clad valley. Trout can be spotted and caught on a variety of flies and spinners. The best stretch of river lies immediately upstream from the mouth at Lake McKerrow but access is very difficult.

From the outlet at Lake McKerrow to Martins Bay there are 4–5 km of snag-infested water that is more suited to spinning. The river is wide, deep and tidal near the mouth but sea-run and estuarine-living browns can provide plenty of sport. In recent years marauding seals and dolphins have reduced the trout stocks.

There are good DoC huts in the valley but tramper-anglers should check with the Ranger Station at Te Anau before visiting the area.

Hidden Falls Creek usually holds a few good browns. A small run of quinnat salmon have strayed into the main river in recent years.

Location and access As for the Lower Hollyford Valley. Trampers should be aware of the Demon Trail along the eastern shore of Lake McKerrow, as windfalls often obstruct the steep track. Park Board huts are available at the top of Lake McKerrow and at Hokuri Creek.
Season Open all year.
Restrictions Bag limit is four fish. Artificial bait and fly only.

This deep lake is over 20 km long and occupies an old drowned glacial valley. It is flanked by steep, bush-clad mountains and can rise by three metres or more after heavy rain. The lake is more suited to spinning but brown trout can be seen cruising the shore, especially around the Hollyford mouth and the mouth of Hokuri Creek. These can be taken on small nymphs or bully imitations. Over recent years seals and dolphins have entered the lake and reduced the trout population.

Pyke River

Location Rises in the Red Hills behind Big Bay, flows into and out of lakes Wilmot and Alabaster, and joins the Hollyford River some 6 km upstream from its Lake McKerrow mouth.
Access Reached by tramping, floatplane, fixed-wing to the upper Pyke strip, or helicopter.
Season Open all year.
Restrictions Bag limit is four fish.

The Pyke is a medium-sized, sluggish, tea-coloured river holding a good stock of brown trout in the 1.3–2 kg range. Fish are easy to spot despite the water colour but logs and snags in the river help trout escape when hooked. The best stretch of river lies 1 km downstream from Lake Wilmot. Access is never easy because of the swamp, flax and scrub, and hordes of sandflies do their utmost to make angling miserable. In recent years some overseas anglers have flown in and floated the river.

Location Both these scenic, bush-lined mountain lakes lie in the Pyke Valley.
Access As for the Pyke River.
Season Open all year.
Restrictions Bag limit is four trout.

Trout are difficult to spot unless the lakes are low and there is plenty of unobstructed shore. Both are lightly tea-coloured and are generally best fished with a spinner. There are areas for the fly angler, such as the Pyke delta at the top end of both lakes, where trout can be seen cruising in clear conditions.

Late in the season spawning fish congregate in these areas, and lure fishing with a Red Setter or Orange Rabbit is very productive. There are good numbers of brown trout in these lakes, with an occasional fish over 4.5 kg. The scenery is superb, especially looking south from the top end of Lake Alabaster, with the snow-covered Darren Mountains reflected in the lake presenting an unforgettable sight.

Kaipo River

Location and access This inaccessible, small to medium-sized river drains the northern Darren Mountains and enters the sea 10 km south of Martins Bay. There is an old deer recovery airstrip on the top flats. The mouth can be reached after a three- to four-hour tramp along a bouldery coast from the south end of Martins Bay.
Season Open all year.
Restrictions Bag limit is four trout, but catch and release is recommended.

Upstream from the top flats there are a few stable pools, overhung by beech bush, that hold good-sized brown trout. Between the top flats and the gorge downstream the river is unstable and holds few fish. There are fish in the gorge but the estuary holds some large sea-run trout that feed on whitebait. Fish stocks can be unreliable.

Cleddau River

Location and access Rises near the Homer Saddle on the Milford Road (SH 94) and has a short, steep course to Milford Sound. SH 94 follows down the true right bank, with access available from the Milford airstrip, at the Lodge, at the rubbish collection area and above the Tutuko River confluence.
Season Open all year.
Restrictions Bag limit is four trout.

At times the medium-sized Cleddau River holds good brown trout, mainly in the lower reaches. These fish are sea-run and generally enter the river in summer when the water temperature rises, but stocks are unreliable. At times very few trout can be found in the river. Fish are easy to spot in the cold, clear mountain water and respond to both dry flies and nymphs. Remember to take insect repellent for the sandflies.

Arthur River

Location and access Rises near the McKinnon Pass and from the Sutherland Falls on the Milford Track. Flows into and out of Lake Ada to enter Milford Sound near Sandfly Point. Access from the Milford Track. There is an airstrip at Quinton Hut.
Season Open all year.
Restrictions Bag limit is four trout. Artificial bait and fly only.

This deep tea-coloured bush river carries good-sized brown trout, but the rainfall (in excess of 6000 mm) and sandfly swarms deter most anglers. The river holds large volumes of water and is not easy to fish except with spinning gear. Quinnat salmon have appeared in the river in February and March but these runs are unreliable.

Lake Ada

Location and access Lies in the lower reaches of the Arthur River. Access from the Milford Track is difficult as the shore is overgrown and swampy. A boat is essential for shoreline access.

Season Open all year.
Restrictions Bag limit is four trout.

A small, bush- and rush-encircled, tannin-stained lake that is best fished from a boat or with a spinner. It holds good numbers of browns, most of which die from old age. Some fish are in poor condition.

Isolated rivers and lakes of Fiordland

Information is very sketchy on many of the rivers entering the Tasman Sea south of Milford Sound. However, though I have visited only a few of these rivers, I can confirm that most of the larger waterways hold brown trout. Many of these are sea-run and enter the estuaries chasing whitebait, so stocks are unreliable. Most of these fish have migrated down the rugged Fiordland coast from the Hollyford River and Lake Ada since 1890, although rainbow fry have entered the Lyvia River via the turbines and tailrace of the Manapouri Power Station in the 1960s. Nearly all the rivers have a short, steep course, are overgrown with bush, have swampy estuaries and rise to alarming heights when in flood. However, they recover just as rapidly.

Access to most of these rivers and lakes is very difficult through this rugged, inhospitable, mountainous terrain, where the annual rainfall is around 6000 mm and the strong prevailing westerly winds, sandflies and mosquitoes deter all but the hardiest of anglers. Most anglers combine hunting with fishing, and use helicopters or floatplanes from Te Anau. February and March are the most settled months to visit these waterways. The following hold brown trout.

- Joes River entering the top end of Lake Ada. The valley can be tramped from the Milford Track.
- Transit River entering the Tasman Sea at Transit Beach, immediately south of Milford Sound.
- Poison River at Poison Bay, also just south of Milford Sound.
- Light and Dark (lower) rivers entering Sutherland Sound.
- Wild Natives River at the head of Bligh Sound.
- Catseye River between Bligh and George sounds.

- George River entering George Sound.
- Edith River draining into Lake Alice at George Sound.
- Stillwater River draining into Lake Marchant at Caswell Sound.
- Large Burn joining lakes McKinnon and Marchant.
- Irene and Windward rivers entering Charles Sound.
- Camelot River at the head of Bradshaw Sound. There are two lagoons on this river, formed by landslides below the Belvidere Falls, and these hold fish.
- Seaforth River and Kintail Burn. These enter Dusky Sound, with the Kintail Burn accessible from the Manapouri–Dusky Sound track.
- Waitutu River draining Lake Poteriteri. Access from the trampers' track along the southern Fiordland coast from Port Craig.
- Lake Hakapoura. This isolated lake lies inland from the southern Fiordland coast. Tramping access available from Port Craig beyond the Waitutu River to the Big River.

The following river and lakes hold both brown and rainbow trout.
- Lyvia River and the Manapouri Power House tailrace at Doubtful Sound. Rainbow fingerlings have somehow negotiated the turbines of the power station and populated the tailrace and Lyvia River. Access from the West Arm–Doubtful Sound road.
- Lakes Thomson and Hankinson beyond the northwest arm of Middle Fiord of Lake Te Anau.

If you are brave or foolish enough to venture into these areas to fish, you certainly deserve the best of luck! There may be a trophy fish.

Lake Te Anau, its tributaries and related waters

Lake Te Anau

Season Open all year.
Restrictions Bag limit is four fish.
Boat launching At Te Anau waterfront and at Te Anau Downs.

This is the largest lake in the South Island, being 61 km long, covering 850 ha and 417 m deep. The western shore is broken up into deep fiords, which penetrate far into the rugged, bush-covered Fiordland mountains. The eastern shore is drier, covered in scrub, patches of bush and pastoral land. Te Anau township, which is on this eastern shore, is a thriving tourist centre offering good accommodation, restaurants and various forms of transport to Fiordland locations. The lake level is controlled for hydro-electric generation by a weir built at the southern end in 1975.

The lake is best fished by trolling from a boat or spinning from the shore, though there are a few spots mainly at stream mouths where fly anglers can fish. Trout can be hard to spot except on sunny days and at shallow deltas such as the Eglinton. There is good shoreline fishing in front of the golf course, and in rough, windy conditions fish can be spotted in the waves. There is good night lure fishing at stream mouths, especially the Upukerora River.

Lake Te Anau tributaries

Many small streams enter the west side of Lake Te Anau, and most have short courses and are heavily bushed. However, some hold fish in their lower reaches and many provide good fly casting from a boat at their mouths. Such streams include the Glaisnock River and Lugar Burn in the North Fiord, the Doon River entering the southwest arm of the Middle Fiord, the Ettrick Burn north of Te Ana-au glow-worm caves, and the Chester Burn in the south fiord.

Clinton River

Location Rises near McKinnon Pass on the Milford Track, flows southeast and enters the head of Lake Te Anau at Glade House.
Access
- By boat from Te Anau Downs to Glade House and the start of the Milford Track. The track follows up the true right bank to Pompolona Hut.
- By tramping a very difficult route over Dore Pass from the Eglinton Valley.

Camping is only permitted away from the Milford Track but permission should be obtained from DoC, Te Anau. At times there may be accommodation available at Glade House.

Season 1 November–31 May.

Restrictions Bag limit is two trout. Artificial bait and fly only.

This magnificent, moderate-sized, clear mountain river holds good numbers of brown and rainbow trout up to 4.5 kg. Fish are easy to spot but careful stalking and an accurate first cast are all-important. Use a long, fine trace but of sufficient strength to hold large fighting fish stripping off 50 m of line with their first run. The river is rock and stone in type, with bush overhanging the water on some sections. Crossings are tricky, and as the water is very clear it is much deeper than it appears. With heavy rain the river will rise, but as the headwaters drain dense native bush the water will seldom become silt-laden. Rather, it may become tannin-stained for a few days, but it rapidly recovers. Most trout when hooked seek the shelter of a hide beneath sunken logs and flood debris so beaching all fish hooked becomes a real problem. Trout will accept small weighted nymphs of both mayfly and caddis varieties. Dry flies such as Coch-y-bondhu, Humpy, Royal Wulff, Irresistible, Elk Hair Caddis and Parachute Adams can bring results. Careful stalking, accurate casting and a drag-free presentation are generally more important than the fly pattern. Don't forget insect repellent!

The North Branch, Neale Burn and Lake Ross all hold good-sized trout for experienced tramper-anglers unafraid of torrential rain and sandflies.

Worsley Stream

Location Drains lakes Sumor and Brownlee, flows east and enters Lake Te Anau at Worsley Arm.

Access By boat or floatplane from Te Anau.

Season 1 November–31 May.

Restrictions Bag limit is two trout.

This remote, medium-sized, scenic river flows through rugged, bush-covered, mountainous terrain that is the habitat of New Zealand's wapiti herd. It holds browns and rainbows up to 4 kg. The river is rock and stone in type and can be forded at selected crossings provided the river level is normal. Most trout can be spotted but all likely looking water should be fished.

The lower reaches are deep and difficult to access except by boat, and the track upstream on the true left bank is rather overgrown and washed out in some sections. The Park Board hut along the beach from the mouth is heavily used, especially on weekends and holidays in summer.

The middle and upper reaches offer stable pools and sparkling runs, and good fishing is available to beyond the Castle River confluence.

The Castle River itself holds a few large rainbows in deep, clear, slow-flowing pools, and these are a real challenge to hook. Use the same flies and methods as suggested for the Clinton River.

Eglinton River

Location Flows into and out of lakes Fergus and Gunn, then south down the famous, scenic Eglinton Valley to enter Lake Te Anau north of Te Anau Downs.

Access SH 94 follows the river upstream on its true left bank, although a walk across tussock flats and through beech bush may be necessary to reach the river. The mouth is usually accessed from a boat unless the river is low, braided and easy to cross.

Season 1 November–31 May.

Restrictions Fly fishing only. Bag limit is two trout. Fishing from any flotation device is not permitted.

This moderate-sized, freestone river offers over 30 km of fishing, with reasonably easy access from the main road. It is a spawning river for Lake Te Anau but also holds resident fish. Rainbow and brown trout averaging around 2 kg are present in good numbers and most of these can be sight fished in bright, clear conditions. The river can take three or four days to clear after heavy rain and often carries snow and glacial melt early in the season. It is best fished early in the season during periods of low water flow. The river is safe to wade and cross at the tail of most pools.

The most productive water lies between Walker and Mackay creeks and below Knob's Flat, although trout are present up as far as Cascade Creek. There are large fish in the gorge but this is virtually inaccessible. The fish are not selective and will respond to a variety of weighted nymphs and dry flies carefully presented. Some trout can be sight fished but all good water should be tested.

There are a number of small side creeks of the Eglinton River that hold fish early in the season.

The East Branch is fast-flowing and unstable in the lower reaches but active anglers will find better water three hours' tramp upstream. The access track is marked near the road bridge.

Lakes Fergus, Gunn and Lochy

Location and access SH 94 skirts the shorelines of all three lakes in the upper Eglinton Valley.
Season 1 November–31 May.
Restrictions Bag limit is four fish.

These scenic lakes offer limited fishing due to their heavily bushed shorelines, but all hold brown and rainbow trout and perhaps a few landlocked Atlantic salmon. They are best fished with spinners or from a boat or float-tube.

Upukerora River

Location Rises in the Livingstone Mountains, flows southwest through patches of bush, scrub and pastoral land, and enters Lake Te Anau at Patience Bay just north of Te Anau township.
Access *Lower reaches* SH 94 crosses the river 3 km north of Te Anau. Walk upstream from the bridge.
Middle reaches Turn off SH 94 onto Kakapo Road 5 km south of Te Anau, then onto Ladies Mile Road. There is a marked anglers' access.
Upper reaches From the end of Kakapo Road through private farmland. Permission is required.
Season 1 November–31 May.
Restrictions Bag limit is two trout.

This small freestone river is also an important spawning stream for Lake Te Anau. It holds mainly rainbow trout averaging 1 kg, but larger browns are present in the upper reaches. Although close to Te Anau township the river holds good stocks of fish, and many of these cannot be spotted in the fast runs. It is well worth fishing all likely looking water as well as sight fishing the edges of runs and looking carefully into the pools. The nor'west wind tends to blow upstream and this can be a real bonus. The river is easy to wade and cross and is a great learner stream.

Provided the mouth is not too braided, there is good night lure fishing. There is an access track to the mouth from the bridge on SH 94.

Upper Waiau River

Location Flows from the weir at Lake Te Anau to Lake Manapouri.
Access
- From Te Anau, Golf Course Road leads to the weir and the out-let. The Kepler Track follows down the true right bank.
- From the Te Anau–Manapouri road there are a number of access points. The two most popular are Queens Reach and Rainbow Reach. There is a basic camping area at Queens Reach, and boat launching facilities.
Season 1 October–31 May.
Restrictions Bag limit is four trout. Boats are permitted for access.

This large, heavy, deep, clear-water river holds a good stock of rainbow and brown trout, but shoreline access is very difficult because of overhanging manuka scrub and beech trees. A boat is a great advantage for access. The lower three kilometres of river upstream from Lake Manapouri are unstable, contain fallen trees and are unattractive to fish. The river fishes best when the water level is low. When the control gates are open and the river is high, most shingle banks and islands are covered with water and the river can only be fished in a few spots with spinning gear. In low water summer conditions, excellent 'blind' fly fishing with dry flies and nymphs can be enjoyed. Rainbows around 1–2 kg are most commonly caught and these fight extremely well. Fish can rise during the day but evening and night sedge fishing can on occasion be spectacular. Recommended shoreline fishing spots include the control gates, the boat ramp, Rainbow Reach and Balloon Loop. Use mayfly and caddis imitations along with attractor patterns.

The mouth at Lake Manapouri is a favoured spot but a boat is necessary as wading is treacherous in the soft silt.

Lake Manapouri, its tributaries and related waters

Lake Manapouri

Season Open all year.
Restrictions Bag limit is four fish.
Boat launching At Pearl Harbour, Manapouri.

Manapouri is a beautiful, cold, scenic lake surrounded by native bush and rugged Fiordland mountains. Regrettably, it was modified in the 1960s for power generation, and during periods of excessive draw-off unattractive sand and mud banks are exposed. The lake is very deep at 443 m, while the mean lake level is 177 m above sea level.

The lake holds brown and rainbow trout and a few landlocked Atlantic salmon. However, the latter are now rarely caught. Fish are difficult to spot along the shore and trollers catch 90 percent of the fish taken. There are a few stream mouths worth trying with a lure but the lake is much better suited to boat fishing.

Iris Burn

Location Rises in the Kepler Mountains, flows southwest and enters Lake Manapouri 3 km west of Shallow Bay.
Access Either by boat or by walking the Kepler Track, which follows up the true left bank to the Iris Burn Hut in the headwaters.
Season 1 November–31 May.
Restrictions Bag limit is two trout.

This small freestone stream is a spawning stream for the lake, but it also holds resident fish, mainly in the upper and middle reaches where the water is more stable. There are only a few fish below the Big Slip, which came down the mountainside and created a shallow lake. There are rainbows averaging around 1 kg in the stream and in the shallow lake but not all are in good condition. The mouth is worth fishing but the rest of the stream is probably only worthwhile as a diversion from walking the Kepler Track.

The tannin-stained Forest Burn and the Freeman Burn entering the north arm also hold a few fish, especially early in the season.

Spey River

Location Rises near Centre Pass on the Manapouri–Dusky Sound track, flows northeast and enters the west arm of Lake Manapouri.
Access Initially by boat, then from the road to Doubtful Sound.
Season 1 November–31 May.
Restrictions Bag limit is two fish.

Fishing has deteriorated since the Doubtful Sound road was built. The water, although lightly tannin-stained, is still sufficiently clear to allow sight fishing. The river holds rainbows averaging 1–1.4 kg, with the best fishing early in the season and beyond where the road turns towards Wilmot Pass.

Grebe River

Location Drains heavily bush-clad mountains, flows north and enters the south arm of Lake Manapouri.
Access
• By boat to the south arm.
• A metalled hydro road from Monowai leaves Borland Lodge, crosses a saddle and descends into the lower Grebe Valley. The road, which is more suited to four-wheel-drive vehicles, follows up the true left bank.
Season 1 November–31 May.
Restrictions Bag limit is two trout.

This small to medium-sized rock and stone type stream is similar to the Spey River but in places it is very turbulent and fast flowing with little holding water. In the more stable pools in the region of Shallow Lake, the river holds mainly rainbows with the odd brown for variety. Trout can be sight fished but the more turbulent sections should be explored with a weighted nymph.

Just over the saddle and before the road reaches the Grebe there are two small tarns across to the left. Both hold fish, with the one furthest from the road reputed to hold a few large browns.

Home Creek

Location Drains swampy land northeast of Manapouri, winds across pastoral land and empties into the Waiau a little downstream from Pearl Harbour.
Access From the Hillside–Manapouri road at a marked anglers' access. This road crosses the creek. The upper reaches can be accessed across the Manapouri Airport.
Season 1 October–31 May.
Restrictions Bag limit is two fish, but catch and release is recommended for this creek.

This small creek holds a reasonable stock of brown trout and an occasional rainbow. The upper reaches are difficult to fish due to dense bank vegetation of flax, willow and scrub, but there are stretches across farmland where fish can be stalked. Unless the day is bright and sunny, trout are difficult to spot in the slightly tannin-stained water. Pools are very short and drag becomes a problem unless one creeps up close behind a fish and places a short, accurate cast first time.

Lake Monowai

Location and access Lies south of Manapouri and northwest of Tuatapere. Access to Monowai from the Blackmount–Clifden road. Turn off a few kilometres north of Blackmount.
Season Open all year.
Restrictions Bag limit is four trout.
Boat launching This is available.

This 22-km-long lake, which is surrounded by heavily bush-clad hills, holds brown and rainbow trout. Unfortunately, the lake's scenic values have been devalued by the dead trees that still poke up above water level, remnants of bush that was flooded when the lake was raised for the production of hydro-electric power in 1925. Shoreline angling is very limited on this lake and the majority of trout are caught by anglers trolling or harling from a boat. The water is lightly tea-coloured. The mouth of Electric River at June Bay and Roger Inlet are favourite spots for trolling. The Electric River holds brown trout for adventurous bush-whacking anglers who have accessed the river mouth by boat. There are three Park huts around the shoreline.

See Waiau tributaries for Monowai River and Borland Burn.

Green Lake and Walker River, just north of Lake Monowai, also hold brown trout. There is a marked trampers' track from Lake Monowai; it is a two- to three-hour walk to the lake.

Lake Hauroko

Location and access Lies south of Monowai and west of Clifden and Tuatapere. Branch off SH 96 at Clifden on the Lill Burn Valley Road. There is a Park Board shelter at the lake. For anglers or trampers wanting to reach the head of the lake, a water taxi is available from Tuatapere.
Season Open all year.
Restrictions Bag limit is four trout.
Boat launching There is a concrete ramp at the road end.

Although larger than Lake Monowai, this lake is similar in that it is surrounded by densely bush-covered mountains. At 462 m, Hauroko is New Zealand's deepest lake. It is best fished from a boat, but beware of the nor'west winds. Although the lake is lightly tannin-stained, it is possible to sight fish for cruising browns in the bays at the road end and picnic area. There are three huts around the shore.

The Hauroko Burn, which enters the head of the lake, offers good fishing for tramper-anglers walking to Dusky Sound.

Location Lies west of Lake Hauroko.
Access
- By tramping the southern coast from Port Craig and following up the Waitutu River to the lake. This trip is for experienced trampers only.
- By floatplane or helicopter.

Season Open all year.
Restrictions Bag limit is four trout.

This long (28 km), remote, bush-surrounded lake holds brown and rainbow trout, but shoreline fishing is very limited unless the lake is low. There's a Fiordland National Park Board hut with six bunks on the southeastern shore. Don't forget insect repellent!

 Lower Waiau River, its tributaries and related waters

Lower Waiau River (below the Mararoa Weir)

Location This large river drained Lake Manapouri before the Mararoa Weir was built below the Mararoa confluence; now this water is redirected back into the lake for hydro-electricity generation at West Arm on Lake Manapouri. Below the weir the river flows south close by Monowai and Clifden, eventually reaching Te Waewae Lagoon south of Tuatapere.
Access *Mouth and lower reaches* SH 96 crosses at Tuatapere and at Clifden. Roads follow down both banks from Tuatapere, with the Tuatapere–Riverton road offering access to the lagoon on the eastern side just south of Te Waewae settlement. King's Island below the Clifden Bridge can only be accessed through private property.
Middle reaches Between Clifden and Redcliff there are a number of access points, many through private property. (Most property owners readily give permission but please ask before fishing.) Some of these are:
- Motu Bush Road off Lill Burn Valley Road on the west side of the river, across private farmland.

- Wairaki River mouth. There is a track to the mouth on the south side of the Wairaki bridge.
- From Glendearg Station north of the Wairaki River.
- From Sunnyside Station on the west bank south from Monowai.
- From Monowai Power Station and the Borland Burn mouth north of the power station, both on the west side of the river.
- From Blackmount Station.
- From Redcliff Station, from a road leaving the top of Redcliff Saddle.

Upper reaches
- From Whare Creek on Jericho Station.
- From Excelsior Creek.

Season Open all year below Tuatapere bridge including Te Waewae Lagoon (excludes the Holly Burn). Above this bridge and upstream to the Mararoa Weir, 1 October–31 May.

Restrictions Bag limit is six fish. Boats or other flotation devices are not permitted between the Mararoa Weir and the Monowai River confluence. Fishing is not permitted within 100 m of the fish pass in the Mararoa Weir.

This once large and magnificent river has been severely modified for hydro-electric power generation. However, water flows have recently been increased to not less than 12 cumecs and this has improved the fishing. Unfortunately, silt builds up periodically at the Mararoa Weir and flushing this downriver adversely affects the trout and the sub-aquatic life. The river holds brown and rainbow trout, with an occasional large sea-run brown entering the lower reaches to run upriver. Fish up to 4.5 kg can be anticipated although most fish caught average between 1 and 2 kg.

At the mouth, in the lagoon and upstream to Tuatapere, most trout are caught on live bait or spinners, especially when whitebait are running. The King's Island area south of Clifden is popular early in the season but access is difficult when the river is high due to bank vegetation.

Between Clifden and the Wairaki mouth access is easier, the river is more spread out and the banks are lower. Fish cannot be spotted so all likely looking water should be covered. Above the Monowai Power Station rainbow trout become the predominant fish, and the river becomes more stable and confined to one channel.

There is good water downstream from Whare Creek, with good numbers of well-conditioned rainbows in the 1–2 kg range. Again, trout are difficult to spot but will rise to dry flies. The river can normally be forded in this upper section but the algae-covered stones are very slippery.

Two swampy ponds in Redcliff Wildlife Reserve hold browns.

Whitestone River

Location Rises in the Livingstone Mountains to the west of Mavora Lakes, flows generally south to join the lower reaches of the Mararoa River in the Mt York area.
Access *Lower reaches* From the Hillside–Manapouri road.
Middle reaches From SH 94.
Upper reaches From Kakapo Road a branch road to Mt Prospect crosses the upper reaches, and through private farmland.
Season Below Prospect Bridge on Kakapo Road, 1 October–30 April. Above this bridge, 1 November–30 April.
Restrictions Bag limit is two trout.

This small, freestone stream draining the Snowdon State Forest is a spawning stream and fishes best early in the season. By mid-December most rainbows have drifted back downstream from the upper reaches. However, it does hold resident browns in the more stable, deeper runs and pools. In long hot summers the river tends to dry and flow beneath the shingle. The majority of spawning fish are rainbows, but some good-sized browns are also present. Most fish can be spotted and stalked as the river normally runs very clear. It is easy to wade and cross.

Mararoa River

Location Rises near the Mararoa Saddle, flows south between the Livingstone and Thomson mountains and enters the north end of North Mavora Lake. Drains this lake and enters South Mavora Lake 4 km to the south. Emerges from South Mavora Lake and continues in a southerly direction for over 40 km before joining the Whitestone River in the Mt York area. After flowing through a gorge the river joins the Waiau River 6.5 km south of Lake Manapouri, just above the Mararoa Weir.

Season 1 October–30 April.

Restrictions Bag limit below Key Bridge on SH 94 is four trout; above this bridge, the bag limit is two trout only. It is illegal to fish from a boat or any other flotation device. Bait fishing is permitted below Key Bridge.

For descriptive and geographical reasons, the river is divided into three sections.

Upper reaches (from the headwaters to South Mavora Lake)
Access
- By boat to top of North Mavora Lake and walking up the river.
- By four-wheel-drive along the eastern side of North Mavora Lake. The track can be very rough and boggy in the first section and difficult if the lake is high.
- By tramping to the headwaters over Mararoa Saddle from the Greenstone Valley. There are two DoC huts for basic accommodation. The first lies on the eastern lake shore 1 km from the head of North Mavora Lake. The second is sited 6 km upstream from the head of the lake.

The Upper Mararoa River drains small tarns in the headwaters and flows down a long, barren, exposed tussock valley. The river flows over a gravel bed and is small and easily crossed in this section. In the stretch of water upstream from the lake there are browns and rainbows averaging 1.4 kg, which are easy to spot on a sunny day. They can be carefully stalked and will take a wide variety of dry flies and nymphs. The Windon Burn, entering from the west, also holds a few good fish in its lower reaches early in the season. If you are prepared to walk up the valley over lumpy tussock there are some good-sized browns up to 3.5 kg, but these are much more difficult to deceive. Anglers arriving by boat to fish the river should realise that the four-wheel-drive track reaches the river about 1 km upstream from the lake. The nor'wester can ruin upstream fishing.

It is a very long walk to the tarns in the headwaters and there can be fishing all the way; at times, the tarns also carry fish.

Between the lakes, the river is deep, clear and quite swift. There are very few fish.

Middle reaches (from South Mavora Lake to SH 94)
Access
- SH 94 crosses the river just beyond The Key.
- The Te Anau–Mavora Lakes road leaves SH 94 at Burwood Station and follows up the true left bank to the Mavora lakes. There are marked anglers' access points off this road. The Centre Hill–Mavora Lakes road joins the Te Anau–Mavora Lakes road at the apex of a triangle. There is access from the Mararoa Station bridge.

At the southern end of South Mavora Lake, the river flows through an inaccessible, rocky, bush-covered gorge. The medium-sized river emerges from this gorge 2 km upstream from the Kiwi Burn swing-bridge. Tussock and patches of beech bush line the banks until the river leaves the bush and flows through pastoral land. As the river drains a stable lake it remains clear and fishable after rain, but it generally fishes best in low water summer conditions. The water is clear and some fish can be seen along edges of runs and in pools, but many will be missed in the deeper, faster sections. The river is difficult to cross in the Kiwi Burn area but the valley widens and flattens out downstream, and in the pastoral section the river braids and fording becomes possible at the tail of most pools. There are good stocks of fish (25 large fish/km) in the 1–3 kg range. Above the Kiwi Burn, 70 percent of fish are rainbows; below the Wood Burn, 70 percent of fish are browns. The Kiwi Burn section is relatively sheltered in a nor'wester. The river suffered badly from a severe flood in 2000.

Lower reaches (from SH 94 to the Mararoa Weir)
Access
- Walk downstream from SH 94.
- South through private farmland in the region of The Wilderness.
- About 1.5 km on the Manapouri side of the Hillside–

Manapouri road bridge over the Whitestone River there is a track on the left that leads downstream to the Whitestone confluence, Flaxy Creek and the top end of a gorge.

- Weir Road from Manapouri crosses the river below a gorge and near the weir.

Above Weir Road bridge the river flows through a gorge, which can be negotiated by fit anglers in low water conditions only. Some of the crossings can be tricky. There are some deep, stable pools, which a few local anglers fish successfully with live bait. Trout are hard to spot in this section but there is some good water for upstream nymph and dry flies in summer. Above this gorge the river braids and flows quite swiftly, with willows and gorse obstructing casting on some sections. However, you are unlikely to meet other anglers on this section of river and there are some good-sized trout present in the more stable water.

A wide selection of flies will take fish on this river. Early in the season when the water is high, the swifter sections can be fished with two well-weighted nymphs and an indicator. Later in summer, attractor type dry flies provide good sport. Even well-sunk Woolly Buggers fished across and downstream can bring results.

Mavora Lakes

Location Between the Livingstone and Thomson mountains, just south and west of Lake Wakatipu.
Access From SH 94 take branch roads to Mavora Lakes from Centre Hill or Burwood Station. These roads join and follow up Mararoa River to the lakes. There is basic camping at North Mavora.
Season Open all year.
Restrictions Bag limit is four trout. Artificial bait and fly only.
Boat launching Small boats can be launched from the beach with a four-wheel-drive vehicle.

These are very scenic high country lakes. North Mavora is 9.5 km long, and apart from beech bush at the southern end is surrounded by tussock- and matagouri-covered mountains. The eastern shore can be readily accessed and there is a rough four-wheel-drive track to the head of the lake. The western shore requires a boat for access as the outlet is deep and swift. Both brown and rainbow trout in the 1.3–2 kg range can be stalked and ambushed around the lake edges with dry flies and nymphs. Many trout are also caught from boats, either trolling or harling a fly.

South Mavora is much smaller, at 2.5 km in length, and being surrounded by beech bush is more sheltered. Fly casting is more

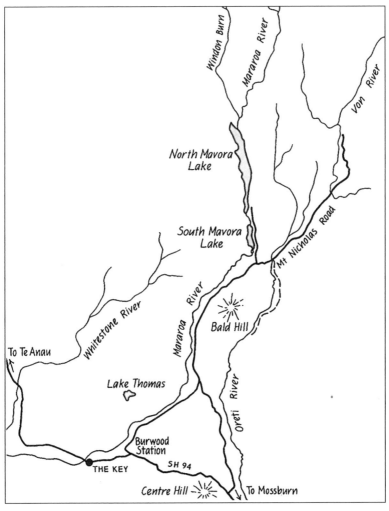

Mavora Lakes

difficult, but at the open northern end of the lake where the river enters there is good fly fishing for cruising trout. The sandflies can be fierce!

Lake Thomas

Location Lies 4 km from Mararoa Station north of The Key.
Access Turn off SH 94 onto Lagoon Creek Road 2.5 km on the Te Anau side of the Mararoa Bridge, then onto Danby Road. Permission may be required before walking the track to the lake. Access is also available through Mararoa Station but the four-wheel-drive track is confusing. A tunnel-shaped haybarn is the reference point.
Season 1 October–30 April.
Restrictions Bag limit is two trout. Non-mechanically powered boats are permitted.

This small, shallow, exposed lake covers 10 ha and is stocked with rainbow trout. The shoreline, which is covered with broom, gorse and flax, makes it difficult to fish, and a float-tube would be an advantage. Fish are difficult to sight, and in strong winds the waves stir up the mud lake bottom. The lake overflows into Lagoon Creek, which drains into the Mararoa River.

Borland Burn

Location Rises in the Hunter Mountains, flows southeast through native bush and enters the Waiau River 1.6 km upriver from Monowai Power Station.
Access From Monowai Road to Borland Lodge and then on a marked track to North Borland Hut. It is a 15-minute walk through the bush to the river. The first stream crossed is the tannin-stained Pig Creek.
Season 1 October–30 April.
Restrictions Bag limit is two trout. Artificial bait and fly only.

This clear, wadeable, rock and stone type stream flows through native bush and holds a limited stock of browns and rainbows in the

1–2 kg range. Fish are easy to spot but become very spooky as the season progresses. Careful stalking and an accurate, gentle first cast is required. Small nymphs and dries such as Coch-y-bondhu, Dad's Favourite and Parachute Adams are worth trying. The stream floods readily but just as readily returns to normal. Carry insect repellent.

Monowai River

Location Drains Lake Monowai and after a short easterly course empties into the Waiau River.
Access Lake Monowai Road crosses this stream 1 km past Monowai village and follows up the true left bank to the lake outlet. There are four-wheel-drive tracks off this road through manuka scrub to the river.
Season 1 October–30 April.
Restrictions Bag limit is two trout. Artificial bait and fly only.

This is a deep, fast-flowing, gin-clear, weedy stream that is over-grown and almost impossible to fish with a fly rod. It holds good-sized browns that are selective and easily spooked. The stream fluctuates according to power requirements, and there are only 6 km of river to fish. It remains clear after heavy rain. Carry a landing net and insect repellent.

Wairaki River

Location Rises in the Takitimu Mountains, flows southwest and enters the Waiau River 10 km north of Clifden.
Access *Upper reaches* Through private land on Mt Linton Station.
Middle reaches Through Eastern Bush via Clifden or Orawia.
Lower reaches SH 96 crosses the lower reaches north of Clifden. There is an access track from the bridge to the mouth.
Season 1 October–30 April.
Restrictions Bag limit is two fish above the power pylons and four below. Bait fishing is permitted below the pylons only.

This small, unstable, flood-prone, shingly river holds minimal stocks of brown and rainbow trout in the middle and lower reaches.

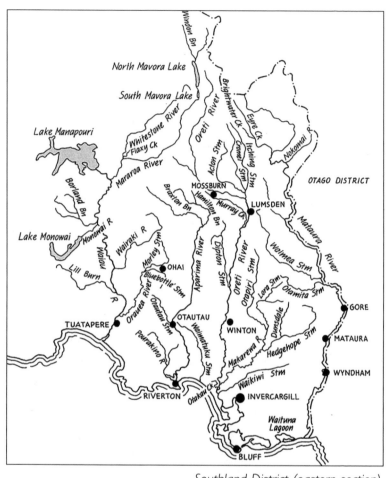

Southland District (eastern section)

The river's upper reaches, which have private four-wheel-drive access, offer more stable water and better fly fishing.

Lill Burn

Location Drains the Kaherekoau Mountains northeast of Lake Hauroko and follows a northeasterly course to join the Waiau River 5 km north of Clifden.

Access The Lill Burn Valley road to Lake Hauroko follows the river upstream on the true right bank and provides easy access across private farmland.

Season 1 October–30 April.

Restrictions Bag limit is four trout.

This medium-sized, lightly tea-coloured stream emerges from native bush and flows gently across pastoral land. The river is choked with willows in parts but holds a good stock of browns in the 1–2 kg range. Only the lower 10 km is worth fishing as fish stocks are low in the bush-lined section.

With a sand and shingle bed, this is a pleasant river to fish as trout tend to cruise in the deep, slow-flowing sections and can be ambushed between the willows. Try small nymphs, mayfly imitation dry flies, Willow Grub, Coch-y-bondhu, and Black and Peacock.

Orauea River (Orawia)

Location Three small streams, the Sharpridge, Morley and Bluebottle, rise from country surrounding Ohai and join to form the Orauea near Birchwood. The main river then flows southwest across pastoral land to enter the Waiau River just upstream from Tuatapere.

Access The Otautau–Tuatapere road and SH 96 from Orawia to Ohai follow the river.

Sharpridge Creek can be approached from Birchwood on SH 96, Morley Stream from Mt Linton Road north of Birchwood, and Bluebottle Stream from Bluebottle Road south from Ohai.

Season 1 October–30 April.

Restrictions Bag limit is four trout.

The main river is slow-flowing and choked with willows in some sections. It holds brown trout averaging 1 kg, which can be spotted in bright conditions, especially early in the season before weed growth from farm run-off chokes the stream. The best water lies upstream from Pukemaori.

All three tributaries hold fish and are worth exploring early in the season, but fish are often difficult to spot and the banks are overgrown in many sections.

Aparima River

Location Rises in the Takitimu Mountains. The headwaters flow east, but after being joined by the Hamilton and Braxton burns south of Mossburn the river turns south across farmland for over 60 km before reaching the Aparima River estuary at Riverton.

Access *Lower reaches* The estuary can be accessed from Riverton and the lower reaches from Gummies Bush and Thornbury bridges. *Middle reaches* Between Thornbury and Wreys Bush the river is spanned by four bridges. Roads follow up both banks between Thornbury and Jacobs Bridge, and there are marked anglers' access points off these roads.

Upper reaches Above Jacobs Bridge access can be gained from the Dunrobin Valley Road across private farmland. The headwaters can be reached by four-wheel-drive from a farm track beyond the old Dunrobin Station.

Season Open all year below Thornbury Bridge. Above this bridge, 1 October–30 April.

Restrictions Upstream from the Hamilton Burn confluence, the bag limit is two trout and only artificial bait and fly can be used. Below this confluence, the bag limit is six trout and all legal methods are permitted.

The Aparima River holds a good stock of brown trout in the 0.75–1.5 kg range (130 trout/km above Wreys Bush, with 50 percent of these being medium-sized). There are larger sea-run fish in the tidal section and in the headwaters.

The lower reaches are tidal to just above Gummies Bush Bridge. Most trout are caught on live bait and spinners but the occasional fish over 4.5 kg is landed. From half-tide to low water is the favoured time to fish, when the trout are more confined to the channels. From Gummies Bush Bridge to Thornbury Bridge the river is very windy, with high willow-covered banks. There are some deep holes beneath the willows, connected by pleasant riffles, and fish stocks are good for anglers fishing blind with spinners, nymphs and live bait.

In the middle reaches the river braids in some sections and is more unstable but there is plenty of fishable water with long glides and ripply runs. This section is very exposed to nor'west winds.

There is excellent water upstream from Jacobs Bridge and although fish numbers are much lower, sight fishing for good-sized browns can be rewarding on a bright, calm day. There are 15 km of fishable water above Jacobs Bridge right up to and including the Pleasant Creek tributary. There are larger stones and rocky ledges in this section, quite different from the gravels of the middle reaches.

Like most Southland rivers the Aparima fishes best in a light southerly wind, although fishing can be good in a nor'wester provided you can find a sheltered spot and can cast. An easterly wind appears to discourage fish from feeding. Mayfly and caddis imitations in either nymph, emerger or dry fly patterns take most fish. In the willowed middle and lower reaches, a willow grub imitation is worth trying in midsummer.

Hamilton Burn

Location The North and South Braxton burns, the Braxton Burn itself, Hamilton Burn and Centre Burn all rise from the northern Takitimu Mountains and join before entering the Aparima River 15 km south of Mossburn and 2.5 km north of Jacobs Bridge.
Access From the Mossburn–Otautau road, the Dipton–Mossburn road, Goodall Road, Waterloo Road and Mt Hamilton Road to the upper reaches.
Season 1 October–30 April.
Restrictions Bag limit is four trout. Artificial bait and fly only above the Mossburn–Otautau road.

Both the Hamilton Burn and North Braxton Burn offer classical small stream dry fly and nymph water for good-sized brown trout, especially in the middle and upper reaches early in the season. There are long slow-flowing sections in the Hamilton Burn, and trout often cruise these pools rather than remaining on station to feed. The banks of willow, broom, gorse and flax allow anglers to stalk these fish with long fine tippets, accurate casts and small flies. This type of fishing can be very demanding, especially when the bank vegetation obstructs casting. Trout can also be very selective at times. It helps to have a friend spot for you, and keep track of fish while you disentangle your fly from the scrub! Wading will disturb fish and it pays to carry a net. The nor'wester can end all fishing. These streams can remain clear when the main river is dirty and unfishable.

Pourakino River

Location Rises from the forested Longwood Range west of Riverton, flows southeast and enters the Aparima River estuary.
Access The lower reaches are best reached by boat. The upper reaches can be accessed from Pourakino Valley Road then Ermedale Road and the Pourakino Walkway, which follows up the true left bank for 8 km from the carpark and picnic area.
Season Open all year below Waipango Bridge. Above this bridge, 1 October–30 April.
Restrictions Bag limit is six trout.

In the lower tidal reaches good-sized sea-run and estuarine-living brown trout are best fished to by trolling or spinning from a boat. The river is sluggish and slow-flowing.

In the upper reaches from the end of Pourakino Valley and Ermedale roads, this small to medium-sized river flows through thick beech bush. The water is heavily peat-stained and unless trout are rising they are very difficult to spot. Bush overhanging the river on some stretches tests your casting ability.

The Gorge Creek tributary also holds browns but is difficult to fish unless you wade quietly up the stream.

Waimatuku Stream

Location Rises from springs and swamp east of Otautau. Flows through pastoral land to enter the sea south of Waimatuku township.
Access To the mouth from Hamilton's Bridge, the middle reaches from SH 99 (Waimatuku–Invercargill road) and from roads north of Waimatuku at Otahuti and Isla Bank. Private farmland may need to be crossed.

Season Open all year below the Rance Road bridge. Above this bridge, 1 October–30 April.
Restrictions Bag limit is four trout.

This small stream has been affected by farm run-off and becomes weedy in summer. It holds good numbers of brown trout averaging 1 kg in stable pools and runs. It has grassy banks, and trout can be spotted in bright conditions. The stream can remain fishable after light rain, but is best fished early in the season before weeds choke it. It is wise to carry a landing net.

The tidal section below Hamilton's Bridge yields a few good sea-run fish to threadline anglers.

Oreti River and tributaries

Oreti River

Location Rises in the Thomson Mountains east of North Mavora Lake and flows south for over 130 km before entering the New River estuary just west of Invercargill.
Season Open all year below the Invercargill–Riverton highway bridge (SH 99). Between SH 94 bridge and the confluence of the Irthing Stream, 1 October–31 March. Elsewhere, 1 October–30 April.
Restrictions Bag limit: from the headwaters to the downstream limit of the 'walk only zone', catch and release only. From the downstream limit of the 'walk only zone' to Rocky Point, two trout only. From Rocky Point to the sea, the bag limit is six trout. Bait fishing only permitted downstream of Rocky Point.

For descriptive purposes this magnificent river is divided into five sections.

Headwaters (catch and release walk section)
Access
- Take the Centre Hill–Mavora Lakes road off SH 94 and the short gravel Oreti Road to a carpark and locked gate. It is

approximately a 16-km walk to the upper Oreti bridge.
- From the upper Oreti bridge on the Mt Nicholas Road, walk downstream.

This section of river is very exposed to nor'west winds and is best fished in light southerly conditions and bright sun. The valley is wide and flat and there is little background shadow to reduce the glare on the water when spotting fish. Trout are very difficult to spot in overcast conditions and many will be spooked. There is a good stock of browns averaging over 2 kg, with an occasional trophy fish possible. The average weight of fish caught has gone down a little since catch and release was introduced, but there is still excellent sight fishing in this section of river. The river flats and surrounding hills are tussock-covered, with the odd patch of beech bush. Crossings are easy on the stony riverbed and there are few trees to hinder casting. Early in the season careful stalking and accurate casting with weighted nymphs accounts for most fish hooked. In December and January mayfly and green beetle imitations are worth trying, while in February large cicada, hopper and attractor type flies can provide great sport. Only a few fish inhabit the river upstream from the upper Oreti bridge. There is a farm track to walk back on at the end of fishing.

Angling pressure can be intense on this section of river. If someone has already parked at the gate, find another stretch of river to fish.

Upper reaches (from the 'walk only zone' down to Rocky Point)
Access There are marked anglers' access tracks off the Centre Hill–Mavora Lakes road. Further downstream below the Windley confluence there is little close road access, and private farmland must be crossed to reach the river. SH 94 runs close by the river at Rocky Point.

This section of river also holds some large browns, especially in the deeper runs and pools above the Windley River confluence. Below the confluence the river spreads out over a wide, shingly riverbed and in long hot summers some fish will drop back downstream to deeper, more permanent water. Early in the season this section of river is well worth exploring, but it is best on sunny days to aid spotting. The riverbed is flat, with no hills or scrub to reduce glare on the water. More walking is required between fish on this section of river.

Middle reaches (Rocky Point down to Dipton)
Access
- From SH 94 between Rocky Point and Lumsden.
- From the Mossburn–Dipton road and SH 6. There are marked anglers' access tracks off both these roads.

The river is more unstable in this stretch and braids out on some sections. The valley is wide, shingly and flat, and spotting trout becomes very difficult. Deeper runs and pools, especially those with one permanent bank, will usually hold fish and although stocks may be higher than in the upper reaches, trout tend to be smaller, averaging around 1 kg.

Likely looking stretches here should be explored with dry flies, nymphs or even soft hackle wet flies. The latter should be fished across and down. This technique is most useful in strong downstream winds.

Lower reaches (from Dipton down to the Invercargill–Riverton highway bridge)
Access Roads follow down both banks, with bridges at Dipton, Benmore, Limehills, Winton, Lochiel and SH 99 (the Invercargill–Riverton road).

There are plenty of brown trout in the 0.5–0.75 kg range in this section of river. There are wide shingly runs and long willow-lined glides. Because the river is often braided and changes course in floods, it is important to find a stretch of river with a stable bank. Fish can be taken on all types of legal bait, spinners and flies. Below Winton the river becomes slower flowing, with willows and mud banks, and is more suited to spinning.

Tidal section (below SH 99 bridge)
Access From a number of roads west of Invercargill and Otatara, Ferry, West Plains and SH 99 bridges.

This section of the river, close to Invercargill, is quite heavily fished both from boats and from the shore. The mouth of Waikiwi Stream is a hot spot, with most fish taken by trolling, spinning and live bait fishing. Trout food is abundant, with small flounder, whitebait, elvers, smelt, bullies, minnows and shrimps. Some very large sea-run and estuarine-living brown trout are caught, including one weighing over 11 kg a few years ago.

Irthing, Cromel and Acton streams

Location These three streams drain the Eyre Mountains north of Mossburn and join near Lowther, just west of SH 6 and 2 km upstream from the Ellis Road bridge.
Access From the Mossburn–Five Rivers road, Ellis, Irthing, Lowther and Selby roads, and across private farmland.
Season 1 October–31 March.
Restrictions Bag limit is four trout.

All three are small, shingly, willow-lined streams that wind across farmland and hold brown trout averaging around 1 kg. The streams are easy to fish but farm run-off and mob stocking of cattle has caused severe bank erosion and general stream degradation. All now readily discolour after rain and tend to dry in summer. The Irthing holds most water, and drift dives have revealed a good stock of small trout. These are spawning streams and fish best early in the season.

Murray and Stag creeks and Dipton Stream

Location and access All enter west bank of Oreti River between Lumsden and Winton. Murray Creek enters opposite Josephville, Stag Creek 6.5 km north of Dipton, and Dipton Stream 4 km south of Benmore. The Mossburn–Winton road crosses all streams.
Season 1 October–30 April.
Restrictions Bag limit is four trout.

Murray and Stag creeks are difficult to fish due to heavy flax, scrub and willows growing along the banks. However, both hold some good browns, especially early in the season. Dipton Stream is larger and the lower 5 km above the Oreti confluence is worth exploring early in the season. Trout can be spotted but are easily spooked. All are important spawning streams for the Oreti River.

 Makarewa River and tributaries

Makarewa River

Location Formed by the joining of the Otapiri, Lora, Dunsdale and Titipua streams, all of which drain the Hokonui Hills. The main river meanders south across the Southland Plains, through the farming communities of Hedgehope, Tussock Creek, Makarewa and Wallacetown, before entering the Oreti River at West Plains 11 km from Invercargill.
Access From roads in the vicinity of Wallacetown, Makarewa, Tussock Creek and Hokonui.
Season Open all year below the Invercargill–Riverton highway bridge (SH 99). Above this bridge, 1 October–30 April.
Restrictions Bag limit is six trout downstream from the Otapiri Stream confluence.

The Makarewa is a slow-flowing, sluggish river that easily becomes eutrophic in summer, with weed growth choking some sections of the river. Trout fishing has suffered from flood control activity, which has straightened and channelled the river. The locals mainly fish it early in the season with spinners and live bait. The lower reaches hold small brown trout and perch.

Otapiri Stream

Location and access Flows south through the Otapiri Gorge and near the farming communities of Browns and Otapiri. Joins the Makarewa just north of Hedgehope. Access from roads north and east of Browns and Otapiri.
Season 1 October–30 April.
Restrictions Bag limit is four trout.

The lower reaches have been channelled for flood control and are not worth fishing. The middle and upper reaches, especially through the gorge, offer good small stream sight fishing for browns up to 1 kg. The water is tea-coloured and the banks are covered with grass, scrub and willows. Wading and crossing on the gravelly riverbed is easy. Some pools are slow-flowing, and these can really test the angler. Stalk carefully, cast accurately and fish with fine gear. Best early and late in the season. Try small mayfly imitation dry flies, Midge Pupa, lightly weighted nymphs and emergers.

Lora Stream

Location Also flows south; joins the Makarewa near Lora School.
Access From Lora River and Lora Gorge roads.
Season 1 October–30 April.
Restrictions Bag limit is four trout.

There are 7 km of fishable water upstream from the school along Lora Gorge Road. The banks are reasonably clear, with some scrub and flax. Brown trout up to 1 kg can be sight fished. This small stream is best fished early in the season before low water flows encourage fish to drop back downstream to the Makarewa. This is another delightful but testing little stream that requires accurate casting and careful spotting.

Hedgehope Stream

Location Joins the Makarewa at Tussock Creek bridge.
Access From Hedgehope Road south of Hedgehope.
Season 1 October–30 April.
Restrictions Bag limit is four trout.

Although this small stream holds browns up to 1 kg, it has been ruined by severe channelling and excavating. Best early in the season.

Dunsdale Stream

Location Joins the Hedgehope Stream south of Hedgehope.
Access From Dunsdale Valley Road east of Hedgehope.
Season 1 October–30 April.
Restrictions Bag limit is four trout.

This small stream, which flows down a sheltered valley, offers 6 km of fishable water upstream from its confluence with the Hedgehope. Gorse, broom and willows line the banks but there are good numbers of small browns, especially early in the season.

Lake Waituna

Location Lies on the south coast at Toetoes Bay, some 25 km east of Invercargill.
Access Take either Kapuka South or Waituna Lagoon road south from SH 92 at Kapuka. There is a walking track from the eastern end of the lake to the outlet.
Season 1 October–30 April.
Restrictions Bag limit is two trout. No boat fishing within 500 m of the outlet, indicated by white marker posts.

This shallow lake is 11 km long and 1.5 km wide. It is tidal when the outlet is open to the sea and contains some very large sea-run and estuarine-living brown trout, with an occasional fish weighing up to 8 kg. The lagoon offers boat fishing, live bait fishing, spinning and smelt fly fishing, with the hot spot being the outlet channel. Best early in the season.

 Mataura River and tributaries

Mataura River

Location Rises in Eyre and Garvie mountains south of Lake Wakatipu, flows southeast to Gore then south to the sea at Fortrose.

Season Open all year below the Gorge Road bridge on SH 92. Above this bridge, 1 October–30 April.

Restrictions Above the Garston bridge, catch and release only. Between the Garston bridge and Black Bridge, 3 km north of Athol, four trout. Below Black Bridge, six trout. Fishing from boats, float-tubes or other flotation devices is only permitted below Mataura Island bridge.

This famous trout-fishing river provides over 150 km of fishable water. It is described in three sections.

Upper Mataura (Fairlight to Cattle Flat)
Access There is access from SH 6 just north of Garston from a side road bridge. Downstream from Parawa, a gravel road running east follows down the river into the Nokomai Gorge. There are many other access tracks across private farmland from SH 6, but permission is required from local landowners.

The upper Mataura River runs over a gravel bed and is willow-lined. Brown trout in the 1–2 kg range are relatively easy to spot under normal conditions and fish stocks are good (40 fish/km at Nokomai, with 40 percent of these a good size). They become more spooked as the season progresses. The upper river is quite small and can be crossed at the tail of most pools. There are deep holes beneath willows, long glides and shallow riffles. Between Nokomai and Cattle Flat the river runs through a gorge but this is normally easy to negotiate and fish. It can be walked in one long day but it is better fished over two or three days. Early in the season the river usually contains snow-melt, but by mid-November the water runs clear; the river recovers reasonably rapidly after rain.

Mayflies and caddis predominate and nymphs, emergers, soft hackle wets and dry flies all take fish. I suggest trying Pheasant Tail and Hare's Ear nymphs, CDC emergers, Dad's Favourite, Twilight Beauty, Parachute Adams, March Brown, Dark Red Spinner, Kakahi Queen and Elk Hair Caddis dry flies, and Purple Grouse soft hackle wet flies. Later in summer, Willow Grub and some terrestrials can be useful.

Middle reaches (Cattle Flat down to Gore)

Access There are many access points, including the Ardlussa–Cattle Flat road, Ardlussa Bridge, Waipounamu Bridge, Pyramid Bridge at Riversdale, Mandeville, Otamita Bridge, Monaghans Beach at Croydon, and Graham's Island on the east bank at Gore.

This is the most popular stretch of river, although the water quality deteriorates and sight fishing is no longer an option. Overseas anglers, especially those from the US, enjoy this section as like many American rivers the water itself must be fished, unless of course trout are rising. The riverbed is still predominantly gravel, the mud banks are covered with grass and willows, and there is a healthy stock of browns that average around 1 kg. However, there is the occasional fish up to 4 kg. Above the Waikaia confluence the river can be waded and crossed in normal conditions, but below this confluence it swells to the point where crossings become more hazardous. Trout can be more selective from this point down and there are some interesting backwaters to explore. Use the same flies as suggested for the upper Mataura, with the addition of Midge Pupa and Corixa, especially in the backwaters. During the 'mad Mataura rise' try a small unweighted dark-bodied nymph or a soft hackle wet fished dead drift. Use a small indicator or even a small Parachute Adams that is easily visible. When the trout are unresponsive try seining the river to determine the food source then operating on a fly with a pair of scissors to match the hatch!

Lower reaches (Gore to the mouth)

Access SH 1 more or less follows the river from Gore to Edenvale on the west or true right bank. However, there is easier access from the east or true left bank, especially between Mataura and Gore. Further downstream there are numerous roads near Tuturau, Wyndham and Seaward Downs, with SH 92 crossing on Gorge Bridge at the top of the tidal section.

The best water lies upstream from Mataura Island, as below this point the river becomes unattractive and channelled. The river is much larger and deeper in this section, with an occasional coal reef altering the character of the riverbed. There are long glides and willows, with very high numbers of trout present. Some of these are large but they often remain difficult to catch. Use the same mayfly, caddis, midge pupa and corixa imitations as above, with even a Black and Peacock for snails. Spin and live bait anglers enjoy good success in these lower reaches, especially when whitebait are running.

Brightwater Stream

Location Flows over private farmland just south of Fairlight before joining the upper Mataura River.
Access Take Fairlight Station Road off SH 6 and ask permission at Fairlight Station.
Season 1 October–30 April.
Restrictions Catch and release.

This is a small, clear, weedy spring creek. Fish must be very carefully stalked and a short, accurate first cast is very important. Use small weighted nymphs, Midge Pupa, mayfly and caddis emergers on long, fine tippets.

Wading is unnecessary but carry a net or fish hooked will escape into the weeds. Trout often remain hidden beneath the banks and weed beds but they usually emerge to feed during the afternoon when insects are more abundant. The Brightwater is an important spawning stream, which fishes best early in the season. It seldom discolours after rain.

Waikaia River

Location Rises in the Umbrella Mountains just east of the Pomahaka River headwaters. Flows south for 50 km, first through native bush and then pastoral land, before joining the Mataura River at Riversdale.
Access The Riversdale–Waikaia–Piano Flat road and side roads off it offer generally easy access to the river. Beyond Piano Flat the Whitcombe Road leads to Whitcombe Flat but leaves the river.

This is a four-wheel-drive road, which can be negotiated in dry weather by conventional vehicles. The Waikaia River Track follows upstream from Piano Flat more closely than this road, and provides better access.

There is pleasant, basic camping at Piano Flat but take insect repellent.

Season 1 October–30 April.

Restrictions Bag limit is four trout above the Glenary bridge and six trout below this bridge. Boats, float-tubes or pontoon boats are not permitted on this river.

This moderate-sized, highly regarded brown trout river is the Mataura River's major tributary. The rugged, bush-clad, inaccessible headwaters upstream from Piano Flat hold few trout. At Piano Flat there is interesting, slightly tea-coloured water that offers sight fishing in bright conditions. Fish stocks are good (40 trout/km) and the river can be waded and crossed at selected sites. Once the river emerges from the bush and crosses farmland sight fishing becomes more difficult and one looks for rising fish. The banks are clay and mud, with willows and grass. There are long glides, deep pools and shallow riffles. Fish average 1–2 kg. The same selection of flies as those described for the Mataura River are effective on the Wakaia River.

Early in the season the Waikaia tributaries Dome Burn and Steeple Burn hold fish recovering from spawning. By Christmas, when these small streams dry, most fish will have retreated downstream to the main river. The Waikaia–Piano Flat road crosses both tributaries.

Waimea Stream

Location Drains the Waimea Plains and Hokonui Hills south of Lumsden, flows southeast and enters the Mataura River at Mandeville.

Access From roads south of Balfour and Riversdale, such as Waimea Valley Road, Nine Mile Road and Crooked Road.

Season 1 October–30 April.

Restrictions Bag limit is four trout.

This stream has been straightened and channelled for flood protection and unfortunately the fishing has suffered as a result. It holds small brown trout, with better fish in a few good stable holes in the vicinity of Fairplace Station.

Otamita Stream

Location Rises in the Hokonui Hills, flows east and joins the Mataura just downstream from the Waimea at Mandeville.
Access *Lower reaches* From behind Mandeville village on the Mandeville–Otamita road south of Mandeville, then the Otamita Valley Road.
Middle and upper reaches From the Gore to Dolamore Park road, then through the Hokonui Hills to Hargests.
Season 1 October–30 April.
Restrictions Bag limit is four trout.

This very pleasant small stream flows over a rock and gravel bed. It is a highly regarded stream, which holds a reasonable stock of browns averaging 1–2 kg. The water is lightly tea-coloured but this does not prevent sight fishing on a bright day. The banks are generally open. The headwaters tend to hold fewer fish but they are larger.

Waikaka Stream

Location Rises from the Black Umbrella Range, flows south parallel to but east of the Waikaia River, and enters the Mataura River at Gore.
Access North of Gore at Willowbank, Maitland, Waikaka and from the Waikaka–Waikaia road.
Season Bag limit is four trout.

The lower reaches of this small stream have also been ruined by catchment works. The best water lies upstream from the township of Waikaka. There are a few good brown trout in these upper reaches, and as the river has a relatively small catchment it can remain clear after rain when other rivers in the district have become unfishable.

Location Rises in Slopedown Mountains and Catlins State Forest Park, flows west and joins Mataura River near Wyndham.
Access *Lower reaches* From the Wyndham–Mataura road.
Middle and upper reaches From Mimihau Road at Burns Road, Venlaw Road and the Waiarikiki turn-off; and Venlaw Station and Kowhai Grove picnic area on the Catlins Forest road. Permission may be required as many accesses are over private farm land.
Season 1 October–30 April.
Restrictions Bag limit is four trout.

Above Waiarikiki there are over 10 km of river flowing through native bush. Although the water is tannin-stained the odd fish can be spotted and they also rise freely. In some stretches the stream must be crossed and waded; care should be taken as although the stream is small, the rocks and stones are very slippery. The upper reaches clear rapidly after rain, whereas below the Waiarikiki Stream the river is often discoloured. The lower reaches cross pastoral land and are choked with willows in some stretches. Most fish taken on the lower reaches are caught on live bait. There are good stocks of fish in this stream but the average weight is less than 1 kg.

Mokoreta River (Wyndham)

Location Drains the hills on the west side of Catlins State Forest Park, flows west and joins the Mataura River 3 km south of Wyndham.
Access From the Wyndham Station–Clinton road, Mokoreta Bridge, Craig Road, Klondyke Road and Wyndham Valley Road. Like the Mimihau, access is often over private farmland so permission should be obtained.
Season 1 October–30 April.
Restrictions Bag limit is four trout.

This medium-sized, heavily peat-stained river offers good blind fishing for browns averaging around 1 kg, especially early in the season before low water flows and weed growth make fishing more difficult. The middle reaches are the most popular, with long, slow-flowing pools, rock ledges, shelves and riffles. Fish stocks are good and although gorse and scrub obstruct casting on some sections of river, there is plenty of water with good access. The river can be crossed in some sections but the rock shelves are extremely slippery. It becomes much easier to fish when trout are rising.

The tea-coloured Mokoreta River in Southland

Appendix: Identification of trout, salmon and char

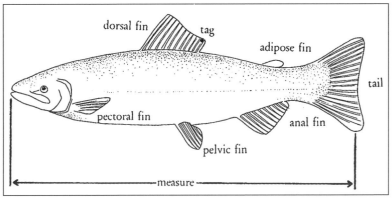

Tagged or marked fish

Brown trout

Salmo trutta, first introduced in 1867 from Tasmania, are the predominant species and are widely distributed throughout the South Island.

Sea-run browns tend to be silvery in colour, river fish yellowish-green with dark brown and red spots, while lake fish have a creamish-yellow body and a speckled appearance.

Distinguishing features include:
- square or slightly forked tail
- blue halo around spots, especially on gill covers
- mouth not black inside
- relatively short and deep anal fin
- tail not densely spotted.

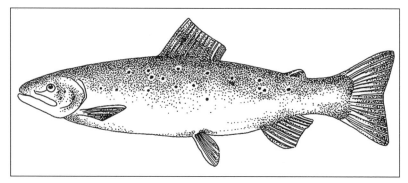

Brown trout

Rainbow trout

Oncorhynchus mykiss, previously classified as *Salmo gairdnerii*, were first introduced from Somona Creek, San Francisco, in 1877. There are no sea-run species in New Zealand. Lake-dwelling fish tend to be more silvery in colour.

Distinguishing features include:
- square or slightly forked tail
- pinkish-rose tinge on the gill covers and along the lateral line, but no spots on the gill covers
- mouth not black inside
- short-based anal fin with 8–12 rays
- dense black spots on tail, head, back, sides, dorsal adipose fins.

The Rotorua 'r' strain bred at the Ngongotaha Hatchery are late-maturing rainbow.

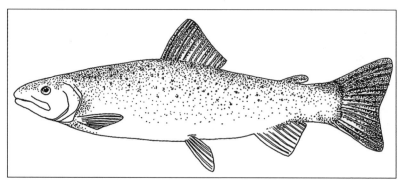

Rainbow trout

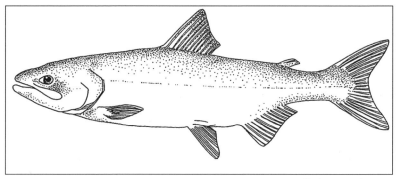

Quinnat salmon

Quinnat, king or chinook salmon

Oncorhynchus tschawytscha were introduced from the west coast of North America in 1901 and liberated into the Waitaki River. They are present as landlocked fish in Lake Coleridge and the southern lakes, and as sea-run fish in many South Island rivers where the sea temperature does not rise above 15° Celsius. Lake fish are much smaller. Sea-run fish tend to darken in colour and lose their silvery sheen as they migrate up rivers to spawn.

Distinguishing features include:
- prominently forked tail
- mouth black inside between the teeth
- long-based anal fin
- hooked snout (the meaning of the word 'oncorhynchus').

Atlantic salmon

Salmo salar were introduced from Europe in 1875 and are present in small numbers as landlocked fish in lakes Te Anau, Manapouri, Gunn and Fergus. These fish are now rare, are generally in poor condition and tend to be long and thin. They seldom grow larger than 2 kg. They resemble brown trout, but have small, slender, dark spots on the back and sides of the head which are not surrounded by paler halos, and there are no pale or reddish spots on their sides.

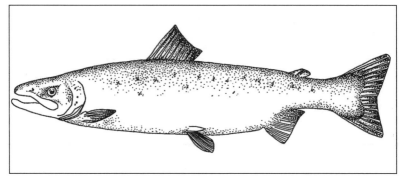

Atlantic salmon

Sockeye salmon

Oncorhynchus nerka, which were also introduced from the west coast of North America around 1902, are found in lakes Ohau and Opuha as landlocked resident fish. There is no evidence of a sea-run habit in New Zealand.

The mouth is not black between the teeth, and gill rakers are long and numerous (31–43).

Brook char

Salvelinus fontinalis, found in a few small lakes and the headwaters of selected streams, were introduced in 1877. Distinguished by their colourful appearance, they have a dark olive-green vermicular pattern on the back, dorsal fin and upper lobe of the tail, and the flank is a silvery-purplish, pale blue colour, while the belly is white tinged with orange. There are also yellow and red spots on the sides. The caudal fin is a little forked and the shortest ray is more than half the length of the longest ray. There is a pale leading edge to the pelvic and anal fins, followed by a strongly contrasting black stripe. They do not usually co-exist with other members of the salmon family.

Macinaw

Salvelinus namaycush, or 'Great Lake Trout', were introduced in

1906 from North America. They are now very rare and only present in Lake Pearson. They have not thrived, as this lake warms too much in summer and the food supply in deep water is poor.

Macinaw are greyish-green on the back and sometimes have a pink flush on the sides. The caudal fin is deeply forked and the shortest ray is less than half the length of the longest. The pale leading edge to the pelvic and anal fins is not followed by a black stripe. They are sometimes mistaken for poorly conditioned brown trout.

Splake

These are a hybrid (cross-breed) between the female macinaw and the male brook char. They have been released into lakes Dispute and Letitia.

Index

Other Fishing Books from Reed Publishing (NZ) Ltd

North Island Trout Fishing Guide
John Kent

The companion volume to the *South Island Trout Fishing Guide*, this practical handbook provides accurate, up-to-date information on trout fishing in the North Island of New Zealand. It is directed towards local anglers and the increasing numbers of overseas enthusiasts attracted by New Zealand's unsurpassed fishing waters. The world famous Taupo and Rotorua areas are described in detail. So are many lesser-known but equally rewarding back country waters. In fact, more than 300 streams and 60 lakes are covered.

New Zealand's Top Trout Fishing Waters
John Kent and Patti Magnano Madsen

New Zealand is a fly angler's paradise as most rivers and lakes have excellent water quality and offer sight fishing to large wild brown and rainbow trout. There is virtually no private water and the licence fees are reasonable. Access to most rivers and lakes is easy and there are wilderness areas providing trophy trout for the adventurous. Many overseas anglers visiting New Zealand have limited time to fish and the wide range of water available can be confusing and overwhelming. This book has been written to make that choice easier and to offer tips on fishing New Zealand waters.

To simplify the anglers' itinerary the authors have grouped the fishing spots in close proximity to a central location so the angler has a choice of rivers and lakes to visit within a reasonable travelling distance. Also included is information on the availability of local fishing guides and fly shops in the vicinity. And, to be well entertained on non-fishing days, various local attractions have also been mentioned.

New Zealand Trout Flies Traditional and Modern
Keith Draper

Written by one of New Zealand's foremost exponents of fly fishing, Keith Draper's *New Zealand Trout Flies Traditional and Modern* is a comprehensive and informative catalogue of the flies, nymphs and lures used on the New Zealand trout fishing scene. An essential reference for fly fishing enthusiasts, it includes patterns of both local and imported design that have become standard since publication of the author's best selling *Trout Flies in New Zealand*, as well as many traditional flies of historical interest and importance.

Richly illustrated with anecdotes and featuring many well-known local fly fishing personalities, *New Zealand Trout Flies Traditional and Modern* traces the origins of patterns and acknowledges the contribution of creators to the world of fly fishing. Entries give details of each dressing, and colour plates show over 400 flies.

New Zealand Fly Tying: The Ten-thumbed Beginner's Guide
Hugh McDowell

You don't need the dexterity of a brain surgeon to tie flies just as dainty and just as deadly as those in the shops. If you can tie a fly to your leader, you can tie the fly itself — and Hugh McDowell has written and illustrated this book to show you how easy it is.

He describes the inexpensive tools and materials you'll need to get started, and then demonstrates step-by-step the techniques necessary to make:
- the big lures unique to New Zealand
- wet flies, dry flies and nymphs
- the new saltwater flies

This lively handbook is packed with handy hints and entertaining yarns drawn from a lifetime's experience of tying flies and catching fish with them.